GRABBING
LIGHTNING

ALSO BY DONALD AND PAIGE MARRS, PHD

Executive in Passage

GRABBING LIGHTNING

A Memoir

The Messy Quest *for an* Extraordinary Love

DONALD MARRS & PAIGE MARRS, PhD

Foreword by James Finley, PhD

BARRINGTON SKY
PUBLISHING

First Edition

Published by:
Barrington Sky Publishing
connect@bsky.com

ISBN: 978-0-925887-01-6 pbk
ISBN: 978-0-925887-02-3 ebk

Book design by Stacey Aaronson
Cover design by Ben Saffran and Emily Denis

Grabbing Lightning is a work of nonfiction and is based on the authors' personal experiences and memories. Certain names and other identifying details have been changed to respect the privacy of those involved, and certain events have been reordered or compressed.

Printed in the United States of America

To all those on the path of extraordinary love.

Our Thanks

With sincere gratitude, we wish to acknowledge the following people whose support and guidance made this book possible:

Jim Finley, author of the Foreword, whose friendship and contemplative vision has been so inspiring for us in the writing of this book and in the living of our lives.

Ron Scolastico, who not only introduced us but then sustained us with his wisdom and persistent encouragement for this project through many years.

The editors and designers who helped us at various stages along the way: David Carroll, whose story-editing ability contributed to narrative crispness and flow. CJ Schepers, whose copyediting skills provided some much-needed clean up of the manuscript. Ben Saffran, who from the other side of the world tirelessly engaged the cover design and gave the spirit of our story its visual presence. Emily Denis, who used her astute aesthetic sense and deep understanding of our mission to bring the cover to its full life (and was so fun to work with). And Stacey Aaronson, who designed the interior pages and who once again used her production skills to make one of our books a readable thing.

And with overflowing hearts, we again thank the friends, family, and colleagues (the generous souls we mention at the start of the epilogue) who read and critiqued the manuscript: Donna Thomas, Susan Scolastico, Kim Pearce, Keith Melville, Marilyn Price-Mitchell, Ilene Morgan, Rebecca Ewing, Deena Arnold, PJ Tyler, Taryn Arnold, and Michael Larson, who also contributed the photo of us on the back cover.

Let the beauty you love be what you do.

—RUMI

Contents

You know you have loved someone when
you have glimpsed in them
that which is too beautiful to die.
—GABRIEL MARCEL

An Awakening Flash

First, I want to start with a little story about how I came to write this introduction.

At a lunch with my friends, Paige and Don, we were discussing our current writing projects. They mentioned that they were making good progress on their book, and as always, we entered a discussion that included our various perceptions of the writing process and the work itself.

Their book's title, *Grabbing Lightning*, and the transformative experience it reflects, is deeply familiar to me, both from personal experience and from my days studying with Thomas Merton. When I started to share my insights about it, they asked me to pause a moment and if it would be okay to record what I was saying.

Then at another lunch quite recently, they reminded me of this and asked if they could read me what I'd said. Upon hearing it, I suggested it would make a nice intro to the book, if they wanted.

Thus, here it is.

The ego lives within a certain range of experiencing itself in daily life as it passes through time.

Above this layer of consciousness lies that which transcends the ego and all that the ego can attain: the realm of the Divine, the realm of the Infinite, the realm of Mystery, whatever name you would give the realm of transcendence.

Beneath that ego layer is the realm of the body, the realm of primordial concreteness that gives body to the ego.

The ego, then, in its tendency to be so identified with the middle layer in which it lives, is estranged from experiential awareness of all that is above it and all that is beneath it.

Then in certain moments of awakening, and in the many ways this can happen, a flash of lightning strikes from the realm above the ego right down through the middle of the person's mind, the middle of their body, the middle of their life, reaching all the way down to the ground. In this way, the ego consciousness is intersected by that flash of lightning.

In the aftermath of that flash, the person is left in a transformed state—a state that relevantizes them or awakens them to what was previously an absolute quality of their ego consciousness. That is, they are transected or transversed by what is above and beneath, but not just in that fleeting moment. Now they have become aware that they are habitually transversed in that way.

Some examples of this . . .

I would first mention Thomas Merton in his "New Seeds of Contemplation." The metaphor he uses is, "For the world and time are the dance of the Lord in emptiness. The silence of the spheres is the music of a wedding feast." And then he says, "We do not have to go very far to catch echoes of that game, and of that dancing. When we are alone on a starlit night, when by chance we see the migrating birds in autumn descending on a grove of junipers to rest and eat; when we see children in a moment when they are really children, when we know love in our own hearts; or when, like the Japanese poet, Basho, we hear an old frog land in a quiet pond with a solitary splash."

When Merton says: "the world and time are the dance of the Lord in emptiness," he is poetically saying that the divinity of the intimate immediacy of what is—that is, all of reality— is the generosity of God. So in this sense, the incarnate intimacy of God in the unfolding layers of love is the unfolding revelation of God's loving presence for us in life and through each other.

In this kind of relationship you can help each other transform within the dynamics of the relationship itself. Instead of reinforcing each other's amnesia or contributing to each other's forgetfulness, you can see that you have chosen the person in whose presence you are helping to habituate each other in this transformed state. And in this awareness, there is a new gratitude and dimension for the relationship.

Later, when I thought more about this introduction, I thought: *No one actually grabs lightning.* Yet in this metaphor, when lightning strikes, it kind of does a number on you through and through, and you can walk away learning to take in what happened and see what's been given to you. Then by calibrating your heart to a finer scale, you see that the lightning was striking at every moment in subtle, subtle ways, and that every little renewed awareness is another lightning strike—like an electric current that keeps the heart open.

So when that clarity strikes, you say to yourself: *Oh my God. What's it asking of me? Now that I see it, I can't put the cat back in the bag again. But I can't just magically walk away either.* This puts you in a very painful place, the price we pay for being conscious. But the price we pay for *not* being conscious is much greater. Trust me I know because I've lived that way. But what's the art-form of listening to the lightning strike? Like AA, do the next indicated thing. If you just do the next indicated thing, you move out of the darkness into the light, away from the darkness you created.

I've known Don and Paige for decades, and this lightning-transected reality is the day-to-day living of their relationship. The journey being told in this book is the journey of creating the conditions in which this lighting strike occurs again and again.

James Finley, PhD, author, and psychotherapist, was a Trappist monk
at the cloistered Abbey of Gethsemani in Kentucky,
where Thomas Merton, world-renowned mystic, was his spiritual director.
Dr. Finley is the author of *Merton's Palace of Nowhere*,
The Contemplative Heart, and other inspiriting volumes, and is
one of three core faculty at The Living School for
Action and Contemplation founded by Richard Rohr, OFM.
Jim lives with his wife Maureen in Los Angeles.

All journeys have secret destinations of which
the traveler is unaware.

—MARTIN BUBER

chapter one

Into the Storm

I can't think of many weeks that were worse than this one.

It was winter 1982, the year that El Niño became a household name in California. Thirty-six hours earlier I'd watched the weatherman forecast a train of storms raging toward Los Angeles from Hawaii. Rain, industrial-strength winds, floods. The most severe to hit LA in decades. I felt a sharp jab of fear. My house was on a hillside.

Several days into the growing fury, a loud crash startled me out of bed. I hurried to the front window and found that a large limb of a Eucalyptus tree had fallen against my carport. Then another loud crash, this one a bit remote.

I paced each room looking for the source but found none. *What the hell's going on?* I turned on the local news. Wind and rain were pounding so hard on my skylights I could barely hear the broadcast. But the images were enough. Entire houses had slid off their foundations into the streets. Dozens of cars parked along Laurel Canyon had been lifted by the torrential runoff and, like riding an amusement park waterslide, were swept all the way down to Hollywood Boulevard. I felt like I was in the cyclone scene from *The Wizard of Oz*.

For once, an LA storm warning had not been exaggerated.

I put on my slicker and boots and stood in the carport away from the fallen branches and flowing water. A rare streak of lightning briefly illuminated the ghostly shapes in my surroundings. I grabbed my flashlight and directed it toward the vine-covered slopes above me. A huge blob of mud and debris was edging over a small retaining wall—like a giant beer belly creeping slowly and inexorably down toward my house.

I made my way to the edge of the property and my heart sank. An earthen berm along the fire road that crossed my driveway had dissolved into a river of molten mud cascading toward the house just below mine. *I could be sued!* I tried to put that thought out of my head. Until the storms let up, there was nothing I could do about it.

Back under the protection of my carport, I took off my boots, draped my slicker over the hood of my car, and went back inside.

SHORTLY AFTER DAWN, THE downpour lightened to a drizzle. I put on my rain gear and walked out to the backyard, bracing myself for what I'd find. A waterlogged piece of the hillside beneath the far end of the pool had given way, sending huge clumps of mud and branches into the street below. This was bad. But there was still nothing I could do.

Midmorning the flat roof on my house succumbed in several sections, and streamlets of water dripped steadily onto the bedroom and living room carpets. I ran around placing pots and buckets to catch the flow. *Drip, drip, drip.* What was next? Nothing would surprise me. For months it seemed that some powerful force was pushing me out of my house. Was this series of storms the final blow? Even if not, the destruction around me was an apt metaphor for my life at that point.

It hadn't always been this way.

IT WASN'T THAT long ago that I walked away from my job as VP, Creative Director for Leo Burnett, Chicago. Burnett was one of the largest ad agencies in the world, and most of my clients were Fortune 500 multinationals. The money was correspondingly lush, but

I'd developed conflicts about the work. I was making ads for Kellogg's presweetened cereals that I wouldn't let my own kids eat, and working on cigarette campaigns for Phillip Morris while trying to stop smoking.

Finally, my better angels prevailed.

I needed to find something more meaningful and responded to a growing pull toward Los Angeles. I told Burnett's Chairman that I was burning out and wanted to produce commercials in our LA office, and for some reason he agreed. I moved out here as an agency producer—a less prestigious, less well-paying job. But it was perfect. I'd have time and mind-space to decide my next steps.

The move from Chicago, I should add, also helped me recover from a failed marriage and protracted divorce.

A COUPLE OF YEARS later, the call came. Either come back to my old position in Chicago or leave Burnett. That's when I walked away from advertising and focused all my attention on screenwriting.

My agent at William Morris circulated several of my scripts around the studios. Feedback, when it finally came in, was always good. But it was never good enough and I hated that my livelihood, my future, was in someone else's hands.

But then I got an excited message from my agent on a Friday afternoon, making it a day I'll never forget. Film director Ridley Scott wanted to option one of my screenplays and had taken it to London to read again over the weekend.

By Monday he'd changed his mind. Another day I'll never forget.

Frustrated and disappointed, I finally had to admit it. Four years of effort, trying to translate my advertising successes into success in film, had come to nothing.

Fortunately, I had a few good contacts in the industry. One led to a stint at Disney and another to a position at Fox, both in production and marketing. Neither was satisfying, and neither fulfilled my purpose for coming to Los Angeles. I declined several other lucrative offers and instead took less money to work with a startup, a multimedia entertainment company.

They called themselves Quantum Leap, and the draw for me was their mission: to produce "conscious films." The opportunity came at a time when I really needed something that felt meaningful, and from what I could tell, their plan combined all the elements I'd been trying to put together.

I was beyond excited. And hopeful.

Just months after I joined them, this well-intentioned, values-driven firm filed for bankruptcy—a blow that made me feel like an airplane that had just crashed into a California mountainside.

The emotional wreckage was profound. With no job, no creative projects, and zero prospects for income, I spent days at my house agonizing over what to do. My nest egg from Chicago was almost gone, yet I had no desire to take writing projects that meant nothing to me, and the thought of going back into an ad agency soured my stomach.

But, I *could* sell my home to finance a fresh start.

In the end, that's what I did. I chose to untether myself from my house, my sanctuary for so many pivotal years, and move into a tiny apartment with a woman I loved but had virtually just met.

SO, THERE I WAS, in my mid-forties, standing in the living room watching rainwater drip into pots and pans. The world around me was turning to mud, and I was powerless to stop it.

But there was a twist.

I'd never been happier. Never more hopeful. Never more filled with love—for everyone and everything that crossed my path.

The problem was I just couldn't tell anyone *why*.

chapter two

The Move

Gears crunched as the moving van chugged up my steep driveway toward the street. A belch of exhaust stung my nose and throat. From the patio, I watched it make the sharp right turn and start down the mountain. Far below, the City of Angels was still emerging from its morning ocean fog. Everything I owned was in that small van.

Back inside my soon-to-be-someone-else's dream house, I checked each room to see if the movers had missed anything. From the closet in the study I retrieved several books, all of which had influenced the early years of my journey. I walked them to the front door and started a pile. Next I found a reel of commercials from my advertising days sitting among several unproduced screenplays. They were all still dear to me so onto the pile they went.

Glancing down the hall toward the living room, I returned to the day I decided to buy this place. I'd just arrived in California and this "glass house" was a gift to myself, my refuge from a career turned toxic and a marriage that felt the same.

Now, in my last moments there, I was flooded with that same satisfied glow of discovery—my first encounter with the mountain air, fragrant with orange and lemon blossoms, and the stately pines and eucalyptus that perfectly framed the 1940s Richard Neutra–style architecture. The raw beauty of the place nearly knocked me over, and it seemed like forever before my legs would take me across the pebbled stone hallway into the sunken living room.

Walls of glass floated on all sides. Light flooded in from a dozen windows, dappling the floor with moving shadows. Whichever direction I turned I was rewarded with a view of the mountains. And in the yard, barely ten feet beyond the windows, the quiet surface of the swimming pool perfectly mirrored the slow-moving clouds above.

Three garden-like acres in the Hollywood Hills with a house of glass and a lapis-lazuli blue sky. I never imagined I'd own something so beautiful.

THE PHONE STARTLED ME out of my nostalgia. I hoped it was Ellen.

"How's it going?" she purred. "Have the movers finished?"

"Yeah, they left a few minutes ago."

"Painful?"

"Sure. But I'm good."

"Good?"

"Hard to explain," I said, gazing out over the pool.

She was quiet a moment. "So, you're heading to my apartment now?"

"Not quite yet." I paced the room slowly, imagining the next owner walking these floors after me. "The movers are stopping for sandwiches and said I had some time before they start unpacking."

"So you're really okay?"

"Yeah, I am. Though I think I'll feel even better when I'm settled into your place."

"Me, too! Hey, I moved some furniture to make a little extra room. It'll be . . . cozy."

"Cozy's good."

"Oops," she whispered, responding to the chime in the background. "Gotta new patient."

"Go ahead. I'll see you soon."

"I love you."

"Love you, too."

I'D MET ELLEN A few months earlier. It was my first acupuncture appointment. The moment she entered the waiting room, our eyes locked and a kinetic surge erupted between us. And just like that, the doors of my heart, closed since my divorce, flew open.

She felt it too.

A friend had recommended her as a talented practitioner, and the thought of getting help from someone steeped in ancient Taoist medicine appealed to my spiritual aesthetic.

She listened intently to my reasons for being there, then to the pulses in my wrists. The needles were more uncomfortable than I'd been led to believe, but it felt like something good was happening. During that first session, perhaps to distract me from my obvious discomfort, she mentioned that she meditated regularly and often attended weekend retreats. *Yep*, I thought. *This could be interesting.*

My fourth appointment with Ellen was my last. We wanted to start dating. Within months our lives had melted together seamlessly, and I began to feel that I'd met a woman, perhaps an angel, with whom I could rebuild my life.

Getting to know each other was, in some ways, like catching up with an old friend. I told her about my advertising career and why I'd moved to LA, and about the many disappointments that followed, including the disaster at Quantum Leap. We even discussed the possibility of my needing to sell the house.

I RETRIEVED THE STACKS of memories waiting for me in the front hallway, arranged them neatly in a couple bankers boxes, and took them out to my car. Then standing again at the entrance to the house, I took a long look at the emptiness and locked the front door for the last time.

Next I walked over to the spot near the driveway where my faithful German shepherd, Stray, had for all those years waited for me to come home. This same spot was now home to his ashes. I rested my palm on the slight depression in the earth and bid him a silent goodbye. I could almost feel his heartbeat in my hand.

It was then I remembered the living treasure that had been with me almost as long as Stray. I walked around the side of the house to the pool where my bougainvillea bonsai sat in the spotted sunlight. It had somehow survived the storm and was still in full bloom with its odd combination of pink and orange blossoms. I picked her up, cradled her to my chest, and we walked back to the car together.

Driving away I realized that of all my remaining possessions, this delicate bonsai was the one I cherished most.

chapter three

Down to the Flats

A parking space opened up directly opposite Ellen's apartment, a rare event that I took as a positive sign. Her building was in an area known as "the flats," a half block from Sunset Boulevard near the famous Schwab's drugstore where film star Lana Turner was supposedly discovered.

With my bonsai in hand, I waited for a break in the almost-incessant flow of traffic and made my way across the street to where the movers were parked. Most of my furniture was staying on the truck, heading for storage. The bulk of my clothes had already gone to Goodwill, including a tux and several three-piece suits, all remnants of my life in Chicago.

Joining me in my new life were some jeans and shirts, a sport coat, and a couple sweaters. My Queen Anne–style desk was already on the sidewalk, along with my two Edward Curtis photographs and a tall, narrow dresser that I hoped would fit somewhere. As I approached the movers, one of them absently handed my IBM Selectric typewriter to his partner who almost dropped it.

"Hey, that's vintage!" I howled. "Have some respect!"

A few people strolled by and gawked at my belongings as if shopping a garage sale. I felt exposed. Nude. The bare remnants of my life were piling up like bones on the pavement, and I couldn't wait for the public part of this to end. I led the movers upstairs and opened the door to Ellen's bright, sunlit apartment. The space had a single bedroom and was spacious enough, though after years of living in my sprawling home on three acres it was as Ellen said, cozy.

"What about this?" asked the guy carrying a wardrobe box toward the bedroom.

"No, right here," I said, pointing to the entryway closet.

A quizzical look creased his face.

"Not in the bedroom?"

"Her closet's full, but there should be room in here."

He shrugged, and I stepped aside so he could set the box where it belonged. While he went downstairs for another load, I carried the bonsai to the bank of French windows at the end of the living room and positioned it carefully on the sill. The windows were generous, but the foreground view was of tarred roofs and air conditioners. In the distance, however, the cluster of downtown LA high-rises was impressive.

I looked into the entryway closet and found Ellen's coats pushed to the far end of the bar, just as one might do for a weekend guest. One by one, I pulled my clothes from the wardrobe box and hung them neatly in their new space. A moment later the chief mover was at the door carrying a chair and lamp.

"Nice place," he said as I squeezed aside to let him in.

"But not quite a house on a mountain top, is it?" I was trying to hide my lingering sadness but was sure I hadn't.

"I move 'em both ways in this town."

Great answer, I thought. At least it made me feel a bit better.

chapter four

Dinner

The choice to let my house go and move in with Ellen was a huge step in our relationship. To celebrate our first night living together, I made reservations at a French restaurant near the heart of Old Hollywood. I'd lunched there many times with studio execs and friends in the industry. It was also where I took Ellen on our first date and she'd loved it.

The maître d' greeted me by name and nodded graciously at Ellen. With menus tucked under his arm, he led us down the stone staircase into a vaulted room that always reminded me of a Parisian café. Rococo paintings covered the restaurant's rough-plastered walls, and a myriad of candles flickering on small, intimate tables turned the room into a romantic hideaway.

Across from me Ellen was radiant. Her skin was deeply tanned and her dark eyes reflected the bouncing fire of candlelight. The space between us was as full of promise as the day our eyes first met in the waiting room, and the depth of possibility took my breath away. We were a couple in love.

Over the next hour we flirted, laughed, gossiped, spoke fondly of friends, and imagined vacations together. We talked about her use of Chinese herbs in her practice, how busy she was, and whether she should move her office to a better location. After dinner, the check arrived with an unexpected tray of tiny chocolates.

"My treat," she smiled, reaching for her purse.

"Hey, I'm not in that much trouble." I laughed and slipped my credit card into the folio. Then I noticed her looking at me as if mulling over whether to say something.

"Go ahead," I said, leaning forward. "What's up?"

"You can read me that well?"

"Enough to know there's something on your mind."

"I don't know . . . we spent most of the dinner talking about me and my work." She hesitated for a long beat. "And I want to hear about *you*. You just sold your house. That's big stuff. Have you thought more about what you want to do next?"

"No new revelations yet, but I'm happy we're together." I reached across the table and took her hand into mine. "I'm pretty content about everything right now."

"You've said that. But what do you want to do next?"

"Well, right now I want to digest all that's happened. It's been quite a year, as you know, so it makes sense to take a beat before deciding anything."

"What about the company you started? And doing some consulting?"

"Yeah, it just feels a little early to push on that. Besides I'm looking forward to having time to write."

Her eyes flashed concern.

"Don't worry. I'll get something going."

"Of course you will, but I'm just curious what you think that might be?"

I shifted uncomfortably in my chair. I didn't want to go into all this. Not here. Not now. But her questions were reasonable.

"That's a tricky one," I said. "Yes, a little consulting, if something shows up. But to be honest with you, and with myself, I feel I need to stop and get my bearings. I've got money from the house and . . . I've been thinking about maybe writing a book."

She pulled her hand away and started playing with a rose petal that had fallen from the single flower in the vase.

"Since we're being honest, I'll admit . . . the reality of you losing your house . . . it really hit me today."

"Tell me about it!" I joked, still raw from the move.

She didn't smile. "I mean . . . when we met, you had this big career in advertising behind you, a fabulous house in the hills. You'd worked in the film business. And, well, I thought I'd finally met a grownup."

Ouch! I sat back in my chair.

"Wait, no, I'm so sorry. I didn't mean that the way it sounded." The edge in her voice had given way to her usual gentleness. "Look, this is probably more about me than you, but today it sank in that you were *forced* to give up your house. And that made me wonder if—"

"If I might not be the guy you thought I was?" I interrupted sharply.

"No," she whispered. "It's just that this situation is familiar. It's a lot like the man I fell in love with when I was just starting my practice. He was a bit older and well-to-do, but right after we got married he started having a few business problems." She made quote signs with her fingers as she said the word "few."

"Then he had a total career meltdown and lost everything. *We* lost everything."

Tears welled up in her eyes as she poured out how much she'd loved this guy and how sure they were that things would turn around. But years passed and they went through all the money they'd both saved. Their divorce was amicable, but the experience left a deep mark. She'd shared pieces of this story before but never the whole thing. Now, sitting in the dim light of this romantic restaurant, it hurt to hear it—for her sake and mine.

"So that's where my head was," she continued. "You had *such* a great career! And you're so employable. Why not take advantage of that now?

I appreciated her faith in me but was growing weary from her probing.

"Look, I haven't lost my ambition," I said, trying to reassure her. "And keep in mind, there's decent money from the house, and I still own those two acres in the Hollywood Hills. So there really *is* enough money for me to take time for myself."

She shook her head. "You seem so relaxed about it, and I don't know . . . almost passive."

We stared at each other across the table. I felt myself falling into an emotional hole.

"I hope you understand," she shifted back to a softer tone. "I love you, and you have so much talent. And so many contacts right now. Why wait?"

"Okay, time out! This is our first night. There'll be plenty of time to talk about this." I hastily signed the receipt. "Why don't we head home? It'll be more comfortable there."

"You're right," she said, standing up and grabbing her purse. "I shouldn't have brought it up."

We climbed the restaurant stairs in silence and drove home in silence. When we entered the apartment, by some unspoken agreement, neither of us turned on the lights. There would be no cork popping tonight.

Ellen retreated to the bedroom, and I went to the entryway closet. *God, I miss my house!* I had no room to go to and no place to pout.

But maybe this is good. Maybe it's time to tell her everything.

"Coming to bed?" she asked in a half-seductive, half-deflated voice.

"It's still early. Can we talk a little more?"

She perked up. "Talking's good."

chapter five

Full Disclosure

I followed Ellen into the bedroom. She settled herself against the headboard and fussed with the pillows to get comfortable. I sat on the edge of the bed, turning toward her.

"Okay," I started. "I know you're upset that I'm not looking for work and that I'm being . . . what'd you call it? 'Passive.'"

She winced. Her empathy was a welcome gesture.

"Well, I want to tell you why I seem so content and what's behind my wanting to take some time before I dive into something."

"Okay . . ."

"So, we've talked about what happened at Quantum Leap, and you know I took that job because I was beyond fed up with the entertainment business. My work at Disney and Fox and other projects all left me feeling hollowed out. And empty. When Quantum Leap came along I resigned from Fox, thinking I finally had a shot at doing something that meant something to me. I was so optimistic. We all were. Anyway, you know what happened there. That loss put me into a very, very dark place—in a hole I couldn't get myself out of."

"Yeah, you told me a bit about that. Sounds awful."

"Well, there was this one day shortly after we closed Quantum Leap. I was out by the pool with Stray, you know the spot, near where I kept my little bonsai? Anyway, I'd been feeling utterly depressed, like I'd come to the end of the road in myself. But sitting there with him, I finally found a moment of peace and thought I could savor it if I meditated."

I paused. She was watching me closely.

"So, I'm sitting there by the pool, eyes closed, trying to relax when, in a heartbeat, the ground beneath me opens up and sends me falling downward into total darkness. Not darkness exactly, more like . . . how can I describe it? Like light that was black. I kept falling and falling and thought maybe this is how death works. You're here, and then you're not here. Then all of a sudden, I was at the bottom of the darkness, landing gently in what seemed like a sunlit field of flowers."

Ellen arched her brows enough to look dubious.

"Let me go on," I whispered.

"Of course."

"It was as if I'd dropped into a place that was . . . it's hard to find words, but it was like the clear light of absolute goodness. Boundless love. Not the romantic kind," I added, squeezing her hand. "It was like I was existing in a state of extraordinary love—pure love. All fears and concerns were gone. Nothing but love existed."

Ellen nodded at this. "Like a near-death experience?"

"It was definitely an out-of-body thing," I smiled. "But rather than a near-death experience, it was more like a near-*life* experience—seeing life as it truly is.

"Then just like that, the experience changed and scenes from my past started appearing. This part was sort of a life review, where I was *in* each scene but also watching myself from the outside."

I paused to adjust my position.

"Over and over, I was being shown how fear had influenced my choices. In the first scene, I was maybe two years old, having emergency appendix surgery, and feeling terrified. The next scene was me trembling when my mom told me that my grandfather had died. Then there was being frightened to spend a night away from my parents. Then the fear of being teased yet again by the kids at school, and by my brother, for stuttering. And my fear of not being popular, of not fitting in. Fear of getting a failing grade. Fear of disappointing the nuns. Fear of going to hell and losing my soul. Somewhere in all that, I started to see just how large a factor fear was in my life."

Ellen's expression was noncommittal but I didn't want to stop to ask what she was thinking.

"And the scenes kept rolling in, chronologically, frame-by-frame: Scene 14: Fear of not finding a career. Scene 15: Fear of not being successful. Scene 16: Fear of *being* successful. Like that, on and on, nonstop: Fear of speaking up, fear of being silent, fear of not making a mark on the world . . . and of course, fear of not making enough money, fear of losing money, fear of not making it in advertising . . . fear of loving, fear of not loving, fear of not being loved . . . fear of losing my house. Then there were fears about the future. Fear of ending up alone and being poor . . ."

Ellen's dark eyes were fixed on me, now shining with what seemed like genuine compassion. A wave of relief ran through my body.

"Was there speaking in any of this?" she asked. "Like hearing a voice?"

"No, not really. I was just *in* this parade of experiences. The meaning was clear. I was enveloped by love, and all those fears— from the nightmare of Quantum Leap all the way back to my early childhood—didn't exist anymore. Fear had lost its foundation."

I moved off the bed, stretched my neck, and started pacing.

"So, with all that, it was impossible to ignore how much I'd built my life from fear. Yet, fear wasn't the biggest thing, though it's sure easier to describe than boundless love. What really got me was *feeling* that we all exist in a universe of love all the time. That there's nothing but love. And that no matter how bad my problems got, my fears were like clouds temporarily hiding the sun."

Standing near Ellen, I realized how intense I'd gotten. And talk about fear . . . I was now afraid of sounding like a lunatic! I took a deep breath and a measured exhale, then sat back down on the edge of the bed.

"From then on, everything was different. I was still the same guy, but I was living in this glow. It lasted months. Everywhere I looked there was love. At the supermarket, the post office, even with the cars driving crazily in traffic. It was so obvious that love is every-where. It isn't just *in* each human heart. It's the very soul of the world." I paused briefly and looked at her. "The intensity of all that passed, but the truth of it stayed with me. And I knew I needed to start making choices a different way."

Ellen reached out and touched my hand. "Why didn't you tell me about this before?"

"Well, full disclosure can be scary. I was afraid that you, or any-body, would think I was crazy to see this as anything more than a fleeting experience. So I told virtually no one. It happened just be-fore we met, and all I knew at the time was that my life would change, and definitely my work. The problem was, and still is, that I don't exactly know how to do that. That's why I need to take a beat."

Her eyes revealed empathy, but then she shook her head. "It sounds wonderful. Beautiful. But I don't see what it has to do with you looking for work now or not?"

My head fell onto my chest. She wasn't getting it. Or if she was, she wasn't liking it.

"What I mean is . . ." Ellen continued, "why would you take a mystical experience, even a big one like that, and try to apply it to your career choices, or making money? I don't get that."

"Okay," I said, modulating my voice to hide my disappointment. "I'm not sure I can even explain it, but *that* it happened to me, and when it happened, I have to think there's a reason."

I got up and started pacing again.

"But forget that experience for a minute. Even before that, I knew I couldn't go back to advertising, or any corporate job. Even to save the house. The good part now is that I have time to find the *right* thing rather than grabbing at whatever."

Ellen flashed a frown but then patted my side of the bed, inviting me back. I settled in next to her, glad for the support of the pillows and headboard.

"I can see how important this is to you," she said after a long silence. "But I still don't know what it gets you. I mean, love is great and all that, but we still live on planet Earth. We still have to work to put food in our mouths and a roof over our heads. I mean, you've got all these world-class advertising skills. You're *so* hirable right now and could do so well. Isn't that what it takes for a happy life?"

My heart sank.

"I'm sorry," I said. "I just can't do the corporate thing again. I've got to find something I can connect with. Some kind of work that meshes with my sense of life now, not that runs counter to it."

"But where does that leave you?"

"I don't know yet. That's the point. I need time to figure it out."

We sat in silence staring at the wall. This turn in our discussion had scared us both. There it was again. Fear. An undertone of deadlock, or perhaps even of a dead end, had stolen our closeness. Then something changed.

"So you really trust this . . . thing?" she asked.

"Totally."

"And you're willing to gamble your future on it?"

"I am."

"Then I'll support whatever you decide to do." She was trying hard to smile.

"Does all this make a difference," I had to ask, "in whether you would have wanted me to move in with you?"

At that she beamed. "No. I'm here for you under any condition. I love you, remember?"

We talked a bit longer in that bland way you do after an intense conversation that's left you drained. Ellen had to get up early, so I encouraged her to go to sleep and said I'd join her soon. I was surprisingly wired and wanted to decompress. We kissed and hugged, and she crawled under the covers.

IN THE LIVING ROOM, I turned the rocking chair so it faced the windows and sat down heavily. The lights from downtown LA blinked in the distance, and my bougainvillea sat peacefully on the window sill, its pink and orange blossoms aglow from a nearby streetlamp.

I'd thought Ellen and I were more in sync. Thankfully there was zero hesitation in her wanting to be with me. We really did love each other, and love meant more than anything.

Our conversation kept rolling around in my head, and I realized that I had many of the same doubts Ellen had. Maybe it wasn't possible to build a life, a career, on something so otherworldly. Especially when I had no clue how to ground transcendent love in the practical world of work. Still, I believed that experience held some secret about how to do that.

REFLECTION

the epiphany

At first, that experience by the pool confused me. But I soon
recognized it as a full-on epiphany that was pointing me toward a
complete life reset. In fact, the life I'm living now began that day when
the intimate experience of love and fear replaced all my beliefs about
how life worked. Life and love had always occupied separate worlds.
Now they didn't.

At the time I had no spiritual, religious, or philosophical
context for what happened to me, no mystic's appreciation of its
significance, and no way to know how to respond. My heart was
clear, but my mind was unprepared.

As the weeks passed, my feelings fluctuated. One minute I'd be
immersed again in pure love, feeling its living presence in my
chest. The next I'd be hit by torturous uncertainty.

Fear would have me take almost any job to save my ego's sense
of who I was, while love kept inviting me to be more reflective,
more trusting. In a most visceral way, I was in a struggle for
personal mastery, and love wanted me to create the next stage of
my life by privileging love.

So did I.

As the journey was unfolding, my fears still had their power
and the path was not without its pain. And it definitely wasn't
straightforward. But love was having its way.

Clearest of all, I now knew my prime directive: When it came to
making choices, I'd do my best to trust the primacy of love and keep
fear from having a deciding vote.

chapter six

Jennifer

I entered Michel Richard's famed boulangerie a couple minutes late and found Jennifer already well ensconced at a back table, nibbling on toast. She was a dear friend and respected therapist to several acquaintances in the film industry, and sometimes a mentor to me.

"You're a little late," she laughed as we hugged. "I'm tight on time today, but how are you?"

"Terrific. Still adjusting to traffic patterns from my new abode. You look great, by the way."

"Thanks! You know I try." She mocked a giggle.

Jennifer's dark, curly hair had a luster that highlighted an innocence in her face. She was tall and attractive, in her late 30s, slender, and always well dressed but not trendy. We periodically met for breakfast, although she barely ate and was often in a hurry to get back for a patient.

"So, my friend," she looked at me over her glasses. "I assume you're all moved in by now?"

"Pretty much."

"And . . . ?"

"Well, we jog most mornings before Ellen goes to the office, so I'm tightening my buns and getting muscle cramps. Otherwise, we're okay."

"Just okay?"

Jennifer had a therapist's habit of shifting into inquiry mode when she sensed something was up. It was off-putting at first but not anymore.

"We're good, we're good. It's just that the neighborhood's noisy and the space is a little tight, especially compared to . . . well, you know. But I'm learning to relax into it."

Jennifer was the friend who'd referred me to Ellen for acupuncture, but their relationship cooled when Ellen and I started dating. Jennifer deemed our romance unethical even though I stopped being a patient beforehand.

Jennifer and I were introduced at a studio party and hit it off immediately. I was especially intrigued by her metaphysical interests and insights. She was the most awake person I knew and we easily spoke about our inner lives. The two of us also shared a common background. We'd both grown up in rural parts of the country and we both hoped to one day return to a slower life.

THE WAITER BROUGHT COFFEE, a warmup for Jennifer, fresh for me, and I ordered a croissant. It'd been several weeks, but I was anxious to tell Jennifer about Ellen's reaction to my epiphany experience.

"Well, I'm glad you finally told her."

"Me too, but it kind of upset her. Especially the part about taking some time before I focus on work again. She also didn't get the connection between that experience and how I make a living."

Jennifer frowned. "Really? Seems so straightforward. Although, I *can* see why it bothered her. Everyone wants to feel secure, and being with someone who's not working is scary. That said, it's important that you integrate the full scope of what's been happening to you *before* you can identify a situation that fits your new sense of things."

"Exactly. I knew you'd understand."

"Then of course," Jennifer continued as the waiter delivered my

croissant, "there's another possibility. Maybe Ellen's doing you a favor by wanting you to get a job right away. Maybe that's the universe
pushing you to do something sooner than you'd planned. Why, I
don't know, but . . ."

"I'm not sure I like where you're going with this," I chuckled,
"but I'll listen."

Some of Jennifer's perceptions made sense. But some didn't. Or
maybe I wasn't ready to hear them.

We refused the waiter's offer for more coffee, and Jennifer
checked her watch. "I'm sooo sorry, I want to talk more, but—"

"Real quick," I interrupted, not wanting to end on this disquiet-
ing note. "Anything new with you?"

"Just Aunt Julie." Jennifer stood up and grabbed her purse. "She
fell again and I'm clearing my schedule to go back to Wisconsin, I
hope for just a few weeks. I'm trying to move some patients to phone
sessions and referring others out."

"Sorry to hear, but I envy you spending time in the country."

"Yeah, that's the good part. Hey, if I stay longer, maybe you can
visit? You know you'd love it there. It's so . . ." She said no more but
her gaze lingered.

We hugged goodbye and held each other tighter than usual. I
didn't like the feeling that she might be slipping out of my life.

chapter seven

Rude Awakening

A few days later I was sitting in the small waiting area outside my accountant's office. He'd summoned me to review my situation after the sale of the house. My anxiety was high, and with no magazines to pass the time, I again studied the array of laminated plaques that covered the walls, each one featuring Milt's full name in bold letters.

When I finally entered his office, the first thing I noticed was that the bookkeeper was almost hidden behind a stack of papers. It felt like an ominous sign.

The receptionist brought in a mug of black coffee and set it down in front of me.

"O-k-a-y then." Milt stretched his arms out to either side as if preparing for a mighty task. "The good news, my friend, is that you got a very hefty price for your house. You bought wisely and this gonzo real estate boom has helped considerably."

We all looked at each other with approving smiles.

"Escrow should've covered all the expenses from the house, but let's see, let's see . . ." He glanced through the papers the bookkeeper kept giving him. "Yes, we're good. The balance on the mortgage, the realtor's commissions, property taxes, some small penalties, but yes, you're good."

Milt then handed me a single sheet, an itemized accounting of

expenses and payments. The zero on the "Total due" line was comforting. "We also finalized our fees," he added, this time handing me
an invoice on his letterhead. "including time spent paying your bills
these last few months when you felt . . . you couldn't."

I stared at it a moment, reminded of how distracted and overwhelmed I'd been in the months prior to the house selling. Their
bill wasn't as bad as I expected. I thanked them both and braced myself for whatever would come next.

Milt's face was usually pretty expressionless, but for a moment it
showed compassion. Or was it pity, presumably for a client who'd
been having a meltdown?

Milt nodded to the bookkeeper who then gathered a few folders
and left.

"So," he said, back to his matter-of-fact self, "the only loose end
is the profit on the house. Unless you intend to buy again within a
year?"

"I don't see myself doing that."

"That's what I assumed, so I ran an estimate of what you'll owe
Uncle Sam. Since you're still in a—let's call it a career transition and
not earning much—there'll be little or no income taxes. Just the capital gains, but you should set that money aside right away. The due
dates are coming up."

The rest of the meeting was brief. He slid a stack of papers toward me, a messy array of bills all marked as paid. Then came a set
of documents with red tags telling me where to sign, followed by
another set marked "client copy."

Finally, Milt pulled a single sheet from the printer and held it
out for me to take. It was another detailed list of figures. My eyes
shot down to the bottom of the page. The net amount made my
blood freeze. It was far worse than anything I'd imagined.

Without a word, Milt took the stack of papers that had gathered
between us—except the current invoice—and slipped them into a
large manila envelope. "Keep these with your tax records."

We both stood up and I thanked him again for his help, especially over the last few months. He responded with a deference that smacked more of politeness than genuine care. I was never happier to leave a meeting.

Only after I was outside in the fresh air did it hit me. *If I wasn't careful, I'd be broke in a year or two.* It made me so sick to my stomach, I thought I was going to throw up.

As I drove away, Jennifer's comment came back to mind. She'd suggested that Ellen's pushing me to find work might be a good thing. As it turns out, she was right. They were both right. I didn't have a choice.

chapter eight

A Path Opens

T he following morning I was a wreck. *Trouble, trouble, trouble* throbbed in my head as I paced the length of Ellen's living room, making U-turns in the kitchen. My whole sense of my new life had been shattered.

Almost worse, I couldn't believe how easily and how completely I'd been thrown off by a single piece of news. How could the last five minutes in an accountant's office obliterate the innermost layer of tranquility that had been with me since that afternoon by the pool?

THE WALLS OF ELLEN'S apartment were closing in on me, so I decided to drive down to the La Brea Tar Pits for a long walk. This city park was built around sinister-looking black ponds of tar that bubbled up from subterranean gasses—apparently once a watering hole and graveyard for thousands of prehistoric animals. Despite the oddness of the place, or maybe because of it, I found it a haven during stressful times.

I parked my car near the museum and started down one of the paths that wound alongside the pools of oozing tar. Life-sized bronze statues of saber-toothed tigers, huge sloths, and other ancient giants lined the walkway and peppered the landscape.

As I approached the large-tusked bull mastodon standing belly deep in tar, I recognized his anguish like never before. This poor creature, frozen in timeless ooze, mirrored the mire of my own frustrated mind. Like him I was stuck in the fear of impending disaster.

As I continued my walk, it dawned on me that while I was frightened, I wasn't stuck. I had options. Several of them, in fact.

Recently, over a salad at the Fox commissary, a studio exec had offered me a job as second-in-command of domestic and international film marketing. Another opportunity was with a friend from Chicago. He ran a large family foundation and had asked me to oversee their interests on the West Coast. Then there was advertising. I cringed at the thought, but all I had to do was say the word and I could partner up with an old pal who'd just started an agency here in LA. He'd already acquired a hefty motorcycle account and wanted my help pitching an international hotel chain.

When I first moved out here I might have jumped at any one of these opportunities, but at this point, none felt the least bit in sync with who I was. Maybe if I was on the brink of being broke, but I wasn't. It was like I'd told Ellen, I'd bought myself some time—just not as much as I'd thought. I finally had a clean slate and my heart kept urging me to reach for love—something fully in sync with the experience of love I'd encountered in my epiphany.

Each time I thought about *how* to find that or exactly what that might be, I ran into the same dead end. I wanted to live a loving life, and I wanted to make money. Good money. How to go about doing that was the mystery.

I RESUMED MY STROLL through the park and noticed a woman ahead walking a German shepherd, a large, courtly animal that immediately reminded me of Stray.

"May I pet him?" I asked.

She smiled her approval, and I knelt down and looked into the dog's moist eyes. I reached out slowly and he moved his head toward my hand. As I scratched behind his ear and rubbed his back, his tail wagged the same way Stray's had. Gosh, I missed that dog. The simple act of connecting with the beautiful creature who was still swishing his tail in pleasure brought me to a peaceful clarity, almost as if Stray himself was comforting me.

"Thanks, old boy." I tussled his head, stood up, and thanked the kindly woman too. A few paces later, I sat down on a bench, and as I watched them ramble off, I marveled at how quickly that dog had soothed me. It was also the first time my heart felt fully open and receptive since leaving the accountant's office.

I closed my eyes and took a few deep breaths. Then, as if talking to an old, dear friend, I asked whatever forces were looking after me to tell me how to build my life from this state, from how I was feeling right then.

To my surprise, after a few more breaths, an answer came. Actually it was a question. *What do you love?*

What? What kind of question is that? It's so naïve!

I laughed at my inner protestations and decided to go with it anyway.

Okay, so what do I love? What does that even mean? I love a million things, don't I?

This was weird, but I had nothing to lose. I reached into my jacket and pulled out a pen and pad. On the top line I wrote: *What do I love?* The first thing that popped into my mind: ice cream. I said the words aloud as I wrote them down.

I love ice cream.

Really? Where could this possibly lead? I kept going.

I love dogs.

How about fishing?

Sure, I loved to fish. I wrote it down.

And meditating? Definitely.

And people watching.

Oh. And making love.

And walking in the mountains with Stray. Sigh. Bittersweet.

Visits with my daughter.

Driving along Mulholland, gazing at the San Fernando Valley below—on non-smoggy days.

What else do I love? What makes me feel love? The ideas were coming more quickly now, and a few passersby looked at me quizzically, thinking I was talking to them. Most didn't seem to notice. Either way, I didn't care.

How about sitting in the park between the fossil museum and the LA County Museum of Art? That's a good one. I wrote it down.

Also, walking by the ocean.

Skylights. I *love* skylights. When they don't leak.

Wool socks, the kind that don't scratch.

Listening to Willie Nelson. Favorite album: *Red Headed Stranger.*

I wrote furiously. One guy stopped and stared at me as if he'd never heard someone talking to himself in a park before. I smiled at him and he moved on.

I did feel a bit self-conscious composing such a private list in public, but something significant was happening. I felt I was being talked to, guided, so I stayed with it. *How about strolling along upper Madison Avenue in New York City,* I asked myself, *preferably in a light spring drizzle?*

I wrote it down.

What about driving along California's coast, Route 1 to Big Sur?

Now I was getting excited.

And I love driving through the Loire Valley in France.

Burgundy wines, red or white.

Helping others. *Hmm. That's different.*

Having deep conversations with like-minded people.

Gregorian chants. I could listen forever.

I stopped and peered up. A flock of crows were chatting loudly in the trees above me. It was getting late. The last rays of sun were casting long shadows onto the now empty pathway.

The chattering of birds. Late afternoon shadows. I mouthed the words as I wrote them both down.

Writing my book. *Yes! Good one.*

Then came the shocker:

Writing ads.

What? Writing ads?! The thought was there before I could stop it. *How could I love writing ads? I hate advertising!*

That one obviously threw me. *Do I write it down?* I tried to analyze it to make it go away. Was this my fear trying to hijack my "love list?" Maybe. But my inner sensing checked out fine. It felt right. Good even. But how could that be? *Writing advertising copy?*

Then I said it aloud just the way I'd heard it. "Writing ads."

I wrote it on the list.

Had I just committed to sleeping with the enemy?

My mind was still fumbling with this conundrum when, yikes! I was supposed to be back at the apartment by now. Ellen and I were having dinner with friends in an hour and I needed to change clothes. Damn! I hated being pulled out of this flow.

I stuffed my pen and pad into a pocket and hurried back to my car. It was a relatively short drive home, but the whole way there that phrase kept going through my mind: *I love writing ads.*

Crazy.

But there it was, capping off the list.

chapter nine

Riding the Flow

I
t was still pitch black when I awoke into a flood of ideas already swirling in my head. I grabbed my pad and stood in the glow of the bathroom nightlight adding to my love list.

I love getting up early.

I love watching the sun come up over the mountains.

I love feeling the fresh coolness of morning air.

I love meditating just before dawn.

I love writing in the early hours of the day.

Shivering in the chilly bathroom, I was having the best time. *Gosh, I love making this list!* I wrote that down too, grateful that a deeper resource was helping me identify what *really* mattered to me. Not what might matter to others or what had mattered to me at another time, but what was important to me now, in *this* time, in *this* place. The simple act of jotting down these loves was helping me feel aligned with some core place in myself—a place I might not have found otherwise. It was breathtaking.

AN HOUR LATER ELLEN and I went for our usual morning jog. The ideas kept coming but I didn't mention the list to her. I didn't want to rouse false hopes before I knew where, if anywhere, this exercise would lead. I also didn't want her critique. Not yet.

Back at the apartment we showered, dressed, and I made coffee and toast for the two of us. After she left for the office, I settled into the rocking chair facing the windows in the living room. My bonsai seemed to be catching fire in the sunlight. So was I.

I love my bonsai.

I love Ellen's rocking chair.

I wrote for several minutes, then without knowing why, I tucked my pad and pen into my pocket and headed out the door. As if on autopilot, I climbed into my car and was soon driving the 10 Freeway toward the Pacific Ocean. Why was I doing this? Ahh, yes. *I love the ocean.*

The parking lot at the Santa Monica Pier was almost empty, but I wasn't alone. Hundreds of people were already at the beach. Some were sprawled out on towels catching the first warm rays of the sun, but most were active—wading in the surf, playing volleyball, riding bikes or jogging along the ribbon of concrete that paralleled the shoreline. *Doesn't anyone in LA work? And where did they all park?*

I walked down to a less occupied stretch of beach and found a spot for myself on a mound of sand just above the wet line. With the sounds of the sea lapping on the shore—ah! another item for my list —I pulled out my pad and pen and resumed writing.

The sound of waves gently breaking on the sand.

Walking along the water's edge.

What else do I love?

Writing my book. (Things I loved most were showing up more than once.)

Writing screenplays.

Having ideas and writing them down.

Writing in general. *I love writing!*

After a few more entries, I noticed that my seaside inventory was taking a different tack than the day before. For whatever reason, my love list now included ways of being productive, not just physical pleasures.

I love being creative—alone and with others.

I love giving birth to an exciting idea and bringing it to successful completion.

Something else was different too. Something beyond the items on my list. I was more absorbed, almost in some kind of trance yet fully present. All I could think was that I'd moved deeper into conversation with some aspect of myself that was pointing me toward something I needed to know. So I asked again, this time aloud: "What do I love?"

I love painting, drawing, architecture.

I love growing things, making bonsais, mulching plants.

I love reading books, reading screenplays, writing screenplays, writing ads.

Whoa! There it is again—writing ads!

What the . . . ?

I'd thought—hoped—that yesterday was a fluke, an echo of the past. But once again those words volunteered themselves. There they were, on paper: "love" and "writing ads" in the same sentence. These words hadn't appeared together since my earliest days in advertising.

In fact, I wasn't sure I'd ever put them together. But now I'd paired them twice in twenty-four hours.

I got up and paced along the waterline. *No way I'm going back into advertising! No matter who's suggesting it.*

Then it hit me.

Writing ads and working at an ad agency are two different things. One is an individual creative act. The other is a job in someone else's business. One is writing from the heart, or could be. The other is peddling a product. One is a gift from the muse. The other is the conniving of a sales strategy. At least, that's what it had become for me.

It was so obvious. Writing ad copy wasn't bad or good. What mattered was the integrity—or lack thereof—in the product being sold and in the message crafted to sell it. Early in my career, the creative fun was all that mattered. Then came success. I only ran into trouble when it finally dawned on me that I'd gained a nice livelihood but had lost my integrity.

Suddenly it was clear. I didn't *hate* advertising. I was *afraid* of it. Afraid that what had happened to me in that environment would happen to me again.

I walked back to my spot on the sand, wondering how I'd missed this critical distinction before.

When I started at Burnett I was an artist. My job was to make the images for someone else's message, and I didn't have to weigh the virtue of the words—not until I started writing them. In my hunger for success, I'd noticed that the writers had the real power so I went in that direction. I loved writing, and at some point I wasn't just writing the ads but developing entire campaigns.

So my problem wasn't with advertising itself. It was how I had to stretch the truth to be successful—like using my creativity on adorable cartoon characters designed to hook kids on sugar-sweetened cereals or persuading people they'd be happier if they smoked our client's cigarettes. I did give myself a break at one point toward the end of my career there. When asked to lead a General Motors campaign to keep gas-guzzling cars selling during a major oil crisis, I refused, insisting I was too busy.

For two decades, I worked with some of the biggest companies in the world and on some of the most popular consumer brands. I'd even been invited to join the leadership fast-track at Burnett. I was at the zenith of my earning power, but I'd lost contact with myself, my essential self. And I was dying inside.

As I sat there on the beach in Santa Monica, I wondered if this was what a recovering alcoholic felt like. The mere thought of doing anything that even *resembled* advertising petrified me. I was sure I'd lose myself—again.

It was that simple. I'd been saying no to advertising because I was afraid of what it would do to me. More accurately, I was afraid that I would let myself become that guy again.

With that, I saw why "writing ads" had volunteered itself onto my love list. It was an undeniable nudge designed to get me to look more deeply at myself, my motives, and the reality of my situation. I wasn't simply a well-trained writer. I was an experienced creative director, skilled in all aspects of marketing. Even so, the mere thought of going back into an ad agency and working on mega clients made me shudder.

A RENEGADE WAVE CAME rushing in. I raised my feet and rocked back to avoid it, but it got me anyway. Wet now but invigorated, I stood up, brushed off my jeans, and resumed my stroll, sandals in hand. As I walked along the water's edge feeling that half-wet, half-dry squishiness under my toes (another for the list), my mind launched into one of its familiar creative outpourings.

I'd been talking with the owners of a small coffee company in the Ojai Valley, just a couple of hours north of LA. These two earnest young men were selling first-rate organic coffee at decent prices and loving it. We'd first met at a spiritual retreat in Ojai and had followed up with a few business meetings. Our conversations about organic products were fun, but mostly I loved the relationship and sharing the brand development knowledge I'd gained over the years. So, a few more loves for my list:

I love using what I know to help people I care about.

I love organic food.

I love helping the owners of a small company who are trying to build something meaningful.

Oh, and I love it when my inner life and my work life are in sync.

Could it be this simple? As simple as working with people who're also trying to express their ideals through their business?

Little rockets fired off in my mind. What if I offered advice to small companies like the Ojai guys? Other companies that sold healthful products? Companies run by honest people who wanted to stay connected with themselves while earning a living and trying to do some good?

I stopped in my tracks, turned around, and walked briskly back toward the pier. With each step I heard the words pounding in my chest: *This is it! This is it!*

Of course, my fears continued to walk with me too. Back in Chicago, being relegated to working with small companies was a sign of failure. Could it really be my route to success? Health food stores with organic products were just starting to appear. That meant my clients would be small and the fees equally so. But did that matter? I had zero desire to work with large corporations again, but could I make a decent living helping tiny startups? I wasn't sure.

Still, the mantra inside me chanted on (mostly) undeterred: *This is it! This is it!*

On my trek back to the car, my eyes fell on two seagulls squabbling in the surf over a carcass of some kind. For them, it was natural, but could I build a successful company without that scrappy, combative energy?

Once again I pulled out my pen and pad, sat down, and started writing. This time it wasn't my love list. It was what I'd want if I got serious about having my own company. When I first formed my corporation, I was at Fox and needed a legal entity for my consulting. Now it was becoming the foundation for a new kind of work where love was the core. Whatever that would look like.

It seemed there was a bigger question. I turned to a fresh page and wrote it down: What needs to be true for my work life to be in sync with my soul, rather than at odds with it?

I definitely needed to find clients whose work reflected their ideals. I wrote it down. People who were honest and didn't misrepresent their products. People who cared about the well-being of their employees, customers, and vendors.

In my old life I barely knew my clients. Now I only wanted

clients with whom there was a fundamental alignment and a genuine connection.

After reviewing my notes, I was convinced that the health food business was the right place for me. At Burnett I'd worked with many food companies, so I was comfortable in that milieu. More importantly, the owners of health food companies, especially organics, would naturally be dedicated to integrity and tend to have heart-based relationships. It was a small, emerging industry but clearly a fit for me.

Wait a minute! I jumped up. *Could the Ojai guys be my first client?*

They fit the profile perfectly, but why would they be willing to pay me for what, until now, had been pro bono? I cringed at the thought of having a money conversation with them. Yet, my mind was already pondering what to say.

I was so excited, my feet were no longer touching the sand. On the drive home, I stopped and bought a bottle of Ellen's favorite Chardonnay.

I shook my head in amazement. I was starting my own business! My own *advertising* agency!

Seriously?

A HALF-HOUR BEFORE Ellen got home that evening, I put the wine in the refrigerator and pulled out a small round of French artisan goat cheese we'd been saving for a special occasion. I arranged the cheese carefully on her best cutting board with some olives and crackers, then added some grapes and carried the assortment to the coffee table in the living room.

The elevator clanged to a stop, and I went to the door anticipating the sound of her key in the lock. Her surprise when she walked in and saw me standing there was exactly what I was hoping for.

"What's all this?" she asked with a lilt as she noticed the hors d'oeuvres and piles of paper stacked on the floor near my desk.

"You'll see."

I retrieved the wine from the fridge, poured our glasses, and handed one to her.

"I love you," I said, my glass touching hers.

"I love you, too." Then after a thoughtful pause she squealed, "You got a job!"

"Nope. Better."

"Better . . . ?"

"I'm going to start my own ad agency."

"Really?" Her eyes opened wide. "That's wonderful, Don! I'm so excited for you! Congratulations!"

"Me going back into advertising?" I chuckled. "Who would've guessed after all my carrying on? But I've been thinking about it and realized I still love certain aspects of that business. So, like you've been saying, why walk away from what I know? From what I'm good at? It's just that I have to do it differently."

I knew I was telling the version of the story she could best hear. But it was still true.

"Wow, I'd almost given up hope. Your *own* agency—what a fantastic idea! What clients are you lining up?"

At that, I took a sip of wine, almost a gulp.

"I want to start small, build this thing by hand, and be sure of my choices. First is finding clients with integrity, people I can have a real relationship with. Like with the guys in Ojai. That's kind of my model. I'm going to call them in the morning and see if we can work out something."

Her smile collapsed and she put down her glass.

"Ojai? Those two health nuts?"

Dead silence. Neither of us spoke for a moment.

"Don, you've worked on Campbell Soup and Kellogg's. I mean, you spent a decade on the Pillsbury Doughboy. Giant companies with big budgets. Nestlé! Why waste your precious time, and all that experience, with a tiny outfit in the boonies?" She shook her head. "I don't understand."

I studied her face for a long time. She wasn't criticizing my plan, she couldn't see the wisdom of it. Or was she seeing something I wasn't?

It felt like the floor had dropped out from under me. Was I taking a wrong turn? Within seconds, I began to share her doubts.

chapter ten

First Client

The northbound 101 Freeway was wide open, and I was at my turnoff before I knew it. Just another twenty minutes to Ojai—a place that became special for me shortly after my move to the West Coast.

The Ojai Valley was both rural and elegant, famed for its spas and art galleries, as well as its orange, lemon, and avocado groves. The towering peaks of Topa Topa stood at the valley's far end, a sanctuary for the near-extinct California condor and the backdrop for *Lost Horizon*, Frank Capra's utopian film about Shangri-La.

When I first started coming here I was still emotionally exhausted from the intense pressures and conflicts of my life in Chicago. Ojai easily found its place in my heart, in part because it was home to the great Indian sage Krishnamurti. He, more than any of the teachers I'd read, succinctly described my need to escape advertising: "It is essential sometimes to go into retreat, to stop everything that you have been doing, to stop your experiences completely and look at them anew, not keep on repeating them like machines."

My first retreat in Ojai helped stitch me back together. After that, I returned as often as I could. On one such retreat, I met Joan Halifax, who later became founder of a Zen Buddhist center in Santa Fe, New Mexico. At the time, Joan taught a group in the Upper Ojai Valley. When she heard about my background, she introduced me to the two young proprietors of a struggling organic coffee company, Dave and Terry.

At the outskirts of town I felt a shot of anxiety. Ideas about my new company were still jelling and I hadn't yet landed on a good way to describe my offering. The truth of it—that I was doing business from love—seemed, at best, fragile and possibly ill-conceived. But a more immediate concern about them remained. Why would these two guys who ran their operation on a shoestring pay good money for advice I'd been giving them so freely? Plus, how could someone like me, with no real knowledge of the health food industry, presume to act as a consultant to these experts?

My mind vacillated between doubt and being enamored by the orange and avocado groves, and I suddenly realized I'd driven past their address. Turning around, I checked the street numbers and retraced my route back toward town.

There it was. Could *this* be their place? We'd always met at a cafe. Maybe this was why. Their office was a storefront that looked half abandoned. More doubts jumped up in protest—about myself and my audacious mission.

I pulled into a graveled parking area and stopped near their paint-chipped front door. Was this really the best place to start my business? Still, who was I to judge? Looking down at my well-worn jeans and trusty Birkenstocks, no one would mistake this bearded guy for a high-powered advertising executive. No chance of that.

My mind flashed back to my very first cigarette presentation at the Philip Morris Company. I was a proud, clean-shaven young man from Ohio dressed in a sharp, three-piece suit and on his first business trip to New York City. I remembered being ushered into the glass-and-chrome executive suite of the world's largest tobacco company. I still knew the address: One Park Avenue, the best number on the best street in the richest city in America. I was nervous, of course. On the outside, I looked the part. But inside, I was still that awkward country kid who went to his job interview at the famous

Leo Burnett Agency wearing white socks under an ill-fitting suit.

Today in Ojai, the stakes felt even higher. I was no longer naïve, but instead of a young man looking up with anticipation, I was a middle-aged man looking up from having hit bottom. I was starting from scratch, alone and without the backing of a big agency, trying to pull together a new career. I trusted that my marketing and advertising expertise would translate into helping small business, even into health foods, but would the spiritual intangibles be relevant to anyone but me?

I climbed out of my car, grabbed my briefcase, and with a nervous sigh, knocked at their front door.

No answer.

I knocked again. Louder. Still silence. *Is this the right place?* After my third attempt, I heard a muffled voice from inside.

"Come on in," someone called out.

I turned the ceramic knob and the door creaked open. I was immediately met with the familiar aroma of fresh coffee.

"Hey, Don, welcome!" Terry called out to me.

Within seconds he was crossing the room carrying two steaming mugs. His partner Dave was on the phone in the back. He nodded in my direction and covered the mouthpiece with his hand: "Be right there."

"Cream or sugar?" Terry asked. He set my cup on the card table in the center of the room and motioned for me to sit.

"Just black," I said, starting to relax at bit. I pulled out a chair, set my briefcase on the floor, and sat down.

Terry and Dave, both in their early thirties, were devotees of biodynamics, the first of the organic agricultural movements, pioneered in the 1920s by the scientist and metaphysician Rudolf Steiner, who had some pretty cool, esoteric ideas about nature. Steiner was also clairvoyant, and it was Terry and Dave's fascination with this integration of spirituality and holistic growing methods that originally drew them to organics.

Terry and I shook hands, while Dave, now off the phone, joined us carrying a warmed plate of home-baked rolls his wife had made that morning. *There are*, I thought to myself, *some benefits to doing business like this.* I was among friends.

"Geez, man, it's been a while," Dave said as I sipped my coffee.

"Yup, it has." I opened my briefcase and plopped some papers on the table. "Been through some pretty wild changes."

"I understand you there, brother," Dave said while Terry shook his head in solemn agreement.

Over the next hour they updated me on gross sales, distribution, and several new product ideas they hoped would lead to some sorely needed growth. Organic coffee was still a relatively new concept, so there was no real competition. The challenge in their case was increasing distribution and building consumer awareness—both of which required funding. The discussion then turned to finding authentic organic coffee. Their favorite supplier was a grower in Mexico whom they'd visited to be sure of his methods. In short, we talked about everything *except* why I was there.

Noon arrived and we decided to move our conversation to a small, outdoor Mexican restaurant that bordered the town's park, home to the popular Ojai summer concerts where famous composers like Igor Stravinsky and Aaron Copland had once performed. The waiter led us to a table in the shade under a giant oak tree, and we ordered lunch and kept chatting. All the while, I waited patiently for the right moment to bring up my proposal.

"Sorry to be gabbing so much today," Terry finally offered. "Talking business with you again obviously got us excited. You mentioned on the phone you had an idea you wanted to discuss? What's up?"

I exhaled a deep breath and announced that I'd decided to start my own ad agency, but that I'd be doing it differently. I described some of what had transpired during my recent walk along the beach in Santa Monica and how it no longer made sense to me to separate my inner life from my professional life—which I knew they understood.

They were both looking at me intently. It was time to get to my point.

"So I'm thinking of you as maybe being my first client." I paused to assess their reactions. They seemed comfortable with what I was saying, so I explained that I, like them, wanted to work with products with full-on integrity, with people who cared about building solid relationships all around, with customers, vendors, employees.

"This way of working together," I gestured to indicate the three of us, "will, I believe, generate a powerful synergy—and that's why I'm calling my new company Marketing Partners."

I took a gulp of water and sat back in my chair, wondering how that all landed—especially the part about them being my first client.

"Great name, Don! And great concept!" said Dave while giving Terry a meaningful glance. "You know, having your input has been a big deal for us. After your call yesterday, we hoped we might all be able to cook something up together."

"The question is," I chimed in but then paused, wishing I had a more finessed way to ask. "How do we make it work financially?"

"Exactly! Our cash flow is tight," Terry added, as I assumed one of them would. "Mostly because we're both trying to live off the business. But when you called, we suspected, and kind of hoped, it might be about something like this . . . so we did some rough figuring."

This, I was not expecting.

As Terry continued I couldn't keep from smiling. "So, we were thinking we could manage a small monthly retainer for your ongoing advertising and marketing help. We can't pay enough to match your expertise, but we hope it's enough to make it worth your while."

I nodded and tried not to reveal what was going on inside me. Relief. Delight that they were eager to work with me. Dread about how low their numbers likely were, but I couldn't bring myself to ask.

Then Dave jumped in. "Since we know the money we can offer

isn't enough for the kind of involvement we think we need . . ." He looked at Terry.

I waited.

"We wanted to also offer you a third of our company."

There was complete silence at the table. I needed to absorb what this meant but my mind was racing. My first impression was negative. This was not what I expected. Or wanted. But might it be a good thing? Maybe in the long term? They obviously weren't making much money, and certainly not turning much of a profit, not yet. And a small retainer sounded—well, small.

"I wouldn't be investing any money, right? Just sweat equity?"

"Just sweat equity," Terry repeated.

"That's very generous, guys. How soon do you . . ." I needed time to weigh the offer, but Terry rambled on about how profit distributions could work when there were some, the amount of the monthly, and other details they'd considered.

Then Dave jumped in again. "Ever been inside a coffee roasting plant?"

"Uh . . . can't say that I have."

"Want to?"

I shrugged. "Never thought about it."

"Tell you what," Dave said. "Before you make your decision, why not meet us at the roasting plant next week? The company we use is in downtown LA. It's owned by a Cuban family who's been working with coffee for generations, and it might be good for you to get to know the coffee business from the, uh, grounds up."

We all groaned accordingly.

"Sorry, man, that's my little on-cue pun," Dave apologized.

"Don't worry," I quipped, "I won't spill the beans."

"Aha!" Dave laughed. "You're already fluent in coffee. That's a good omen. But think about it. Being part of the roasting and packing process, you'll get hands-on experience of this business from the inside. You know, the manufacturing side of it."

I mulled it over for a moment. Despite the unappealing prospect of tossing around heavy bags of coffee, I couldn't say no. "Sure, let's do it!"

The three of us walked back to their office, but I wasn't listening to any of the small talk. My mind was busy. *I have a client!*

But did I really? Did I want a piece of their company? I wasn't at all sure about that. Did I want to go to a coffee roasting plant? Not really. And about that modest monthly retainer? Disappointing. Anything else on my mind? Yes.

I have my first client!

IT MIGHT NOT HAVE looked like it to anyone else, but to me, this trip to Ojai was a huge win. Terry and Dave were a couple of guys scratching out an income, yet there I was, driving home with an expansive feeling in my chest that couldn't be about money or prestige.

This win was deep inside me.

I had no real reason to feel *this* good, but I did.

new alchemy

At this point in my journey, I was pretty sure of myself when it came to marketing and brand development. But the distinct sense that I'd taken a significant step in a more subtle game is what had me so fired up.

I was still feeling my way forward, but having a paying client was a tangible advance. It was the first time since that experience by the pool that the practical universe said yes with something truly measurable.

It was also the first time after eight years of watching promising situations end in disappointment that I'd landed on solid ground. Actually, I felt like I'd created this solid ground—or co-created it with larger forces—which made it feel more enduring.

Of course my fears were still with me. Lots of them. It was all so tenuous. Perhaps I shouldn't have been so optimistic, but I was.

Until that client meeting and the turning point it represented, I was alone in my imaginings about how my new business might work. Grading my own papers, really. But now there was at least some evidence that this idea was viable, and I dared to believe I had the beginnings of a working model that could be extended.

And if this perception held, it meant that I'd found a way to earn a living while staying in touch with my soul.

What I couldn't see at the time was that my enthusiasm was being fueled by something beyond my awareness—the early workings of a new alchemy that was already transforming my life. And me.

chapter eleven

Planting More Seeds

W hen the alarm buzzed the following morning, I was already awake, thinking about Ojai and how to grow my business. Ellen vaulted out of bed and hurried to the bathroom. A couple minutes later she was kneeling next to me, kissing me in a serious way.

"I'm proud of you," she exclaimed. "Proud of what you're trying to do."

"Hmm," I said. "Wanna climb back in for a bit?"

"Sorry," she said pulling away. "I can't. I'll be late. But listen," she added as she stood up, "I really am proud of you for starting your own company. I just wanted to tell you again in case you have doubts about my feelings in all this."

Her support was a welcome sign, and she *did* need to head to the office, but refusing to get back in bed for even a minute hinted at the ambivalence I'd detected the night before. Over dinner, I'd told her all about my meeting with Dave and Terry, and while her first remarks were positive, she also repeated her negativity about *them* being a client. Now this morning she was all smiles and optimism. These mixed signals weren't just confusing—they amplified the pressure I was already feeling, trying to make business choices that would ultimately give both of us what we wanted.

"I'm so happy you started your business," she chimed yet again as she was leaving the apartment.

AFTER SEVERAL ROUNDS OF circling through the post office parking lot, I gave up and parked at a nearby strip mall. Inside the post office I made my way around the snaking line of people waiting at the windows and opened my mailbox on the far wall. My reward was a stack of bills, mostly from selling the house.

"Damn," I muttered to myself, feeling a jab of anxiety in my gut. At the top of the heap was a tuition reminder for my daughter Sarah's boarding school, and below that an invoice from the moving and storage company—both hefty amounts.

I slammed the box shut, locked it, and flipped through the rest of the mail at a nearby table. A credit card statement was thicker than usual (a bad sign), plus there were final gas and electric bills, and invoices from the roofers—all trailing remnants of a dream I no longer possessed. I stomped out of there angry and feeling intensely sorry for myself.

A couple of deliberate exhales relieved some of the tension, but when I reached my car it all came back. A chrome strip near the rear bumper was loose and hanging. Then I saw the fresh scrape on the fender.

Frustrated and even more angry, I spun around and made eye contact with the security guard. When I pointed toward the damage he shrugged his shoulders as if to say: you take your chances parking at a strip mall, and oh by the way pal, you shouldn't even be parking here in the first place.

Crap. He had a point.

BACK IN THE APARTMENT I plopped down heavily at my desk. My vision of taking it easy for a while had been swept out to sea and was replaced by the practical world of survival pressing in on me from all sides.

"Okay," I said to myself. "Let's do some business."

I stood up and dialed the phone.

"Hello, Terry?"

He recognized my voice immediately and told me how much they'd enjoyed our meeting.

"Me too!" I agreed. As Terry told me that they'd closed out the quarter and discovered an unexpected increase in sales, my fingers crawled through the pile of bills on my desk. He and Dave were so encouraged, they were ordering additional bags of green coffee for the coming month.

"That's great news," I answered, hearing an opening to talk about fees. "And listen, I've been thinking about your offer. The monthly draw . . . is that a fixed number? Think it could be increased a bit?"

My eyes closed as I waited.

No, it was their best offer. In fact, he and Dave had taken a cut in their own salaries to put it on the table.

"Ah, I understand, and I really appreciate that," I said. "Anyway, I'm calling to let you know that I'm ready to start working with you guys whenever you want."

"For real?"

"For real."

"So, you're really on board?"

"Absolutely."

"Can you come up tomorrow?"

"Sure, what time?"

Terry and Dave's jubilant yells were the last sounds I heard as I hung up the phone. My work with my first official client had begun.

Okay, what now?

A few months earlier, I'd met the owner of a natural-foods trade paper at a small-business conference. We'd liked each other instantly and decided to stay in touch. On a hunch I dialed his number and told him that I was doing some marketing consulting. Without hesitating, he agreed to send me a list of local health food companies in the LA area. *Now that was easy.* Hopefully, a good sign.

Ideas for a prospecting letter had been forming in my mind for days. Now it was time to write it. I pulled out several sheets of paper and started scribbling. My first few drafts emphasized my years of experience with large corporations and the big food brands I'd helped build. Hours later, the only result was a sore neck and a pile of crumpled pages scattered around my desk.

After a trip to the bathroom and a fresh cup of coffee, I realized that I had to face the unavoidable question: How do I motivate the owner of a small natural products company to hire a consultant with a history of working with mainstream giants? Especially when health food companies and mainstream giants were natural enemies?

After suffering through several days of writer's drought, I was still baffled by how to make my expertise relevant to my intended target. I even considered asking Ellen for help. *Hey, I'm the advertising guy, I should be able to write my own sales letter.* Trouble was, each time I typed the word "values" I couldn't finish the sentence. In all my years of writing ads for big corporations, the selling message had never once used that word. Or "ethical" or "integrity" or "ideals." Back then, it was all about "new and improved" or "free" or "act now, you owe it to yourself!" Argh. It made me queasy to even think about those years.

ON THE FOURTH DAY, while standing in the shower, I had an idea.

I dried off quickly, threw on jeans and a T-shirt, and headed to my desk. I grabbed a piece of paper, and from the center drawer, retrieved the fountain pen I'd bought while working at Leo Burnett. Until that moment, I'd only used it for writing personal letters, usually to say thank you. I filled it with fresh ink and set to work. Instead of composing a formal prospect letter for potential clients, I decided to write as if I was penning a note to a friend.

The logjam cleared and the words flowed. I described my experience with large food corporations and explained why I'd stopped working for them. I talked about how much I respected the health food industry and the good things they were doing to improve the quality of food available to consumers. I also stressed how at this point in my career, I wanted to share what I'd learned with people who were trying to do business in a forthright and ethical manner.

In less than an hour it was drafted. Just three brief paragraphs.

I typed it up and read it aloud, then made a few minor changes and typed it again, leaving the salutation and signature areas blank to be filled in later with my pen. I took the original to the shop that had just printed my new business stationery, and several days later I was hand-addressing and signing each one. I even managed to get them to the post office before the last pickup of the day. The fate of my new enterprise was now in the lap of the gods.

When I got home I called Ellen and told her the letters were in the mail. She was thrilled and insisted we celebrate over dinner, which we did—and more.

I was on my way.

A WEEK PASSED. Then two. Then two more and not a single response. I considered making a few phone calls but told myself that the letters needed time to do their work.

Despite this self-assurance, a swarm of gloomy fears besieged me. *Somebody should've replied by now, shouldn't they? Was my letter too short? Too confessional? Was writing letters a bad approach? Maybe it was an old list with wrong addresses? Was my experience with mega-corporations that offensive in the world of natural foods?*

A definite maybe to all of the above.

This was harder than I anticipated. For Ellen, too. At about the two-week mark, her concerns showed up in gentle prods and not-so-subtle questions. "How's your little business going? Anything new?"

PLANTING MORE SEEDS 55

There was, however, one good thing about the lack of response. It gave me time to work on my book.

DESPITE UNSETTLING DOUBTS—Ellen's and mine—I still felt confident. An inner voice kept assuring me that my job now was to be patient. Years before, when I was writing screenplays, a similar mailing landed me a respected agent. It also yielded other important connections to people in the industry who I'd never have met otherwise. No good reason that strategy wouldn't succeed again, so when I wasn't working with the Ojai guys or overly fraught with worry, I relished the time to write.

On one of those delicious days, Ellen arrived home unexpectedly. She came over to the desk, bent down to kiss me on the cheek, then abruptly pulled back.

"That doesn't look much like a follow-up letter," she scolded, reminding me of the nun who'd caught me drawing pictures in my math notebook.

"It's my book outline," I replied.

"Your book? You're really writing a book? Now? Don't you think your time would be better spent looking for clients?"

During exchanges like this, I tried to remain strong. And calm. I knew Ellen's fears were talking. The pain from her husband's financial downfall was obviously still in play. I felt for her, but it was difficult to contend with her fears on top of my own.

chapter twelve

Summer Storms

You know those people who move through life on a steady upward slope of success who seem invincible in the face of challenge? For a while I was one of them—or thought I was—and some of our closest friends still were.

Two of them (who I'll call Gabe and Daniel) fit this profile. I loved them both, but sometimes it was painful to be around them.

Gabe was an actor—charming, smart, and drop-dead handsome. Daniel was his well-to-do, also gorgeous partner who did some stage and film producing and managed some family properties. They'd been in Ellen's life for years and were like brothers to her. Sometimes she'd accompany the two of them, or just Gabe, to film openings and glamorous studio events. Understandably, she idolized them both.

The only problem was that being in close orbit to their lifestyle seemed to amplify Ellen's discontent. I felt the pain of comparison too, but believed my efforts would prove themselves in the long run.

Ellen was not so convinced. My refusal to reenter the corporate world was, she insisted, needlessly miring us in a Spartan-like existence. She tried to be supportive but as her frustrations grew, she started snipping at me in front of our friends.

One such outburst came the day of Gabe and Daniel's "wrap party" luncheon at their house. It marked the end of production for what later became a hugely popular movie. Gabe played the lead and was taking a few weeks off before the pressure of the talk-show circuit began. Their other guests had gone home, and the four of us were lounging around the living room chatting casually when Daniel excitedly interrupted.

"Guess what?" he said, standing up. "We're thinking about buying a house on Carbon Beach!" (Now sometimes called "Billionaire's Beach.")

Since Gabe and Daniel had been in their current home less than a year, their desire to buy again so soon, and in such an exclusive part of Malibu, surprised us both.

"Aww, I love this house," Ellen declared with a touch of apprehension, and to my ear, envy. "It's exquisite. And so close to where we live."

"I know, but you two will have your own room there," Daniel assured her. "Besides, we might keep this house and use the new place for weekends."

"You guys are amazing!" Ellen's tone was full of adulation, and she moved closer to Daniel as he started describing the new property—where it was on the coastline, why Carbon Beach was *the* preferred beach in Malibu, and how easy it would be to remodel.

"Wow, you guys really know how to live," Ellen burst out. "Maybe you could give *us* some lessons!"

Her emphasis on "us" was accompanied by a sidelong glance at me. Gabe and Daniel laughed. Perhaps they genuinely found her comment funny, but to me it was a poorly veiled barb. And painful.

The following week brought a repeat performance. Ellen and I spent Sunday with other close friends at their hilltop home in Topanga Canyon. This mountain-to-sea community at the edge of LA was eclectic, but their house was spectacular. Greg was a high-profile therapist with a number of celebrities and entertainment execs in his practice. Beth, a dedicated mom, was Ellen's closest woman friend. We often visited them for tennis and a swim followed by grilling dinner on their deck. Sometimes we'd spend the night.

"This is so lovely, you guys," Ellen said gesturing to the view. "Wish we could stay over tonight."

"Why don't you?" Beth asked eagerly.

"Can't. *One of us* has to get up early and go to work. Ya know, that earning-a-living thing."

Greg and Beth both looked at me empathetically, then at each other, and simultaneously started clearing the table.

AFTER WHAT WAS MOSTLY a fun day, our goodbyes were subdued and the drive home quiet. When I glanced over at Ellen, I noticed the familiar way she chewed on her lip whenever she was about to vent.

"What's up?" I asked, thinking it was better to invite it rather than stew in anticipation.

"Oh, just thinking about going home to our cramped little apartment."

"Yeah. I miss having a house, too."

"And a pool," she jabbed.

Silence.

Then several minutes later, "How's your business going?"

From her tone, it was obvious that she was trying to adjust her mood, and I was grateful for that.

"Good," I replied. "Things are coming along with the coffee guys."

"Any responses from your letters yet?"

"Nope. Not so far."

That ended our driving-home conversation. On the surface, her questions sounded sincere, but it felt like a serious storm was brewing.

chapter thirteen

Sprouts

Despite our tart exchange the night before, I woke up awash in a sense of well-being. Ellen's alarm wouldn't go off for another couple hours, and I relished having the place to myself.

The apartment was dark as I tiptoed through the living room to my closet where I hung up my robe and put on jeans and a soft sweatshirt. After a quick moment communing with the half moon still hanging in the sky, I settled into Ellen's rocker and let my eyes close to start my meditation.

Soon the room fell away and thoughts of recent experiences began marching through my mind. First was a deep pang of loss over the financial meltdown that had cost me my house. Next was the struggle to find clients. After that, a sense of pride for being able to sustain my daughter through prep school, and hopefully, despite my crumbling resources, to send her to her dream college, the Art Institute of Chicago. I acknowledged each one as if a passing stranger, real yet ephemeral, then let it move along on its way.

Finally, my awareness was clear of all such thoughts, and a euphoric emptiness emerged. I luxuriated in this feeling for who knows how long until suddenly a colorful image appeared on the blank screen of my mind.

At first, I was taken aback by the oddness of what I saw. *Why this?* But there it was, crisp and photographically clear, a tray of tiny green sprouts much like the flats of seedlings I'd cared for as a teenager while working summers at a plant nursery. Atop the emerald stem of each sprout were two oval leaves looking as proud and perky as Mickey Mouse ears. The plants were too young to reveal their destiny—giant sequoias or backyard clover—but their self-assured vitality conveyed their message.

This forest in miniature, I intuitively understood, was proclaiming that the earth was reawakening in my life and new growth was sprouting. Years of decline were coming to an end and the future was offering buds of promise. The scene then faded and my spirit lifted its face to the warmth of the morning sun.

LATER IN THE WEEK, I came home from a meeting in Ojai to a message from Jennifer.

She'd be traveling to the Midwest again. Her aunt had taken a turn for the worse and was likely approaching her final days. This was sad news, especially given how close they were, but the heavy, even ominous, undertone in Jennifer's voice surprised me.

After listening through some details, I understood. Unless conditions changed, Jennifer might stay on the farm permanently, even beyond her aunt's passing. She ended the message with her hope that I'd come out there after she was settled and said she'd be in touch then.

The thought of Jennifer moving to another part of the country left a gaping hole in my chest. She was an important conversation partner and ally in my spiritual search, and the idea of her living far away made me realize how much I cared for her.

In a flash of fantasy, I pictured visiting her and perhaps even lingering for a while. Just the thought of being in a rural setting again and sharing time with someone who also loved nature sent a surge of liberation coursing through me. In that kind of quiet, spacious locale I'd be able to write. And think. And share ideas. And we could continue our deep discussions about our innermost lives. Since we'd met, Jennifer had reached out frequently, especially when she'd read a new book or had another out-there perception. Now I was wondering if there was more going on than I knew.

Could this be the new potential the sprouts in my meditation were suggesting?

THE FOLLOWING MONDAY MORNING, an incoming call jolted me out of writing a difficult scene in my book. It was exactly nine o'clock, a perfectly decent time for a call, but I resented the interruption. Then it occurred to me that it might be a response to my letter. I grabbed the receiver but fumbled it several times before getting it to my ear.

"Oops, sorry, Marketing Partners," I stuttered.

"Hi there, this is Ben Pattner," a merry voice replied. "You wrote to me?"

"Oh, yes. Hello, Mr. Pattner." I vaguely remembered his name and grabbed the mailing list from the corner of my desk and looked for his company.

Ben Pattner was, it turned out, the owner of a medium-sized vitamin and health supplement company in the San Fernando Valley. He seemed open and genuine. He was also talkative, which I appreciated because it gave me time to pull my head out of my book and get focused on business.

In the next fifteen minutes, my new potential client managed a vivid chronicle of his company's history, goals, and current problems. He then went on to tell me about his personal consulting practice, antique teapot collection, and why he was a vegetarian. When he finally got around to asking me about myself, I was well prepared to describe my marketing experience in a way that was relevant to his problems. He seemed impressed enough, then after a brief pause added that he hoped I could help with another problem—his grandson.

Did he want me to work with his grandson, not him? I could already tell I had a good connection with Ben—a top criteria for choosing clients—but if he was having trouble with his grandson, maybe I would too.

I told Ben I'd be happy to discuss it, and he invited me to his office the following week.

After the call ended, I sat frozen on the edge of my chair. Then in an explosion of excitement I dialed Ellen and blurted it out: "I got my first callback! And a meeting!"

She yelled the news to the other women in her office, and I was privy to shrieks of joy in the background. Ellen was happy. I was happy. My first response! Finally.

Maybe this is what those sprouts were about.

A FEW DAYS LATER, I booked a cozy room in Laguna Beach overlooking the ocean, a bed-and-breakfast to keep it economical. It turned out that our room had once been a garage, but it didn't matter. We were in love. Things were turning around for us.

chapter fourteen

Ron Scolastico

Ellen and I entered Gabe and Daniel's house hand-in-hand, a bouquet of white mums cradled in her free arm and Gabe's favorite Chardonnay in mine. It was his fiftieth birthday and they'd invited us over for an intimate lunch, along with an old friend Mark, a physician from Orange County.

As a surprise gift, Mark brought with him a transpersonal psychologist, Ron Scolastico, to do a full life reading for Gabe. After introducing his guest, Mark announced that we were all welcome to have our own readings if we wanted—Mark's treat (a gesture that reflected his generous spirit).

"Is he a psychic?" I asked.

Mark flashed a patient smile. "More like a gifted clairvoyant, a channel who provides guidance to people all over the country. He does his readings while in an altered state of consciousness. You interested?" We both knew it was a rhetorical question.

"Great gift, old friend," Gabe offered in his deep baritone voice. "Thank you."

With that, Mark led Scolastico to Gabe's study to start setting up. Apparently each session would be recorded so we could listen again later. The birthday boy would be first, then Daniel, then Ellen. I wanted to go last so I'd have more time to figure out my questions.

While Gabe was having his reading, the rest of us followed Daniel's directions and pulled together an informal but elegant buffet. About forty-five minutes later, Gabe strolled out a bit bleary eyed but fell back into party mode without saying anything about his experience.

Daniel hastily positioned the last platter on the table. "Go ahead and eat everyone—but don't you *dare* do the cake without me!" When he emerged about an hour later, he was a bit subdued, which was odd. Daniel was perpetually buoyant and talkative.

What's going on in there? I didn't dare ask aloud.

When Ellen came out from her session, she sat down next to me. I leaned over. "So," I whispered in her ear, "what'd you think?"

She motioned with her face and hands that we'd talk later and then rejoined the group.

"Okay, Don, you're up," Mark announced, pointing toward the study. Scolastico was seated in Gabe's chair, and a second chair was facing him.

Ron, as he invited me to call him, was a gentle and unassuming man, and I was instantly at ease. He would, he explained, turn on the recorder then close his eyes and say a brief prayer. Then there'd be a few minutes of silence while he was entering the state of "deep attunement" from which he would, at some point, start speaking. I must've had a quizzical look on my face because he further clarified that he'd be attuning to an "all-pervasive, all-loving consciousness" from which he could access a source of insight and wisdom unavailable to his normal awareness. The session would begin with an "opening," some observations about me and where I was in my life, and after that, I'd be invited to ask questions. The reading would last about forty-five minutes and end with a few final comments.

Ron closed his eyes and as he said his prayer, his breathing deepened. I took a few slow breaths myself and noticed that his head was now tilted to his right and nodding as if experiencing something pleasant. When he finally began to speak, his voice sounded a bit different from his normal speech. His words came slowly yet fluidly and easily slipped past my skeptical defenses.

The session began with a litany of experiences from my early years and recent past, revealing a breathtaking familiarity with even the most subtle aspects of my inner life. Then there was a mind boggling description of my soul's reasons for my being born and what I intended to accomplish in this lifetime, including how far I'd come and the challenges I was still working on.

I was glad Ron's eyes were closed. Mine were filling with tears.

As I listened, utterly absorbed in everything being said, long-forgotten events and experiences became vivid again but in a new light. Ron, or whatever source he was drawing upon, described how those episodes, both positive and negative, had contributed to the person I was today. I was especially interested in his description of my being guided from early childhood, as everyone is. It reminded me of the guardian angels I'd learned about in Catholic school. He also talked about my persistent desire for spiritual realization throughout a number of incarnations, and the many forms this desire had taken at various stages in my present life.

About ten minutes into this opening, I was told that my current emphasis on love was a manifestation of my own divine nature and that I could trust this desire as the creative epicenter of my very being.

"You may bring forth your questions now, so that we may be of greater service to yourself." Ron then sat in silence, eyes still closed, his head still nodding slowly.

I was stymied at first and just sat there. It felt like all my questions had been answered, and more. Then I remembered the notes I'd jotted down. There was plenty I wanted to know. I asked about my desire as a teenager to enter the monastic life . . . about my failed marriage . . . my conflicts with advertising that had changed the course of my career . . . and, if there was any deeper purpose behind my financial meltdown.

Each answer came without hesitation. Each was clear and insightful. And each unveiled a context, a level of awareness that was larger than the one that had formed the question.

Wow.

I looked at the clock and guessed that my next question would be my last. I scanned my notes and summoned the courage to ask about my epiphany and what it really meant—if anything. I also described it as my out-of-body experience by the pool to be sure he knew what I was talking about.

The beginning of the answer explained that the conclusions I'd already drawn were essentially accurate but that there was something about the litany of fears I hadn't yet understood. Apparently, I wasn't just afraid of certain experiences, my fear also showed up as anger, impatience, rigidity, self-doubt, criticism of others, and general negativity. And, if I so chose, I could create more of what I desired by attending to those more covert expressions of fear in addition to what frightened me.

Now I was even more grateful that Ron recorded these sessions. There was obviously more in that answer than I could grasp in the moment, and I knew it held important insights about countless areas of my life, including, I suspected, my relationship with Ellen.

I thought Ron might stop there, but he didn't. He went on to say that my unusual experience had provided "a hole in the mirror" to give me a glimpse into the larger reality that exists behind our ordinary awareness. He also spoke at length about human love being an expression of "divine oneness." This perspective perfectly reflected feelings I'd been having for a while and any remaining barriers between his words and my heart instantly dissolved.

There was a brief pause, a subtle shift, and then what I assumed was the wrap-up that Ron said to expect. But whatever this part of the reading was, I dropped into a state I hadn't felt so palpably since that day by the pool. After what seemed like an eternity, I heard: "And for this time in earth, this speaking has ended."

Ron then lapsed into silence. I closed my eyes and waited.

A few minutes later, the sound of his movements brought me back. He was stretching his arms and legs as if waking up from a good night's sleep. When he appeared to refocus, I asked a question about one of his answers.

"Sorry, Don. Once I'm back here," he gestured to the room, "I may remember an image or an impression but not that kind of detail. But it sure felt deep."

That was an understatement.

AS I RETURNED TO the party, like the others, I had no desire to talk about my reading. In fact, I was still in somewhat of an altered state and would've preferred an hour or two of solitude to savor my experience and listen to the recording.

Ron joined the group for a light lunch, and Mark excused himself to pack the recording equipment. When they were ready to leave, I thanked them both and told them how much I'd enjoyed the session. Ron, in turn, thanked me and mentioned that he'd be back in LA in a few weeks and asked if I'd like to meet for breakfast or lunch. Apparently Mark had mentioned my background at Burnett, and someone else Ron met in Chicago had suggested he look me up in LA. Interestingly, that someone else turned out to be my ex-wife. Ron and I exchanged numbers and he promised to be in touch.

As they walked out, it struck me that the Ron who was leaving with Mark was a regular guy, while the Dr. Scolastico who channeled that wisdom was a true mystic—an Edgar Cayce or Rudolph Steiner in the flesh. I really hoped we'd meet again.

OVER THE NEXT WEEK I listened to the reading several times. What struck me most was the vast dimension given to various events throughout my life. As someone with a metaphysical bent since childhood, I'd sensed larger meanings beneath seemingly ordinary happenings, but nothing like this. Not even close.

But sometimes when I'd listen, even when those deeper meanings *seemed* true, I wondered if they really were. There was no question that the session left me feeling expanded, which I'd come to see as a reliable sign that something was valid, but time, ego, and fear can do strange things to even the most compelling of insights. And it didn't help when I discovered later that the readings had little if any lasting impact on the others.

Despite my ambivalence, whenever I revisited what I learned in the reading, I was again grateful and trusted that this encounter was important, whether something came of it or not.

invisible bridge

I couldn't deny it. The presence within Ron's words knew me intimately and sweetly, and I loved that it touched me in much the way my epiphany had. The synergy between that experience and his words is something I never could have anticipated.

As it turned out, that experience prepared me to recognize the deeper intelligence in Ron's words. And now, the reading was expanding my grasp of the deeper intelligence in my epiphany.

Powerful, yes, but it took its own brand of courage to trust these unorthodox forms of guidance—and I couldn't always find that courage. Making choices without the usual kinds of evidence was like inching myself across that proverbial invisible bridge. There was no supportive logic—only a distinct sensing that the next step was safe and true.

Paradoxically, I'd never felt so supported. It seemed I'd found a new ground of being somewhere within myself. I felt more secure and more connected, yet I couldn't bring myself to discuss such things, even with those closest to me. Perhaps it was my own shyness. Or was I embarrassed? Perhaps their silence meant they were feeling the same.

Whatever the reasons, this precious journey of awakening was in some way separating me from those around me, and I kept feeling that I was living the best part of my life alone.

Sometimes that made me sad. Mostly, though, I cherished the privacy in which I was incubating my new life.

chapter fifteen

The Coffee Roasters

My Ojai partners called with an announcement. Their latest shipment of green coffee had arrived at the roaster. And, the cans would be wearing the new label I designed. Their excitement was infectious and like nothing I'd experienced with clients of my past. We set a date to meet, and they gave me the address of the plant in a manufacturing area just south of downtown L.A.

The company that roasted, ground, and packaged their coffee was a family operation started by a once-wealthy Cuban landowner whose family had been forced to flee their plantation during Fidel Castro's communist takeover. The family's patriarch was in his sixties when he'd managed to bring his wife and four teenagers to safety in Southern California.

When this formerly successful businessman started looking for employment, the only work he could find was as a busboy in a Hollywood restaurant. Eventually, he was able to purchase a small commercial coffee-roasting machine and started selling his products to local vendors. Over time, the family bought a small building and began roasting Middle Eastern coffees for nearby restaurants and coffee houses, filling the needs of this and other niche markets with their high-quality products. The business grew from there and this family company was now also selling coffee to restaurants throughout the LA area.

BY THE TIME I reached their address, the sun was already scorching—not an ideal temperature for working around the blazing heat of roasting machines. Plus I'd been warned that the plant wasn't air-conditioned. When I spotted Dave and Terry, they were stacking boxes just outside a large factory door. They waved for me to join them and Dave pulled two freshly packed cans from a carton and proudly displayed our new label. I was glad they liked it, but mostly I hoped it would give them the sales boost they wanted.

After about an hour working with them, I retreated to the company's air-conditioned office to escape both the heat and the loud roar of the enormous roasting machine. Inside, I was greeted by two of the founder's sons I'd met when I arrived. They looked to be somewhere in their thirties.

"Dave tells me you designed their new coffee label," the eldest brother, Pedro, said smiling.

"Yes, I did," I replied.

"Will you design a new label for us?"

This request surprised me but I inquired further to be polite.

"What did you have in mind?"

"It's our espresso label," José, the other brother explained, handing me one of their cans. "We'd like to get into the supermarkets but think the label needs some design improvements."

"I actually like this label," I said after a quick look at it, "and don't think design is your problem."

"What do you mean?" Pedro frowned.

"Well, as you know, the supermarket shelves are dominated by national brands. Espressos are a tiny niche, and there are already two large international players out there."

Pedro took the can from me. "So instead of redesigning it, could you help us get our product into the supermarkets?"

I was completely taken aback by this turn in our conversation.

My mind raced to form a response. I assumed their espresso was high quality, but it was *not* organic. And they were talking about getting into supermarkets, not health food stores. Big chain supermarkets!

They couldn't have known it, but they were asking me to break a solemn vow to stay away from such things. Again, I wondered if this was how a recovering alcoholic might feel when invited to partake in something that had ruined him before.

I smiled at the irony of my predicament. Rather than extricating myself from the relatively modest task of designing a new label, I'd gotten myself invited to help launch a product. I was certain that if I started working for non-health food companies I'd get sucked back into mainstream advertising—and I was not going to let that happen.

How do I get out of this gracefully?

"I'd like to help," I said, "but I don't believe there's room for another espresso in the supermarkets." I assumed Terry and Dave had told them about my background and hoped my credibility would dissuade them. But in case it didn't, I added, "Besides, right now, my hands are pretty full with my health food clients."

They both nodded that they understood, but Pedro persisted. "Perhaps then you could get us some research about the current supermarket situation so we can take a closer look at it?"

I didn't know how to reply.

"Take your time, Don. Think about it," José said, laughing with a big grin. "You can let us know before you leave today."

I couldn't help but laugh with them. They were two very likable guys. But now what?

I was trying to decide whether to give them an unequivocal "no" right then or wait until I was walking out the door. Then I heard Dave call my name. He was at the open door motioning for me to come over. I excused myself and joined him outside. We quickly addressed his concerns about the schedule for the rest of the day, and I took the opportunity to tell him about my conversation with Pedro and José, including my hesitation about being pulled off my natural foods' strategy.

"Look man," Dave said, "it's up to you but it sounds like such a small project. And if you're concerned that helping them would be a conflict of interest, it's not. We're organic. They're in a different business. They're good people. You might enjoy them."

Dave was right. It was a small research project. When I went back inside and saw the brothers standing there, it hit me. I could happily do this for them as a favor for a friend. I wasn't sure why this felt right, but it did.

"Sorry about that, but sure, I'll see if I can get some numbers for you," I offered as if I had no doubts.

"Thank you," Pedro said, shaking my hand. "We appreciate that very much."

"The only thing is that this may take some time."

"That's fine," José said, a smile lighting up his face. "We know you're busy."

"Don, if you don't mind my asking," Pedro said, "how much do you think it'll cost?"

"Not sure exactly, but it shouldn't be much. I'll pull the numbers on one or two local supermarket chains and let you know what I come up with."

"Perfect," they said practically in unison.

In just that brief exchange, I learned several things about these two brothers. They were both open and likable. Pedro was thoughtful and had a gentle authority about him. José had a winning charm and was highly engaging. They obviously made an excellent team, and I felt surprisingly comfortable about doing this limited project with them.

We shook hands and said goodbye, and I walked outside feeling that I might've just met new friends.

AS SOON AS I got into my car, the second-guessing began.

So much for my health food strategy, I grumbled to myself.

But it's just a one-shot deal, I argued back.

When I got back to the apartment, I called a market researcher I knew from my studio days and asked if she could get scanner data on espresso sales from a couple of local supermarket chains. She was happy for the work but was juggling several other assignments and would get to it as soon as she could.

Good. Distraction handled. Now I can get back to building my own business.

chapter sixteen

Two New Clients

My appointment with Ben Pattner, the gentleman with the vitamin and health supplement business, took me to a manufacturing neighborhood in Glendale. Ben greeted me warmly and ushered me into his spacious, yet carefully cluttered office. He offered me tea, and we sat amid stacks of journals and what appeared to be research papers and samples of herbs. Still vigorous in his late seventies, he had a bookish face and warm eyes.

Ben thought he was interviewing me, and he was, but I was also interviewing him. All of my senses were open and attuned. I was listening for who he was as a person, with particular attention to learning about his values. His business, he explained, had two parts. First, it was a natural health products company that sold to health food stores nationwide. He wanted to turn that part over to his grandson, which was why he needed my services—to improve the company's sales and marketing so that Ben could someday step aside, preferably soon.

The second part of the business was Ben's personal consulting practice, based on his extensive knowledge of herbs and indigenous plants. This was his true passion. He read endless foreign publications searching for local and regional reports of healing, hoping to discover obscure remedies he could make available to people who'd exhausted mainstream options. Ben was aware that he could be in risky territory with the authorities, but his desire to help people who were struggling with illness outweighed any sense of jeopardy.

I had two distinct reactions to his heartfelt and carefully reasoned position. First, I admired his commitment to his business and his reasons for being in it. Second, I wanted to avoid even a hint of association with his personal healing practice. Ellen's sparse use of herbs with her patients had sensitized me to the potential implications. He may have been comfortable with such a risk, but I wasn't.

After touring the administrative offices and expansive warehouse, he took me to the sales department to meet his grandson. There I listened for anything that might make me want to *not* work with him, but I felt nothing either way. Back in Ben's office, he matter-of-factly revealed his marketing budget for the national sales side of the business and the retainer he could pay me. Both were larger than I'd expected.

As he walked me to the door, he put his hand on my shoulder and asked if I was available to start right away. *You have no idea!* I thought.

SCOLASTICO FOLLOWED THROUGH on his promise to be in touch. He left a message saying he'd be in LA the following week for some client sessions and would love to get together, if I was free. I checked the calendar and called him back. We agreed to meet for lunch at a garden café that Paul Newman owned. (Rumor had it that the blue-eyed man himself occasionally stopped by to fire up his own Kobe beef burgers.)

At the restaurant, we found a quiet table under the massive California Oak that shaded the patio. I was reminded of my meeting in Ojai and couldn't help but wonder if the shade of oak trees was auspicious for my meetings.

Over heaping salads, we spoke about how we'd each found our way here from the Midwest and what had drawn us into our careers.

I found Ron's story riveting, and he seemed equally impressed with mine—particularly my choice to walk away from a multinational advertising career in search of a more meaningful way to work and live, and that I was now writing a book about it.

During the course of conversation, Ron talked about wanting to spend more time in LA to expand his practice. I encouraged him and offered our apartment as a temporary place to hold readings on the days Ellen was at the office, although we didn't have a room for him to stay overnight.

As we were paying the bill, he mentioned that some of his clients had health-related businesses and that if any ever needed marketing assistance, he'd send them my way. I thanked him and we got up to leave.

Once again, I appreciated that Ron was so down-to-earth. In this setting no one would ever guess the enormity of his otherworldly talent. I walked back to my car feeling even more grateful that Mark had brought Ron to Gabe's birthday gathering.

ELLEN AND I HAD cause to celebrate again—a second response to my new-business mailing. Damian, the owner of a holistic bakery that produced organic breads and muffins, wanted to talk to me. He already had national distribution in health food stores—a positive sign—and as if to dissuade my fear, announced that he loved that I'd worked with Pillsbury and Kellogg's.

"That's why I called you," he said over the phone. "I've been wanting someone with national brand experience to help get us into the supermarkets."

"Well, I'm glad you called," I replied upbeat, excited at the opportunity.

This is interesting, I thought to myself. *Why am I not balking at supermarkets now?* I immediately realized that my commitment to avoid all things mainstream (and my rigidity, if I was being honest with myself) was undergoing a refinement process. My focus was on the quality of the product and the client's values, not on their distribution channels. Hmm.

"I figured anyone at your level," he went on, "who'd worked with those corporate giants wouldn't be interested in a small company like ours. Then your letter came."

I chuckled and told him that Kellogg's was once small too, started by a doctor who believed in the healing properties of grains.

"We won't go into what happened to that company over the years," I continued, "but I believe that health-oriented bakeries are an important part of a whole new cycle of health awareness."

Damian agreed and asked if I could meet him at their plant sometime later in the month. We spoke a few minutes longer, which gave me the opportunity to hear how he saw his business fitting into his way of life. By the time we got off the phone, I understood him to be more than an astute health-oriented businessman. He was also a man with strong personal convictions.

I leaned back in my chair and let a fresh surge of well-being fill me. I had the sense that a spring rain was beginning to fall, nourishing my baby sprouts.

chapter seventeen

Good News, Bad News

When I arrived at a nearby restaurant to meet Maggie, my ever-enthusiastic market researcher, she was poring over the report she'd compiled. Even before I sat down, she apologized about this taking so long then started chirping about her findings.

"I was able to get data on the entire coffee category from *all* the Ralphs supermarkets in LA, so this info should be pretty representative of the other chains in town too. And you were right, Don, there's no room for another espresso."

Maggie pointed to a row of numbers with the names of several European brands that dominated this small segment.

"To be frank," she said, "as far as I can see, hardly anybody around here drinks the stuff."

I agreed. At the time, cappuccinos, lattes, mochas, and other espresso-based drinks hadn't yet captured the American palette. They were still considered the province of Bohemian coffee houses and Italian dinner tables. Of interest to me personally was that the coffee category hadn't changed much since my days on Nestlé's Tasters Choice, but mostly, I was relieved to find that the market assessment I'd given Pedro and José was accurate.

"Now want to hear some good news?" Maggie teased, pulling out a second report from her bag and sliding it across the table. "More like sensational news! At least I think so."

She was so energized she jumped up and came around to sit next to me.

"First, check out ordinary canned coffee sales." She pointed to a summary of the segment. "It's huge, right? And mostly national brands. But look at this. Right here," now calling my attention to a single row of numbers. "There's a new category—fresh-roasted whole bean coffee in bags. It's not ground and it's not in cans! There's only one brand in Ralphs right now, but look at the growth!"

I studied the figures. She was right. The product was leaping off the shelves. But whole bean coffee? In bags? It didn't make sense.

"How do people grind it?" I asked.

"Exactly! So here's the ingenious thing. I visited one of the stores and there's a large grinder right on their point-of-sale display. You do the grinding yourself, on the spot, in the store. It takes about thirty seconds, and you take home *fresh* ground coffee in a bag!"

She jumped back to her side of the table, leaving me to stare at the numbers.

"This could really be something," I muttered.

"Exciting, right?"

I nodded and tried to look pleased, but my mind was already forecasting the challenges. They'd need a free-standing display in each store with electricity for the grinder. And regular cleaning and servicing. It was an opportunity, all right. An expensive one. But the numbers were undeniable—this was a significant new product idea if ever I saw one.

Anyone who'd traveled to Europe came back thinking that American coffees were as weak as dishwater. Introducing grind-your-own-whole-beans might just make sense to a Cuban family with such deep roots in coffee. But could they afford the investment? And would they want to take on the risk? There was a *huge* difference between selling coffee to local shops and restaurants, and in effect, installing a small retail center in supermarkets, each with its own grinder and a variety of whole bean coffees on a lighted display.

Yikes! What'm I doing? I couldn't believe how easily my mind grabbed hold of the challenges and opportunities that come with mass marketing. I was right to be cautious about my proximity to this world. *Slippery slope. Slippery slope.*

"This is great work, Maggie. And astute reading of the numbers." I genuinely appreciated her contribution and didn't want my conflicts to diminish her enthusiasm. "Thank you for pulling all this together. I'll show them and see what they say."

As soon as I got home, I called to schedule a meeting. I couldn't wait to deliver the news. This project hadn't taken much time but it was occupying considerable mind-space, and I wanted my whole self available to focus on my health clients and to follow up on some other inquiries that had come in. And if I had any time left over, I wanted it for writing.

THE PHONE RANG JUST as I was about to leave for the Natural Products Expo. It was José.

"Glad I caught you," he said.

"Hi, José, what's up?"

"Well, you're committed to health foods, right?"

"Yes," I replied, detecting an agenda behind his question.

"You said you liked the integrity of the business, right?"

I barely knew him but suspected he was setting me up.

"Uh, sure. I like what they stand for."

"And I believe you mentioned you and your friends from Ojai were displaying at the health foods show today in Anaheim?"

"That's the plan. Why do you ask?"

"Well, a couple of days ago two different organic coffee companies from back East dropped by our plant and bought coffee to sample at the show you're about to attend. Just thought you'd like to know."

"Really? I didn't know you had organic coffees."

"We don't," he laughed. "That's the point! Those health food companies of yours intend to pass off our regular Colombian coffee as their organics."

"Did they *admit* they were going to use your coffee as their own?"

"That's what they said," he laughed again. "They even found humor in it—telling people how much better organic coffee tastes." José was definitely having fun with this.

"C'mon, you're kidding, right?"

"Unfortunately not." His demeanor was now serious. "We like the Ojai fellows and thought you'd want to know this about their competitors. Check 'em out and see if I'm not telling the truth."

DISAPPOINTMENT AND SHOCK reverberated through me as I headed south to Anaheim. My strategy of working in the high-principled health food business was taking an integrity hit.

Dave and Terry were at the booth as planned and I immediately briefed them on the call from José. They couldn't believe it. After a bit of back and forth, we decided to leave our display unattended for a few minutes to visit the vendors José had named.

One company's booth was just a few aisles away. A well-dressed young man stood next to a giant poster showing a group of smiling South American growers holding baskets of green coffee beans. He beckoned us over and invited us to taste his "organic" brew.

"Well, what's the verdict?" he asked after we'd all taken a few sips.

"Tastes as good as a Colombian," Dave said with a straight face. Terry was about to burst out laughing and had to leave the booth.

"Actually, it's grown high in the Andes, in special volcanic soil. Pure organics. It matures more slowly there than in most other coffee exporting areas of the world. You can't find this stuff anywhere else in the States."

"Yeah," Dave said. "And certainly not from a coffee roaster in LA."

The guy blanched and walked away.

The phony sales pitch was brazen. And deeply disillusioning.

It was the same basic story with the second vendor. We declined their samples and went back at our booth where Terry and Dave pondered what this meant for them and the burgeoning health food industry, and what to do about it, if anything.

All this deception was a tough blow for me too, but for different reasons. My assumption that this community operated on iron-clad integrity was, well, an assumption. Was I being naïve about the health food industry as a whole? Were these two coffee sellers just isolated cases?

My partners thought so, but I wasn't convinced.

chapter eighteen

"Hi, This Is Paige"

Early Monday morning, Ellen and I left the apartment together. She was heading to work, and I was going to the post office.
Just back from an intimate weekend getaway, our goodbye was warm
and tender. For a while now, we were both happier and less stressed.
My small handful of clients was paying off in more than one way.

When I returned with the mail, I dropped it on my desk and
checked my bonsai to see if it was thirsty. After giving it a small
drink, I relaxed into the rocker in front of the windows and closed
my eyes. The phone rang but I let it go to voicemail. I wanted to
savor the afterglow of our weekend.

That lasted maybe ten minutes.

I got myself a cup of coffee and hit the play button on my answering machine. It was a woman's voice. She lived in Newport
Beach and was looking for help with a line of natural skincare products imported from Switzerland.

Why's she calling me? I don't know anything about skincare. I was
certain I hadn't mailed my letter to any skincare companies. Then I
heard her say she'd been referred by Ron Scolastico.

Hmm.

I'd already met with two people Ron had sent my way. One had
an interesting idea and adequate capital but hadn't developed the
product yet. The other had a viable product but zero funds for mar-

keting. The skincare situation sounded more solid, but even if not, there was no way I was going to ignore a referral from Ron.

I sat forward and dialed. A bright, perky voice answered.

"Hi, this is Paige."

She thanked me for calling so quickly, and when I asked about her connection with Scolastico she chuckled and told me the following story.

"Well, I saw Ron last week, and just as he was coming out of his altered state and had barely opened his eyes, he looked right at me and said, 'You have to meet Don Marrs.'"

"That's all he said?"

"Pretty much. As you know, he's not exactly talkative until he's fully back, and even then . . . I'd asked a couple questions about my business, but all he said about you is that you're this 'big marketing guy' and I should call."

I got a good hit listening to her but wasn't ready to suggest a meeting. Given the geography between us and my previous experience with Ron's clients, I thought it best to interview her by phone. But before I could ask my first question, she was interviewing me. What type of marketing services did I offer? What kinds of clients did I work with? Which did I prefer? What was my background?

Her forthrightness could have been off-putting, but curiously it wasn't. To respond to her litany of questions, I drew from my prospecting letter. When I got to the part about my years on large multinational brands, I highlighted the two that were related to her business: Camay soap and Secret deodorant. I paused and waited for the buoyant response I now expected when a potential client heard all that.

Instead, she was silent.

"Uh, so, tell me about your business. You said Swiss skincare?"

"That's right. We, my husband and I, have the US rights to a really pure line of skincare products from Switzerland. And unlike most of what's out there, ours is super simple. Only the products you actually need—a cleansing cream and two moisturizers for the face and a similar set for the body."

This might be important to women, but it's Greek to me.

I got that Paige was passionate, even sincere, but I wasn't sure a simple line of natural skincare products was a big enough idea to make a dent in that ultra-competitive market.

"That's sort of interesting," I said, wishing I could be more enthusiastic. "But to get them noticed in a crowded marketplace, you'd need a dramatic story. Some unique hook."

"You mean like the fact that these products have no chemicals, no fragrances, no mineral oil," she teased. "Or the fact that there aren't any toxins or carcinogens in them? Or that they're packaged in glass to avoid the harmful effects of plastic? Or that unlike the products in the department stores that might say they're natural, ours have no preservatives whatsoever? Is that dramatic enough?"

"It very well might be." It took effort to keep from laughing at her feistiness. She was certainly earnest, but that didn't erase my cautions.

"Could you talk to me about your budget?" I probed as gently as I could.

"Can I ask you something first?"

"Of course."

"You talked about working with some big companies." She hesitated a moment. "That might be a problem for us."

Huh?

"As you can tell," she continued, "values are important to me. To us. Call it being ethical or holistic, or however you describe such things, but one of the main reasons I chose to work with this company is the integrity behind this line. And *how* we do business is as important as the quality of the products themselves. Sorry if it sounds like I'm preaching . . . what I'm trying to say is that I want all aspects of my work life to reflect my inner life, and I thought I should mention that up front."

Oh my God. She's reading from my script!

"Don't get me wrong," she added. "Money's important. But I wanted you to know that working with like-minded people is high on our list, and coming from Ron . . . gosh, I hope you're not put off by all this," she offered, perhaps reading my silence as a negative reaction to her frankness.

"Not at all. Quite the opposite. I only work with natural product companies. Mainly for the same reasons you mentioned."

"Good to know," she replied, although she didn't sound convinced.

"I need to run in a minute," I said, wanting some time to think, "but it seems we have several things in common. Maybe we could meet at some point and—"

"That would be great! How's next Wednesday?"

Caught off guard, I checked my calendar.

"Would you be willing to meet halfway?" I asked.

"Of course. I'm familiar with the restaurant at the Hilton near LAX. Does that work for you? My husband Tim and I can be there midmorning. Around 10:30?"

"That's perfect. I'll see you both then. I'm salt-and-pepper, by the way."

"Good to know. I'm a redhead."

chapter nineteen

Whole Beans

My spirits were high when I parked my car at the coffee-roasting plant. My briefcase was packed with the supermarket research, and I strutted into the building with the confidence I used to feel walking into a meeting when I knew I was carrying a breakout ad campaign.

The receptionist directed me to Pedro's office where the two brothers were waiting for me. They greeted me warmly and called their sister, Leonor, and a third brother, Paco, to join us. Each ran a different part of the operation. This was definitely a family business.

I started by delivering what was apparently a boring overview of the canned coffee market. A few pages in, they were squirming with impatience, so I jumped ahead and showed them the meager espresso numbers.

They all looked disappointed.

"Don," interrupted José, "you said on the phone you had *good* news?"

"I do," I replied, fumbling for the final page of my presentation. "Look at these sales figures for this new line of whole- bean coffees."

They were immediately heads down, engrossed in the numbers. Then almost simultaneously, they lit up with excitement. They recognized the prize.

José looked at me with raised eyebrows and nodded. Pedro kept pouring over the comparative data. Leonor and Paco started chatting about what they were seeing.

"At the present moment," I interjected, "only this one company has a whole bean coffee in Ralphs, and as the numbers show, they're selling a lot of product. You'd have to check the other chains, but if you really want to be in the supermarkets, it looks like this is your chance."

A flurry of questions followed, some of which I could answer, some not. They were fascinated by the idea and understood its implications. This was a rare opportunity for a relatively small player to edge their way onto supermarket shelves. They also saw the risks.

"Marketing espresso to local restaurants and specialty stores is one thing," Pedro said with the full gravity of his position. Then looking straight at me, he added, "But the investment of entering supermarkets with a whole new type of coffee is quite another."

The others nodded in agreement, as did I.

"But," he continued, "it's also very, very interesting. We'll look at the numbers to see what it would take."

"Before I leave you to it," I nodded, "I'd like to say something. At the moment, you have a significant advantage. You're small and can make choices quickly. The national brands are going to see this data too. Maybe they already have. At some point, they're going to come in, guns blazing. But because of their size, they're going to be slow to act. If you're interested you'll want to move quickly."

We talked a few minutes more and Pedro thanked me for doing the research. He then wrapped up the meeting by saying they would give it a serious look and get back to me.

"Sure. I'd be curious to hear what you decide," I smiled and started packing up."

"Wait a minute," José protested. "If we go ahead with this, we'd be counting on you to help us market it."

He glanced at the others. They were agreeing with him.

My stomach tightened. I'd walked into the meeting aware that this might come up and had prepared to give them my definitive no. But in that moment, I couldn't get the words out. I liked these people and didn't want to end our meeting on a sour note.

"Let's see where you are after you review the numbers," I finally said. "I have a lot on my plate right now, but we'll talk."

We said our goodbyes, and the mood as we parted was even warmer than the hellos.

I'd anticipated that the meeting would be good but expected to walk out of there with this project behind me. Instead it remained an open question.

This was starting to feel like one of those birthday candles you can't blow out.

chapter twenty

Skincare, Really?

I punched the "Lobby" button, and on the short ride up from the garage noticed an expansive sensation in my chest.

"A booth for three, please," I said to the hostess. "I'm a bit early, but if a young couple comes in looking for salt-and-pepper, it's probably me."

"Is that them?" she asked, pointing to a corner booth where a man and woman were unpacking small bottles.

"Yes, that's them. Thanks."

I approached the table and we all shook hands. Paige was an attractive redhead with fair skin and a face full of freckles. She appeared to be in her early thirties, and her husband, Tim, about the same, maybe a little older. He was gracious enough but a bit remote.

We spent more than the usual time on small talk, perhaps due to the Scolastico connection. At some point Tim interjected, "Sorry, but could we get on with business? We'd like to avoid having to battle your crazy LA rush hour on the way home."

"Me too," I replied. "I see that you brought samples?"

"Yep, this is the whole line." Paige pulled the five smallish glass jars from the side of the table and positioned them with labels facing me. "I told you it was simple. And here's the current brochure."

The waitress showed up and took our orders.

I picked up one of the bottles for a closer look. The packaging was more sophisticated than I'd expected, as was their brochure. From a quick glance it was clear that the copy needed help, but I wasn't equipped to assess it—or their potential for success. This market segment was too far outside my expertise for impromptu commentary.

"Do you have any experience with natural products like these?" Tim asked, presumably sensing my cautions.

"All of my current clients sell natural products, mostly organic. But my big agency experience with women's products was with Camay and Secret for Procter & Gamble."

"Procter & Gamble?" Tim snickered. "The epitome of natural."

"Precisely," I nodded. "That's one of the main reasons I left."

I then gave a brief bullet-point overview of the problems I'd had with big corporations and the quality of their products, my short stint in the entertainment business, how learning to meditate was part of my journey—all of which led me to offer my Fortune 500 marketing experience to smaller businesses selling healthy products.

"So that's how I got here," I concluded. "How about you? How'd you get into natural products?"

"We got involved in *this* situation," Paige said, "because someone I'd worked with referred me to the manufacturer. I knew nothing about skincare and I rarely use makeup, but the purity and simplicity sparked my curiosity. So in a sense, my interest in natural products started back in college. Art was my major but I was fascinated—no, captivated—by my courses on comparative religions. Mostly Eastern."

Her face brightened as she spoke, but I couldn't fathom how she was going to connect natural products with religion.

"Something about those philosophies . . . about harmony internally and externally." Paige was gesturing a wide infinity symbol, and Tim moved her water glass beyond her reach. "So, I think the part of me that resonated with that perspective saw these products as part of that same synergy. Does that sound totally weird?"

"No, not at all," I replied, aware that if a potential client in Chicago had offered that explanation, I'd be figuring out how to end the meeting. Instead I was intrigued. "What about you, Tim? What's your interest in this?"

He shrugged. "Nothing esoteric like that for me. I'm on the practical side of things—operations, computer systems. Paige handles the marketing and talking to customers. But I do admit, I like this stuff—especially that it doesn't make the house smell like a bordello." We all laughed.

"So I have another question," Paige said, turning to me. "I get why you'd want to stop helping the Proctor & Gambles of the world, but—?"

"Yeah," Tim interrupted. "How does a big-time player like you get interested in small potatoes like us? Did your fees shrink, too?"

Some part of me liked Tim's snarky sense of humor.

"Uh, let me try that a different way," Paige jumped in. "We're still in the very early stages of development. We want to be profitable, of course, and we want to grow, but we're not aiming for huge. Is that okay with you?"

"Preferable at this point in my career. My interest now is using my expertise to help owners of small businesses with healthy products. And I want a more personal engagement with owners rather than the big corporate thing."

They both nodded.

"Can we go back to something you said on the phone?" I asked, looking at Paige. "About your wanting your work life to reflect your inner life. Did something happen that made that so important to you?"

"Interesting question. Hmm, well, in one sense I feel like I've always been this way. But I think my conscious focus began around the time I was studying Eastern religions. That's when I started seeing the unity in everything, or at least having language for it. But before that, there was this weird experience in a watercolor class. The professor had us all meet in a nearby park. It was one of those perfect Southern California days. Bright, cloudless. Once we were all settled around this massive old tree, he told us to put aside our painting materials and announced that we were going to meditate first. Then he asked us to close our eyes and do some rhythmic breathing and to 'just be.'

"Then at some point, maybe fifteen, twenty minutes into it, he asked us to come back into our bodies and start painting. I remember feeling very relaxed and far away. At first, the thought that it was time to open my eyes had no effect on them. They wouldn't budge. A few minutes later, when they finally complied, everything around me was shimmering—tree trunks, branches, leaves, individual blades of grass. It's hard to describe but they were all vibrating with this silvery, translucent light. Everything was so alive. It felt like I was witnessing some hidden pulse of the universe." She tilted her head and studied my face.

"That's quite an experience."

"It was, but I didn't know what to make of it. It was so . . . real. Later, I understood it as a mystical experience and figured it was the real reason I took that class in the first place. I'm a lousy painter." She laughed. "Three-dimensional art is more my thing, but I had to take at least one painting course. You just never know where any given choice will lead you."

"Isn't that the truth!" I replied.

This is definitely not the usual new-client meeting.

I was beginning to understand why Ron had connected us, but I needed to know more about their experience in business. "Say, earlier you mentioned that someone you used to work with recommended you to the skincare manufacturer? What work were you doing?"

"Nothing related to skincare," she smiled. "I was working for *est*. It was part of the self-help—"

"Sure, I'm familiar with *est*," I interrupted. "I took their main training back when it was the thing to do in LA."

"Like a lot of us, right? Well, I worked in the Newport Beach office and was the center manager when I left."

"You left that for this opportunity?"

She and Tim exchanged a knowing look. "Nope, there were several years between *est* and skincare."

"Am I sensing a story?" I looked back and forth at them.

"Paige had quite the yelling match," Tim grinned, "with Werner, the big boss himself."

"True, but that's not why I left . . ." She paused and removed her teabag from the pot. "In fact, I think my reason for leaving has some similarities to why you're here doing this instead of the big corporate thing."

"Really?"

"I think you called it a values conflict, but before I explain, overall I saw *est* as a practical yet spiritual system that helped a lot of people. Me included. If someone asks me about it now, I tell them it's perfect for those of us who need the proverbial hit over the head with a two-by-four to wake up."

We all laughed.

"Seriously, though," she continued, "it *can* be a great wake-up call. It certainly was for me. Plus that's where we met," she smiled at Tim. "So *est* was important on several levels, not the least of which was the crash course I got in business and management. I'm still grateful for that, for all of it really. Personally and professionally. The challenging part—and this is what might resonate with your experience—shortly after I was hired, I started seeing certain things that didn't sit well with me."

"Really?" I asked, now more intrigued but not surprised.

She sipped her tea for a long moment, then looked at her watch, then at Tim.

"Let's just say the view from the inside wasn't what I expected. It's kind of a long story, but—"

"She's right," Tim chortled. "It's a *long* story! Maybe we could review the rest of our materials so we can all get on the road?"

I MOTIONED TO THE waitress for a fresh round of coffee and tea. When she returned, she left the check and said she was going on break.

Paige then walked me through clippings of PR they'd received and gave a succinct overview of their sales history. No question, they had a quality product presented in a classy way and a small but growing business that would benefit from some help.

"Your product line looks good," I told them, needing time to think. "And we're in sync about how to do business. I just need to consider if it's a fit for me."

"Absolutely," Paige agreed. "Us, too."

While we waited for the elevator, Paige reached into her bag. "Here, why don't you take these samples. They're good for guys too. Or for your wife."

"Girlfriend," I corrected. "But thanks, we'll try them."

"And if we do work together," she added, "I'd be curious to hear more about your transition out of corporate life. I'll bet that's a story too."

"Someday, I'll let you read about it," I blurted.

Ack! I'm nowhere near ready to let anyone to read a word of my book —much less a potential client.

"You're writing a book?" Tim asked.

"It's a long way from being readable," I backpedaled.

"But you'll let us read it when you're finished, right?" Paige smiled.

"Given my relationship with my typewriter, it could be years."

"Typewriter?" They chimed in unison.

"Hey, I love my typewriter!" I knew I was about to be ribbed.

"You really oughta get a Mac," Tim said, his tone slightly accusatory.

"I don't know what I'd do with it."

They exchanged glances.

"Where'd you say you found this guy?" Tim asked, thankfully with a smile.

"Hey, play nice." Paige suppressed her giggle and turned back to me. "Mine is set up for writing—hint, hint—and for client communications and designing promo stuff. Tim's got all of our distribution and sales tracking on his. They're good for a lot of things."

"Sounds perfect for your purposes," I said, now feeling the age difference. "I like things simple."

The elevator door opened and we all stepped in.

"Oh, almost forgot," said Paige, looking at me. "Can you give us a few of your references? Our investors will ask for that."

"Sure, I'll get you some names next week."

Investors? A wave of tightness rippled across my shoulders. That would radically change the chemistry. *And references?* The Ojai guys, yes, but my other clients were still so new. Could I toss in the coffee roaster family? *Shit.*

The elevator stopped and I let Paige and Tim step into the garage ahead of me. The three of us exchanged warm goodbyes and went our separate directions.

I paid for parking and pulled onto the street, wondering if I'd ever see them again.

chapter twenty-one

The Marrying Maiden

As soon as I got back to the apartment, I reached for Ellen's well-thumbed copy of the *I Ching*. I wasn't convinced that this so-called "Book of Changes" could divine the future, but I was unsettled enough to give it a try.

I rummaged through the dish on her dresser and found Ellen's trio of old Chinese coins. Before casting them, I closed my eyes and asked the book's higher wisdom to give me any insights about the situation with the skincare company. I shook the coins and tossed them onto my desk six consecutive times, jotting notes in my steno pad about how they'd landed. Then I opened the book and located the appropriate hexagram.

Kuei Mei translated to "the marrying maiden." *Hmm. Did they, did it, not hear my question?* I read on. This symbol was composed of two subsections: "the arousing thunder" and "the joyous lake."

I took the book and my coffee to the rocking chair and pondered the text. Some of it seemed like it *might* be relevant. But it could be interpreted in so many different ways, and nothing jumped out or resonated.

Disappointed, I got up, stretched, and traded my coffee for water. I was about to put the book away but decided to check the interpretation in "The Commentaries." A single sentence made the hexagram make sense.

"The Marrying Maiden," it said, "describes the great meaning of heaven and earth. If heaven and earth do not unite, all creatures fail to prosper.

These profound words, spiced with the perfume of Taoism, prompted a welcome expansion in my chest. I read them again and again: "If heaven and earth do not unite, all creatures fail to prosper."

This was another way, perhaps a better way, to describe my hope for my company and why I was approaching it as I was. *When heaven and earth are united, when spirit and matter are aligned, we all prosper.*

Now I understood why it seemed natural to spend the bulk of our first meeting discussing our inner lives instead of skincare. Paige and Tim were also trying to unite spirit and matter in business. Paige had almost said as much.

I closed the book and then my eyes, and imagined working with them. *We're all breathing the same spiritual oxygen!* With that perception, a vivid image appeared before me: a vast range of snowy mountains, as high and forbidding as the Himalayas. At first I was alarmed but quickly realized that the threatening breadth of these looming peaks needed a second look.

With gentler eyes, the mountains were no longer ominous. Instead they symbolized a rarified upwelling of inspiration. Paige and Tim were precisely the kind of people I'd hoped to work with when I envisioned my company. I just hadn't known to describe it this way.

I returned the book to Ellen's dresser, tossed the coins back into their dish, and walked out of the room thinking, *This feels like the beginning of a high adventure.*

reading signals

High adventure. This was one of those times when a cosmic finger pointed to my experience as if to say, "Hey, pay attention to this!"

Honoring this type of input from what I'd come to call my "inner guidance system" was an inward-looking practice of checking my intuition and trusting that this resource had something valuable to contribute. This was especially useful when navigating the confusing twists and turns that kept showing up in my work and in my life. My inner guidance system was usually subtle with its signals but also dynamic, and even directive at times.

Then after my epiphany's tutorial on love and fear, the language of my inner guidance system got simpler. More refined. And more insistent that I keep developing my understanding of love and fear.

This included recognizing less obvious, covert fears, like self-doubt, self-righteousness, and double-thinking, all of which kept clouding my judgment. It also included being more sensitive to the unmistakable presence of love—which in this case appeared as the sense of high adventure.

What a lift it would be if I could discuss the mystical aspects of business with a client! And who knew what might unfold when two or three minds tapped into the creative power of love. Wow.

Of course, I still had my doubts—and a new fear. Was it hubris to think I knew enough about merging heaven and earth to act as someone's advisor?

Worse, what if this approach failed to produce tangible results? What if prospering when heaven and earth unite didn't apply to business?

chapter twenty-two

New Momentum

The low rumble of thunder woke me up. A flash of light and a loud clap followed. Ellen moved slightly, and I inched closer to the warmth of her body.

A few minutes later, the alarm buzzed and I tapped her shoulder lightly. She murmured "mmmhuh" but didn't budge, so I touched her again with more emphasis. After hesitating a moment, she rolled out of the sheets, grabbed her sweats from the floor, and headed for the bathroom.

"Beverly Hills or Fairfax?" Her words were muffled by the toothbrush in her mouth but I knew what she was asking.

"Beverly Hills," I yelled, groping for my running shoes under the bed. "I think it rained last night."

We had two favorite places to jog. If the morning was dry, which it usually was, we ran on the clay track at Fairfax High School. After a rain, or in the winter when it was still dark, we jogged on the well-lit gravel path along Santa Monica Boulevard in Beverly Hills.

Dampness hung thick in the air as we parked on Carmelita. After a few minutes of stretching, we ran side by side in rhythmic cadence. Our mutual silence allowed my mind the freedom it needed to roam. Of course it went right to the skincare people and the possibility of working with them. And that led me to wonder what to tell Ellen.

I was fairly certain she'd spark to the idea of a natural skincare line from Switzerland but *knew* that if I described it as a husband-and-wife startup her mood would deflate and fast.

"Careful. Puddle ahead," Ellen warned.

"Thanks. I see it."

I also wished I could tell her how exhilarated I was at the prospect of working with people who, like me, cared about merging their spiritual and business lives. However, I wasn't prepared to again hear that I was off-base about that.

Ellen was so proud of the spiritual roots of acupuncture. It was one of the top reasons she'd chosen it as her profession. She spent a week or more each year at spiritual retreats. She meditated periodically and thought of herself as being on a spiritual path. Yet she couldn't, or wouldn't, consider the existence of an underlying unity between a person's work life and their spiritual life. Perhaps most people didn't see that connection, but her?

We obviously didn't need to be in sync about everything to be in love, but it still baffled me that she believed spiritual principles were of no use in the practical world of business.

NEAR THE END OF our run, as we slowed to a walk, Ellen slipped her hand into mine and I felt the unspoken closeness that the mere touch of our skin evoked.

"I may have a new client!" The words came leaping out of my mouth. "It's a natural skincare line from Switzerland."

"Really?"

"Their products seem good," I went on. "Made with pure ingredients. No preservatives. No perfumes."

"Very cool!" she said, apparently catching a bit of my enthusiasm. "I hope it works out."

We got into the car and headed home. I took the absence of further commentary to mean that I'd succeeded in saying enough but not too much about my excitement. Then as we pulled up in front of our building, Ellen broke the silence.

"So, tell me more about it. The skincare situation."

Sometimes her instincts were uncanny.

"Well, it's interesting," I replied. "Like I said, it's imported from Switzerland, but here in the US, it's marketed by a husband-and-wife team. They've gotten some good national PR in *Elle* and other women's magazines. I just met them yesterday. They gave me some samples for us to try."

"Really? I'd love to!"

"Great! I was hoping you'd test them. I'm no expert on this stuff."

"That's an understatement," she teased. "But you seem pretty hyped about it."

"Yeah, I really am hoping to work with them. They're a referral from Scolastico."

Ack! Shouldn't have added that part.

I glanced at Ellen's face and saw the frown I was expecting.

"Uh, what are you thinking?" I asked.

"Well . . . I guess it sounds like it has potential. A Swiss company expanding into the US. But . . ." she added as she opened the car door, "it's women's skincare. I'm surprised you're that interested."

"Yeah, me too, but I'm pretty excited to see where this will go. By the way, they say the products are unisex, for men too. But mostly I'm excited because working with them feels like a new kind of momentum."

A few minutes later, we were back inside shoving our running clothes into the washing machine and chatting about plans for the coming weekend.

chapter twenty-three

Sarah

The baggage claim area of United Airlines was crowded as usual, and I couldn't help but think of all the times I'd greeted my daughter here at LAX over the years. Sarah, now a young woman, was on break from her studies at the Art Institute of Chicago.

When I spotted her riding down the escalator, I was stunned. She was taller and even more gorgeous than I remembered. We embraced happily and chatted pretty much all the way back to the apartment.

As we neared Ellen's neighborhood, my stomach started burning. This was Sarah's first trip to LA since I gave up the house. I'd always promised her that she'd have a home with me in California, but now it was a living room sofa—another painful reminder of my failures as a dad. Truth was, I was ashamed and hoped that she wouldn't think the worst of me.

Thankfully, there was a parking spot right in front of the building. It was light years away from entering the property down a long driveway to an architectural house, but at least I didn't have to endure walking her through a busy neighborhood carrying her luggage. Once inside the building, my nervousness ratcheted up. The elevator seemed creakier than usual and the corridor darker than two hours ago. The hallway carpet was now a seedy rag, the kind you see in cheap hotels, and our apartment door was a horrendous green.

Why hadn't I noticed any of this before? And what could my art-student daughter be thinking? Holding my breath, I unlocked the door and stepped aside so she could enter first.

"Oh, Dad, I love your new place!"

"Glad you like." I allowed myself a deep exhale. "It's mostly Ellen's."

Sarah dropped her purse on the sofa where sheets, pillow, and blanket were neatly stacked. She then sat down and bounced a bit, and after brushing her hand across the white flannel cushion, looked up at me with an approving smile. My heart ached as I watched her gracious charade.

I was reminded that something more essential than a house with her own room was holding us together. During the difficult divorce years, Sarah had never judged me or taken sides. There was something strong in my daughter. And a loyalty that bonded us despite the circumstances. We never discussed it, but I knew we both felt it. Still, I wished she hadn't been exposed to so much conflict at home and often wondered if the dark mood she periodically disappeared into was a remnant from that time.

THAT NIGHT, THE THREE of us went to dinner at Hymie's Fish Market, a wonderful seafood restaurant near the Fox Studios. Ellen was a gracious hostess all evening, other than snapping sharply at Sarah for lighting a cigarette in the car (a familiar reaction for a re-formed smoker, one that I didn't disagree with).

The two of them had met only once before when we'd traveled to the Bay Area for Sarah's prep-school graduation. Other than a slight, perhaps understandable formality between them, they seemed to get along.

On our way home, Ellen mentioned that Gabe and Daniel were flying to New York for several days to see some Broadway shows.

"They'd like us to go with them," she said louder than needed, as if to invite Sarah into the conversation.

I glanced in the rearview mirror. Sarah was leaning against the door, gazing out the window. If she heard Ellen, she pretended not to. I turned up the music a bit, hoping to postpone this potentially radioactive topic for when Ellen and I were alone.

"So, what do you think? New York, with the guys?"

"Could we discuss this later?" I asked quietly.

"We'd be there less than a week . . ."

I glowered at her and she turned away.

"It sounds like a great trip," I replied as gently as I could manage, "but I'm not sure it's a good idea for me to be out of town right now, what with taking on those new clients and all. Maybe next time?"

"It would be so fun to see some shows with them," Ellen pressed, again a bit too loudly. "Let's get out of our routine for once and really play."

I couldn't believe she was being so persistent. Everything in me was screaming *no!* I'd worked hard to pump life into my fledgling business and being gone for even a few days would bring a handful of creative projects to a halt. Plus, money was better but tight, and spending several thousand dollars on entertaining ourselves seemed . . . wrong. Things were finally turning around for me and I didn't want anything to jeopardize that.

"Please, can we talk about it later?" I asked, trying to indicate with the tilt of my head that I didn't want this tension in front of my daughter. I checked the mirror again. Sarah was still gazing out the window, hopefully focused on the music rather than the front-seat drama.

"C'mon . . . let's go," Ellen continued, although this time in a forceful whisper. I shot her one of my frozen faces and she stopped, but from the collapse in her shoulders, I knew I'd gone too far.

Back at the apartment, we helped Sarah make up the sofa, then retired to the bedroom. In a low voice, I told Ellen I was sorry for snapping but that I resented her using my daughter's presence to try to manipulate me.

She understood immediately. We hugged for a moment, both of us trying to restore our closeness—something I was grateful we were learning to do.

Sadly, though, we got ready for bed in silence and kept as much distance between us as the queen-sized bed allowed.

DURING THE REMAINING DAYS of Sarah's visit, the two of us spent as much time together as I could pull from my clients. My wiser-than-her-age-daughter had accepted my new life without uttering an ounce of judgment. Although I knew from her silences that it wasn't entirely comfortable for her.

Putting Sarah back on a plane was a cheerless moment for me, as it always had been since her first visit as a young girl after the divorce. Tears welled in my eyes as I watched this child-woman disappear through the gate.

chapter twenty-four

Mainstream

Several days later, José left a message saying they had another question, presumably about something in the research reports, and would I please call back as soon as I could?

I put my case down and dialed. José picked up on the first ring.

"We're ready to make a decision about the whole bean project. When can you come in to discuss helping us?"

A bolt of fear slammed into my gut and I froze. I hoped he didn't detect that this simple request had sent me into near panic. He couldn't possibly know the magnitude of the question he'd posed: was I ready to abandon my health-products strategy?

Then I heard some distant part of myself agree to a meeting the following week.

I SET THE PHONE down and began pacing the length of the apartment. If they became a client I'd be back in the old game—back in mainstream advertising. The coffee isles were filled with some of the largest corporations in the country. One had even been a client at Burnett.

Why didn't I give him a polite "no"?

Because I couldn't. My attraction to these people was almost instantaneous, and this feeling only strengthened with each encounter. And being honest with myself, I felt more connected to them than to some of my natural-foods clients. Still, going back into a world that had burned me out? It felt like an invitation to hell.

I plopped myself down on the rocker near the window. Immediately my thoughts jumped to the La Brea Tar Pits, where I realized I could trust myself to be guided by what I loved—and when my love list led to my new business strategy.

There was no question that I was drawn to this coffee family, but liking my clients was only one aspect of my plan. What about the natural foods part?

Damn. Why didn't I decline José's request on the phone?

The answer bolted into my mind. The underlying basis of my new business was to live a *love-centered* life, not an organic-centered life.

Good point, I thought. *Really good point.*

Then I went back to what drew me to the Ojai guys. It was their dedication to expressing their ideals in their work. For them, that meant selling natural foods. But for me, the appeal was their integrity and personal commitment to expressing their values in their business practices.

Could I also say that about the coffee roasters?

I didn't know them well enough, but my Ojai partners had spoken so highly of them. In various conversations, I'd heard how particular, even finicky, the family was about the quality of their product and how well they treated people in all areas of their business. So far, that was my experience of them, too. And talk about integrity, it was José who playfully alerted me to the less-than-honest practices of the so-called organic coffee companies at the trade show.

Even with this new layer of clarity, I wasn't ready to make a choice about taking them on as a client. However, I had lost my rigid need to work *only* on natural products.

WHEN THE DAY OF the meeting arrived, I was still undecided. Ellen and I jogged as usual, and as usual, she got ready first and left for the office before traffic got too heavy. I was on schedule to leave after rush hour and had time for a long shower.

Steam was already obscuring the mirror when I stepped in and let the hot flow cover me. Within seconds, my mind and body relaxed and I recognized the fear that had been confounding me.

It had to do with trust.

The aspect of advertising that had gutted me in the past was that to achieve power and position, I often went against my values and sold products I didn't believe in. The circumstances were different now, but could I trust myself not to fall back into old patterns?

That was the key to my hesitation. Fear. I was afraid I couldn't trust myself, afraid that I might betray my values again, betray myself again. That's why I'd been holding so tightly to my original strategy, to work only with natural products, as if that would keep me safe.

The clarity I gained while standing in that foggy shower was that my fear was only a fear. That my fear was unfounded. That I *could* now trust myself not to betray myself again.

BY THE TIME I arrived at the roasting plant, the morning was already hot. Inside wasn't much cooler.

As I approached Pedro's office I was comforted to hear the excitement. José motioned me toward an empty chair and I listened intently to upbeat descriptions of how they could manage the costs and logistics of a new supermarket brand.

Then suddenly, the mood turned serious. The meeting was now about me. Would I help them launch it?

I took a beat and checked myself. Was I still certain about my choice?

I was.

"Of course, I'd be happy to," I said, all remnants of fear and indecision gone, replaced by that telling sense of expansion in my chest.

Once that decision was made, our banter lifted into a kind of celebration. From there our ideas merged seamlessly. We planned a small test for twenty-five supermarkets. It was a significant commitment to a new type of coffee and a significant risk for a small company to enter a world dominated by big brands, but they were resolute.

Despite some new-product jitters, it was obvious that we were all confident about our choices. I would begin work immediately on brand positioning, potential names, packaging, and ideas for freestanding displays.

NONE OF US KNEW it then, of course, but a remarkable adventure had begun. This modest start was a significant move in what turned out to be an American success story.

fundamental flaw

You'd think that deciding how to respond to an invitation from a family business wouldn't have been so tortured, yet the process of getting to that wholehearted "yes" was one of the most grueling in the early days of shaping my company. And ultimately one of the most liberating.

That insight in the shower (about my fear that I couldn't trust myself to be true to myself) did more than simply free me to work with them. It became one of the best choices I ever made.

But there was more.

No longer clouded by my fear of being untrustworthy, I saw a fundamental flaw hiding in my business strategy.

When I remembered that my core choice was to adopt a love-centered strategy for my business, not a natural-products or organic strategy, I was dancing on the boundary of a deeper truth:

Love has no form and love can take any form.

With this awareness, I understood that I needed to worry less about my clients' credentials and more about what was going on inside of me. As long as my choice was made from a loving heart, I could trust that I was on safe ground.

Choices needed to be practical too, and smart, but never without love.

This opening of understanding cleared the way for me to play in a wider, deeper world. Much more than I could fathom at the time.

chapter twenty-five

Kindred Spirit

S orry it took so long," Paige began the call, "but we finally got to that list of references you gave us. And we'd like to work with you —assuming you're still available?"

I refrained from blurting "YESSSSS!" and told her that I'd be happy to have them as a client. I considered asking who they'd spoken to, but instead suggested we meet a few days later at the same place near the airport.

I arrived early and asked for a large booth so we could spread out. A few minutes later, Paige walked in carrying a soft leather briefcase.

"Since Tim's not interested in marketing," she said, sliding a few folders onto the table, "he decided to stay home and catch up on some things. Hope that's okay? He says hello."

"Tell him the same. I sure understand wanting time to get stuff done. Say, before we talk business," I paused while the waiter dropped off menus and asked what we wanted to drink, "I'd like to hear more about your time working with *est*."

"Okay . . ." Paige replied with a quizzical look. "But why the interest?"

"Well, I mentioned I did the training, so I'm curious on that count. But mostly I'd like to hear about the conflicts you said you ran into. And how you handled them."

"It's kind of an involved story," she cautioned.

"I've got time if you do." My curiosity about *est* was genuine, but my real purpose was to understand her values better, something I thought prudent even though I was now past my concern about working with them.

Paige moved her folders from the table to the seat beside her.

"So, my first exposure to *est* was pretty powerful. I was in my junior year at Pitzer. You know, one of the Claremont Colleges? And a friend took me to hear Werner Erhard speak. We were in this massive ballroom at the LA Convention Center, but the impact was very personal. He was up there talking about how we each 'create our own reality' and about 'transforming the world.' It's hard to describe, but there was this resonance between what Werner's saying and my . . . ideals."

"Spiritual ideals, right? Given what you said previously?"

"Right. To me the training sounded like a shortcut to enlightenment—certainly faster than the many lifetimes my class in Eastern religions says it would take. It's kind of embarrassing now." Paige grimaced. "But that night, I was hooked. When Werner stopped talking, I went straight to the nearest registration table and signed up. Then right after the training, I jumped into the first graduate seminar. *Be Here Now*, it was called. Same title as that book by Ram Dass, which I loved."

"I know it well. A classic. You were still in school at that point?"

"Yeah, wrapping up my senior project. Then as soon as I graduated, I started assisting, you know, volunteering, and to me it was holy work. Less than a year later, they opened their Newport Beach office and I got hired to run two departments—Production/Logistics and the Graduate Department."

"Impressive."

"Maybe. But what excited me was that I was barely out of college, working with like-minded people, all of us trying to change the world, and I'm getting paid for it. Mostly though," her voice softened, "I remember the distinct feeling that I'd found my home. Of course, it was super-long hours and little pay. But still, I was one happy camper."

"Even though you ran into . . . whatever it was you ran into?"

Paige's face lost its cheeriness. "This gets to the conflicts you're asking about. Pretty early on, I started noticing stuff . . ." Paige pulled her teabag from the water and poured herself a cup. "Basically all those inspired ideals Werner talked about, which I also saw in the training, were less evident in the day-to-day of the organization. You probably remember the training's strict, almost militaristic manner?"

How could I forget? I thought.

"Let's just say the organizational management style was similar. Frequently harsh. Not always, but often enough. Looking back, it shouldn't have surprised me. I guess I was more focused on the message, at least as I understood it. So while part of me is *thrilled* to be doing the work, I'm also upset. A lot. That's when I decided to write to Werner."

"Really? To tell him what?"

Paige winced. "Essentially that, based on what I was experiencing, his intentions weren't being realized—that was the jargon at the time—and that I assumed he didn't know because if he did, all that harshness wouldn't be happening."

"He responded?"

"Yeah, he wrote back fairly quickly. He said he appreciated my observations and that I'd reached out. Plus some other stuff I don't remember now. And, of course, the letter ended with the usual 'thank you for sharing!'"

She smiled, and I smiled too.

"So basically he ignored you," I said, as the waiter set our breakfasts in front of us.

"Perhaps," she shrugged her shoulders, "but I felt like he heard me and understood."

I looked at her, but she was already absorbed in moving her sunny-side-up eggs onto her hash browns.

"Did things change?" I asked.

She shook her head and put down her fork.

"About six months later, I'm in a regional meeting of department heads. About eight of us are sitting around a conference table and I figure this is a good place to raise that issue—about how we treat people at times being inconsistent with Werner's intentions. I don't know *what* I was expecting, but my manager, a woman I liked and admired a lot, snaps at me, 'Get with the program or get out!'"

"Whoa. In front of everyone?"

"Yup," she nodded slowly. "But that was out of character for her, which is why I'd felt safe bringing it up in the first place. In this instance, though, I guess you could say that her outburst—her threat—was a perfect demonstration of the point I was trying to make."

"Did you tell her that?"

"Gosh no. I was too stunned to think, let alone respond."

Paige nudged her virtually untouched breakfast away.

"As rough as that was, something even more troubling happened in that meeting. I didn't see it until later, but to make the choice to stay rather than 'get out,' I had to muzzle my inner voice. You know, that little voice that nudges you when something's off?"

"I know it well."

"I figured you did." She took a sip of tea. "Anyway, from there, it was back to working my ass off. And not too long after that, I got promoted to center manager. The *sad* part," she sighed, "as Tim will tell you, is that *my* management style got sharper—and I don't mean sharp as in smart—I mean sharp as in critical. I'm not saying *est* caused me to be that way. I obviously have it in me . . ." Paige blanched and looked away as if witnessing something uncomfortable. "I even yelled at an assistant in public once. More than once. Thankfully, though, one day I'm walking through the office, and it occurs to me that my staff is way harder on themselves than I could ever be —and that what they need from me is support, not criticism. And certainly not more pressure. Duh, right?" Paige rolled her eyes. "It was such a small realization, but it turned me around. And things got simpler. And easier. Well, less stressful. I stopped leaning on people in that punishing way and started asking how they're doing and how I could help them succeed. It seems so obvious now, but at the time, and in that environment . . ."

"It took some courage?"

"Maybe, but I saw it as being in sync with our purpose, our mission if you will, which I believed in." She poured the last of her tea and I motioned to our waiter for more hot water.

"Shortly after that, I got lucky. A pair of management consultants were hired for a pilot project with the LA staff, and for some reason they interviewed me. I loved what they were about, so I lobbied the higher-ups that it made sense to include Newport Beach since most centers were closer in size to us than LA. And they bought it. Almost immediately, my staff and I were using better communication methods and getting more done, and with a ton less struggle and stress. We were hitting or exceeding all of our targets, every week. My enrollment manager even had the time to finish grad school!"

Paige took a deep breath. She seemed invigorated.

"Okay, fast forward. We're almost at the incident Tim mentioned. Every year there's a center managers' conference in San Francisco, and I was *so* excited about this one. Between meeting our targets and a happy staff working less hours, I think we're finally performing the way we're supposed to—and I'm *sure* someone will want to know how we're doing that."

"Did they?"

"Well . . ." she shrugged playfully, "the first inkling of how clueless I was came during the opening reception. I was chatting with one of Werner's close advisors, explaining a little about what we've been doing to get those results, and after a few minutes he says, 'Better keep that to yourself,' and walks away."

"Yikes."

"Yeah, but I'm undaunted. He's just one guy and I fully believe that someone high in the organization will want to hear how we can be more supportive and kind, and still be successful. Logical, right?" She smiled. "So the next morning, about thirty of us are gathered in this lovely conference room. Werner's maybe five minutes into the meeting when he goes quiet and scans the group. Then he shouts over our heads: Where the f— is Carl? Or something like that. I don't usually mind that kind of language but—"

"I've heard worse."

"I'm sure, but there was something startling about it in that context. From there, Werner went on about being on time and keeping agreements. Finally someone volunteers that Carl—he managed one of the bigger centers—had the flu and had taken the first flight that morning, but it was late because of fog. Then Werner starts up again. Something about it being idiotic to think you can fly into San Francisco early in the morning and expect to arrive somewhere on time. And then something about why the hell Carl created being sick in the first place."

"This was your first up-close look at him? At Werner?"

"No, but it's my first sighting of *this* Werner. The room was dead silent, and I'm thinking: *Ohhh, this is not good . . . trashing a highly respected center manager, or anyone for that matter, in a room full of . . .*" She shook her head.

"Pretty intense."

"You could say that," she laughed, "but only for those few minutes. Werner just resumed the meeting, completely calm. Then about an hour later Carl walks in quietly, looking like he should've stayed home, and Werner welcomes him and asks how he's feeling and tells him to take care good of himself."

"Not surprising."

"Yeah, but I've got a knot in my stomach that wants me to bolt from the room, but the rest of me wants to tell someone how well our project with the management consultants is working."

"So, you were still hopeful?"

"I guess, but mostly I felt determined. Then later that afternoon, there was this small awards ceremony, and our center was honored for most consistently hitting our targets and being most profitable. I think we were the only one in the black that year, but either way, it occurs to me that this might give me enough credibility to talk directly to Werner. I had no idea how to make that happen, but . . ."

Paige smiled and put her teabag into the fresh pot of hot water.

"But these conferences always include a dinner with Werner. This one's at his home—the *Franklin House* as we called it—and it starts with hors d'oeuvres downstairs, but he's not there. Later, we're ushered up this lovely spiral staircase to a top-floor room with a low ceiling, old beams, candlelight, and a huge U-shaped table that's elegantly set. Everything is visually *perfect*, which of course the artist in me loves."

I nodded.

"Just inside the doorway, we're each handed a card with a little seating map, and mine shows me sitting next to Werner."

"Seriously?"

"Yeah, seriously. I was honored, of course, but super nervous so I kept telling myself: *This is good, I'll have his ear*. Werner makes his way to our table at the far end of the room and I get a warm greeting, but after we're all seated, he turns to the center manager to his left and . . . well, it sure looked like flirting to me."

Paige shuddered deliberately as if to dislodge the image.

"However," she continued, "what happened next is what got me. This parade of assistants enters the room, and all conversation is hushed. Each is carrying two plates, except for one guy headed straight for us, obviously to serve Werner. I'm watching this fellow, and he looks so proud and happy as he sets this beautifully arranged meal in front of Werner. But, as he's walking away, Werner starts yelling, and I remember feeling pushed back by the power of his voice. He's laying into this poor guy for putting his plate down with the carrot tips pointing the wrong direction, or something like that. I mean, even if it *was* a mistake, seems like it could've been handled later or at least by calling him back to discuss it quietly."

Paige shook her head. She looked more sad than angry. "But now I get it," her voice softer. "The tone of the organization comes from the top. The stuff that feels so gruff to me doesn't *mis*represent Werner. It seems to reflect him perfectly. At least this part of him."

"So . . ." I grinned. "Not exactly the time for a thoughtful conversation about what's happening in your world."

"Understatement," she laughed. "For the rest of the conference I'm preoccupied and confused. Other than those two incidents, Werner's generous, charming, and passionate about doing good work in the world—and I can't help but think that *this* is the real him. So I figure that he, like everyone else, trips up and reacts without thinking at times. And I figure *this* means that the reactions I'm having trouble with don't express *his* real intentions, either. So I still think that what's messed up can be fixed. And *that* leaves me determined to get on the phone with him after I'm back."

Paige exhaled, shrugged, and smiled.

"You can be persistent, can't you?"

"When I believe in something. So back in Newport Beach, after a few weeks of ranting to my regional manager about needing to talk to Werner, she gets fed up and arranges a call. When the big day arrives, I'm ready with my notes." Paige made the shape of an index card with her fingers. "The call comes in right on time, but after I get out a sentence or two, he breaks in and tells me that he doesn't care if I stand on my head as long the results keep coming in. Then he hangs up."

"Really? That was it?"

"I guess he'd said what he wanted to say." She shrugged again and smiled. "But of course, I hadn't. After that, I was like the pit bull that got hold of my ankle when I was a kid and wouldn't let go. No way I'm quitting until I give it my best shot.

"Anyway, after more machinations with my manager, another call gets scheduled, this one for a Saturday. Tim and I had plans to be out in the desert that weekend with friends, but I didn't care. I was taking that call wherever I was."

"I can't imagine what you'd want to say to him after all that."

"Well, it was perfectly clear to me," she said happily, "I still had my notes! But just like that other call, I'm a few sentences in, and Werner starts up in that pounding voice of his. I really tried to listen and respond, but he kept interrupting and raising his voice. Then I'm raising my voice . . ."

She stopped and drank some water.

"I can still hear it. And feel it," she added, holding her hands over her belly. "Then after about half an hour of that, I was exhausted from the tornado of words. I held the phone away from my ear, literally at arm's length, and I remember shaking my head and thinking: *This is almost funny.* When I put the phone back to my ear, I broke in and calmly said that I really didn't want to have a yelling match with him and that I should probably put my thoughts into a letter. Then it's silent on the other end, but he finally says, 'Okay, tell me again.'"

"So your moment arrives."

"It does. And he sounds so completely genuine, I tell him that from my perspective the heavy-handed, critical approach to managing people is undermining the organization and its purpose. I described some of the changes we'd made with help from the consultants and how those changes were helping us get the results everyone liked so much. Plus, wasn't good communication and treating people well at least *part* of transforming the world? It takes me maybe five, ten minutes to say what I want to say, and he listened to it all. But when I stop, he tells me he has a concern—that the staff in Newport Beach has become disloyal to him."

"Whoa."

"Yeah, that took me *totally* by surprise. And it's the *last* thing I want him to feel, so I tell him that I really don't believe this is the case but that I'll look at things from that perspective. I also assure him that it's definitely *not* the case with me. Quite the opposite—that I'm doing all this, including working so hard to have this conversation, precisely because I *am* committed to the work."

Paige finished her water in a single gulp.

"I don't recall his response. I was pretty fried. But the profanity was gone, his tone was lighter, and I'm basically on the phone with a completely different human being."

"Good for him," I said.

"I thought so too. But then, he says something even *more* surprising. He tells me that we, meaning the whole organization, have to keep doing things the way we've always done them because that's how you create people who can transform the world."

It took a moment for that to sink in. "So, his style is deliberate?"

"That's what I took it to mean. And I remember thinking: *Well this explains a lot!* It was one of those super-surreal moments you never forget. I was pretty taken aback, but somehow I had the wherewithal to say the exact words in my head: 'I disagree.'"

Paige paused and studied my face. I assumed I looked surprised.

"And then," she chuckled, "something even *more* unexpected happens. He tells me he thinks we're onto something in our center and that it's where we need to go as an organization. But before I can respond, he tells me to set up an appointment to come to San Francisco to talk more. Then there's a quick goodbye, and that was it."

"Wow, whiplash. It sounds you got to him."

"Well, in the moment it felt like that, but I have to believe he'd been getting input from many others, including the consultants. And he was certainly aware of our stats. So I assume I was just one voice of many and that he was already thinking in that direction. I don't *know* any of this, but that's my guess.

"As you can imagine, I was trembling when I got off that call. And not just because it was so intense. In my twenty-something mind this was about *way* more than the fate of *est*. I believed in the mission to transform the world—as if the entire fate of humanity was at stake!"

We both laughed, then she added, "Nothing like idealism mixed with limited life experience."

Good observation, I thought. "So what happened in San Francisco?"

"Well . . . that evening, Tim and I were at dinner with our friends, but I'm off in my own world, in this powwow with Werner, daring to imagine having an impact on the organization as a whole." Paige grimaced then looked away.

"But while I'm picturing all this wonderful stuff, that inner voice of mine suddenly interrupts with: *This is done*. That's all it says. *This is done*. But it speaks with such authority and feels like such a gentle statement of truth . . . I didn't question it. I simply understood that whatever *est* was for me was now complete. So there was no point in my going to San Francisco. I knew that *est* was my past, not my future. My ideals hadn't changed. And I wasn't even disillusioned about Werner or *est*. Quite the opposite. I just knew it wasn't my path anymore. Weird, huh?"

"Not at all. I've had my life turned around by my little voice several times. Plus I understand wanting to move on and do your own thing."

"Ya know, I had no sense of wanting to do my own thing. I just knew that whatever that period was about for me was done, so I gave two months' notice for a smooth transition."

Paige looked at her watch.

"Got time for one more question?" I asked.

She nodded.

"What's your sense of what that was about now?"

"Wow, that's a single question with a bunch of answers. But there's this one thing, something that syncs up with my original experience of *est* being spiritual. It also relates to my favorite book from college, a little book we read in my Eastern religion class, the

Crest Jewel of Discrimination by Shankara. Have you heard of him? The Hindu sage? Anyway, he writes about being discriminating in the best sense of the word, about discerning what's real, what's true, versus illusory. And after I left *est*, that type of self-inquiry became the core of my inner process. At that time, it was about discerning what felt true and enduring from my years there, and what didn't."

"Hmm. Like in what way?"

"Well, for a long time after I left, I'd catch myself thinking or doing or saying something that seemed *est-y*, and I'd ask myself: *Do I really believe that? Does it still ring true to me?* Sometimes it did, sometimes it didn't. These private little moments kept showing up, and I kept teasing apart the stuff that felt right to me from the stuff that felt off—like certain beliefs and ways of handling things.

"Then at some point, this process became almost automatic, noticing when something had that subtle resonance with a larger truth versus when it felt . . . like I said, off. I remember driving along one day and having an image of teasing a thin strand of arsenic from a luscious dark chocolate cake."

"You mean *est* was like arsenic for you?"

"Oh gosh, no! The whole yummy cake was *est*—and an experience I wouldn't trade. But for me there was that thin strand of yuck, the ways of being that I thought didn't belong there. For others, I assume it was perfect as it was."

"Nice metaphor."

"Thanks," she chirped.

Paige pushed her plate to the edge of the table and pulled her folders back up from the seat. "Quick break?" she asked.

"Definitely!"

BACK AT THE TABLE, Paige ran through a tight dissertation on the Swiss skincare company and her overall plans. She then outlined their thoughts on next steps. For cost considerations she wanted to try fleshing out the marketing plan outline I gave her, but we agreed that I'd take a pass at writing a new brochure.

This part of our meeting was crisp and purposeful, done in under an hour. We took the elevator to the garage, and when the door opened at her floor we exchanged courteous goodbyes.

When the door closed I was left with my thoughts. It felt good to have her as a client. Even more, I was excited about having a client who was a kindred spirit.

chapter twenty-six

Planning Greece

I entered the Bank of America on Sunset Boulevard just as the doors were opening, deposit slip and checks in hand. The monthly income from clients was feeding my sense of security, but the buoyancy in my step was from something else.

Prior to this, my life in California had been primarily funded by savings from my big agency career in Chicago. That money had bought my house, paid my expenses, and kept my daughter in school. Now the money from selling the house was supporting my new business startup. In essence, my work in Chicago was the lifeblood of all my attempts to develop a new career and a new life in California.

Finally, after so many years of being tossed around and enduring some outright failures, my day-to-day efforts were being financially reciprocated. It felt like a vote of confidence in my new way of working, basically a thumbs-up from a larger reality.

I CALLED ELLEN'S OFFICE to confirm our dinner plans, but before I could ask, she blurted, "Hi, wanna go to Greece?"

I felt like she'd thrown a bucket of cold water on me.

"Uh . . ." I didn't know how to respond, but it didn't matter. She kept talking.

"Daniel and Gabe are clearing their schedules, and I know I can clear mine. Think you can take two or three weeks off? Please say yes. I *really* want to go! It'll be so romantic."

"Three weeks?"

What about my clients? screamed in my head. Those relationships were thriving but they were also new. Even fragile. *I can't take an extended vacation now—not if I want to keep things on track!*

"Uh, when are the guys planning this for?" I finally asked.

"Summer, so we have a little time and—oh, darn, hang on."

Her other phone was ringing, but she was back in an instant. "Sorry, it's sort of an emergency. Talk more when I see you?"

She was off the line before I could reply, but I was glad to end the call. I needed time to think.

Something about a Greek trip had been mentioned about a month earlier in one of Daniel's spontaneous "wouldn't it be fun" eruptions. His and Gabe's enthusiasm for adventure was infectious, especially for Ellen, and the three of them had often traveled together before I was around. It was now obvious that some serious planning had unfolded in the meantime.

Several hours later, I finished my work and drove to Ellen's office. It was her day to see patients in the evening, and as usual, I was picking her up to grab an early dinner nearby, this time at the Good Earth restaurant in Westwood.

Instead of our typical exchange about the dramas of the day, the conversation started with Greece. Ellen bubbled on about the fun we'd have, the islands we'd visit, the private ship the guys were planning to charter—all while I kept trying to fit her enthusiasm into my business schedule.

"Why so quiet?" she finally asked. "Aren't you excited?"

"Sure, it sounds like a fabulous trip."

"But . . . ?"

"But you guys are deep into planning and I don't even know yet if I can get away. It would've helped to be included earlier."

"You're right. Daniel wanted to keep things low-key in case it didn't pan out. But I'm so sorry about that. Really." She reached across the table and squeezed my hand. "But what do you think? Can we go?"

Her explanation relaxed me a little. "Like I said, the trip sounds fabulous and you know I've always wanted to see Greece. But the timing, it's not exactly ideal."

I leaned back as the food arrived.

"We don't even have firm dates yet. How could there be a problem with the timing?" she asked, her cheerfulness gone.

"Well, you've been urging me to get back to work, and now that I've got clients, you want me to bolt out of here for three weeks?"

"But we're going in the summer. People take vacations. Your clients will understand."

"It's easier for you," I replied. "You have an ongoing practice. I'm just getting started. Even if my clients do understand, that kind of absence will definitely interrupt the momentum . . . and the goodwill. And you know how hard I've worked to build that."

We ate in silence for several minutes. I knew I was handling this badly, raining on her parade. And mine. I'd always had a warm spot for Greece but couldn't see how I could make *this* trip work.

"Well, let's keep talking about it," she said softly. "Maybe we can figure something out. Remember, the dates aren't set yet."

In that moment, Ellen went from a steamroller coming at me to a compassionate partner—and I was once again sitting across from the woman I'd fallen in love with. With her simple shift to gentleness and understanding, I had room to quiet my fears and started seeing things in a different light. This trip to Greece could be our chance to be together in a way we hadn't for a very long time. Or ever. And I'd been wanting to feel a deeper connection to her. Maybe getting away like this would help us do that.

"Okay," I said, welcoming the expansive feeling rising in my chest. "An opportunity like this might not come along again, so yes, let's plan to go. But let's make it *our* trip. Like you said, it'll be romantic. I just need a bit of time to figure out how, and if, I can make it work. A trip like this will be good for us. We'll enjoy Greece as a couple."

"Exactly!" she said, clapping. "That's exactly how I feel. We'll be with a few other people, but this will be *our* trip."

She looked at me long and earnestly, her smile now radiant. "Sorry, I have to get back to the office. But wait up for me if I'm late?"

"Of course."

chapter twenty-seven

The FDA

My first big presentation to Damian at the bakery was in a few hours. I'd been working on new packaging for their organic, whole grain breads for about a month, and all my design options were lined up single file on the living room floor. It was a striking difference from the cork wall and generous counter at Burnett, but I knew the work was as good and a perfect fit for the brand positioning we'd agreed on.

With this display at my feet, I was mentally running through my presentation, but the phone kept ringing. Not wanting to break my concentration, I let the calls go to voicemail. When I was satisfied with my plan, I gathered the labels into a neat stack and tucked them into my briefcase. Heading to the door, I noticed the message light flashing. It was Damian. There was something slightly alarming in his voice and my stomach tightened. He was forced to postpone our meeting, he said, and asked if I'd call him back right away.

"Damian, it's Don. I got your message. Your labels look great!" I said cheerfully when he answered. "When do you want to reschedule?"

"Oh, I dunno," he answered with a doomsday laugh. "The FDA just shut us down."

"What?"

"Yup, they closed the plant. And I don't know when I'm gonna be able to reopen."

"What happened?"

"An inspector showed up for one of their drop-in visits and found a few dead moths and some rat shit in our flour bins. They're picking on me. No big deal, though."

"Wow!"

"Yeah, those guys . . . but maybe you can help."

I couldn't imagine how.

"Do you happen to know a lawyer who's familiar with the FDA?"

"Actually I do. My attorney's partner was an FDA agent. I'll get his name for you."

"That'd be great. I guess this *could* turn into a real problem. They've cited me several times before, so I'm in their crosshairs. I don't know if they're just targeting me or what."

Then in a hushed voice he added, "Wanna know the real truth in all of this? It's the work of the devil."

The devil?

"Okay, well, I'll call my attorney and get back to you when I have something."

I CALLED MY LAWYER'S office and had no trouble getting the ex-FDA agent's name. I dialed the bakery and left the information with Damian's secretary. Then I sat down heavily, replaying Damian's comments in my mind.

Cited several times before. They're picking on me. Work of the devil.

What had I gotten myself into? A "health" food bakery closed down by the FDA several times? And forget the FDA, why wasn't *he* appalled at rat droppings and dead moths in his flour? And what about him thinking it's no big deal?

My trust in Damian melted like movie film in a hot projector. His beliefs were his business, and I understood from working on food accounts that ingredients can get contaminated despite best efforts, but he wasn't taking responsibility for it. It seemed his only worry was being shut down.

How can I work with this guy?

I pulled the designs from my briefcase and plopped them on my desk. My mind was muddled with disappointment and shock. Finally, I put away Damian's labels in the file cabinet, on hold for a packaging conference that would likely never happen.

THE FOLLOWING DAY I returned from a meeting with the Ojai guys and found that Jennifer had called. She was still with her aunt and wanted me to phone her as soon as possible. I punched in her number and after several rings she picked up.

"Hi, it's me," I said. "Are you okay?"

"Oh, I'm good. I've been thinking about you these days and wanted to check in. We haven't talked in a while."

Relieved that all was well but a bit puzzled that she'd called just to say hello (a very un-Jennifer thing to do), I pushed my chair away from the desk and angled it toward the bank of French windows. The bougainvillea blossoms on my bonsai shined brilliantly against the city's gray downtown buildings.

"So how's it going there? I miss our pastry dates."

"Well, trying to manage a farm is a bit . . . well, you know me. This is way outside my expertise. Plus my aunt's sicker than I thought."

"Sorry to hear. How are you holding up?"

"Okay, I guess. I feel for her, but I've never been much of a hands-on caregiver. It is beautiful here, though. You'd love it. Forty acres of forest, open fields, two horses, a few cows, and happy chickens for eggs every morning. Plus, there's a great little herb garden right outside the back door."

"Sounds idyllic, especially given my life these days."

"Really? What do you mean?"

"One of my health food clients just got closed down by the FDA. They found rat droppings and dead moths in their flour, and this wasn't the first time. And, he thinks the devil did it."

"Oh dear! Have you resigned the account?"

"Not yet. But this cuts pretty deep."

"What did Ellen say?"

"Haven't told her yet. But she'll have a field day with this. She never bought my criteria for choosing clients."

"Seriously Don, why don't you come here for a few days? Think about things. Work on your book. You've always talked about how much you love the country."

Her invitation had its appeal. It would definitely feel good to get out of the city. And I did miss our conversations.

"It's temping. More than you know. But I can't. Maybe in a different life."

"Or another time in this one?" she toyed.

We both laughed, then I heard a sudden scuffling sound on her end of the phone.

"Oh my God! Gotta go! It sounds like Auntie's fallen out of bed. But can we talk again soon? I'd really like that."

"Of course. Take care of yourself."

"You, too. I miss you."

Then she was gone.

chapter twenty-eight

Paige's Plan

T he hostess at the LAX Hilton restaurant smiled when she recognized me and led me straight to a booth where Paige was waiting. The emotional jarring from the bakery's run-in with the FDA was still with me.

"Are you okay?" Paige asked as soon as I joined her. "You seem a little—"

"Oh, I'm fine," I assured her, caught off guard by her quick intuition. "Just thinking about something. Nothing important."

I glanced at the menu, and a few minutes into our conversation, I did feel fine. Lighter. And that sense of "high adventure" was back.

After the waitress took our orders, Paige put two stacks of paper on the table and pushed one toward me. "Here's our marketing plan, such as it is. It was a lot of work, but you know that. Just more than I thought."

"How far did you get?"

"About halfway, maybe a little less."

"That's great," I said, flipping through the pages. I had no idea what to expect. This was her first attempt at this highly complex job.

I reached into my case and pulled out the new brochure I'd written.

"Here you go. Given your timeline, I'd like your feedback today.

So why don't I walk you through it briefly, then you can study it while I read the marketing plan."

SECTION BY SECTION, I scanned through her document—market research, target market, her brand's positioning—and when I got to the competitive analysis I stopped. Her work revealed a level of detail that I hadn't witnessed since Chicago.

"Whoa," I said, forgetting that I was interrupting her reading.

"What's wrong? Not thorough enough?"

"It's very thorough. Where did you get all this information?"

"Well, the library had Standard & Poors and I tracked down most of the other resources you suggested. All of that was helpful for the positioning and competitive analysis sections, but I got a lot of insight from going to stores and looking at different cosmetic displays, and the salespeople were pretty open to my questions. It seemed like the only way to get the answers the plan asks for."

"You really dug for the data, didn't you?"

"Well, I figured you weren't asking for me to guess."

We both laughed.

"This is impressive, and obviously too much for me to absorb sitting here. I'll read it at home and get back to you before we leave for Greece. So what did you think of the brochure copy?"

"It's good. I like it. But would you be okay if I pull it through myself? It sounds a little . . . masculine."

We both laughed again.

"Sure, have at it!"

"So, three weeks in Greece," she said, tucking the brochure copy into her case. "I envy you. I'm sure you'll have a fabulous time."

"My first extended vacation in I don't know how long. I *better* enjoy it."

We spoke a little more about her next steps for completing the marketing plan, and when the check came I gave the waitress my credit card.

"Another meeting today?" Paige asked, noticing that I'd glanced at my watch.

"No, the script typist is expecting me. She finished some more chapters."

"Typist?" She raised her eyebrows. "Really? I thought you were getting a Mac." Paige shook her head in mock despair.

"Soon," I said, closing my briefcase.

We got up from the table and walked out of the restaurant toward the elevators.

"So, how's your book coming?"

"Good, but slow." I wanted to reduce any exception that there'd ever be something for her to read.

"You're writing about leaving the big corporations, right?"

I nodded, and there was silence for a moment.

"Well, I'd really love to read it," she said as we stepped out into the garage.

Yikes. Paige's curiosity, put to such good use in her marketing plan, was now focused on me and I felt exposed.

"Besides," she teased, "how are you going to be a big author if you won't let people read your book?"

"You've got a point there," I smiled.

I walked her to her car and watched as she backed out, wishing once again that I'd never said anything about my writing.

DRIVING BACK TO THE apartment, my discomfort at the prospect of Paige reading my manuscript grew more intense. If I chose to talk about that period of my life in a conversation, that was different.

But the whole story? No way I'm gonna let her, or any client, read the gory details—even if those failures did get me to where I am now.

Still, I had to admit I was a little flattered. From what I could tell so far about who Paige was, she was precisely the kind of person I hoped the book would reach. She was both practical and idealistic, as well as spiritually oriented, and she was trying to live all of it in her work.

But her reading it? That could cost me a client.

chapter twenty-nine

State Busts Ben

W hen I arrived at Ben's for our regular Wednesday meeting, his parking lot was overflowing with a small armada of black sedans, some wearing government plates. One visitor's spot remained and I took it.

The receptionist nodded toward a vacant seat in the lobby, her usual smile noticeably absent. Within minutes, Ben emerged and motioned for me to follow him. When we passed the conference room, I couldn't help but notice the gaggle of official-looking men in dark suits rifling through what appeared to be old files.

As Ben stepped aside to let me enter his office, he attempted a smile but failed.

"I'm under investigation by the State of California for practicing medicine without a license," he said, nearly collapsing into his chair. "It's absurd."

He leaned back and loosened his tie. I sat down, feeling an uneasy compassion for this good man.

"Ben, I'm so . . ." the words caught in my throat. "Have you been charged?"

"No. Yes. I'm not sure." He closed his eyes and rubbed his forehead. "They just walked in and demanded to see my client records. Then they tell me they'll be here all week! And of course my lawyers have to be here with them."

"That's rough." My response sounded hollow to me, but in that moment it was the only sign of empathy I could think to offer.

"I'm not writing prescriptions or anything like that!" he blurted out, his voice rising. "I'm just turning people on to herbs that indigenous peoples around the world have used for thousands of years. Herbs that are approved in most countries! Someone must've complained to the AMA or God only knows who. And now the California militia is rummaging through my office."

In one way he was right to be outraged. Ellen and her colleagues prescribed all kinds of Chinese herbs and no one bothered them. *Although*, I thought, *maybe that's yet to come.*

"For the last twenty years," Ben went on, now speaking a tad softer, "I've given myself over to helping people. Men, women, even children, all of whom show up because their physicians have run out of answers. How is this a crime?"

A tone of defeat had crept into his voice.

"You know, Don, it's the damned pharmaceutical companies and their lobbies. They don't like competition no matter how small. Especially herbal remedies they can't own. The growth of the natural products industry is scaring them."

I agreed with a lot of what he was saying, and it was much easier to hear his rationale than Damian's about how vermin droppings ended up in his flour. But bottom line: Ben knew he'd been operating in uncharted territory.

"What're you going to do?" I asked. I felt sad for him. He truly was well-intended. But I wondered why I was there, why he hadn't called off our meeting.

"My lawyers tell me I have to stop the consulting part of my business immediately, which is cutting my heart out. I *love* helping people who have no other place to turn. It's become my life."

His hand trembled as he reached for the glass of water on his desk, and his face was now flushed. I hoped this invasion of suits wasn't having a serious impact on his health.

"My first impulse was to fight," he said. "And if I was younger I would. But I don't have it in me anymore. My lawyers think a legal battle with the state could attract the Feds, and I can't . . ."

"Ben, is there anything I can do?"

"Yes. So, here's what I wanted to talk about today—my grandson. I want you to put all your attention on getting him ready to run the vitamin side of the business. He's . . . he's, well, I'm not convinced he's capable of doing the job, but I promised his mother, my youngest daughter . . . and honestly, I'd like someone in the family to keep this thing alive. But I think it'll take somebody like you to help him make a go of it."

Ben stood up. "Hell, I'd give it all to him today if I thought he was ready. But with all this shit happening, I don't know, we might be forced to shut down anyway."

My heart sank. I loved working with Ben. I'd met with his grandson on several occasions, and Ben's cautions were well founded. Talking to the grandson, it was clear that he was bored with sales, didn't care much about natural products, and didn't have a molecule of his grandfather's heart. Then, in an unguarded moment the last time we met, he revealed that he planned to sell the company when Ben died. I'd been struggling with what to do with this information, but this turn of events made it even harder. It would be painful to say no to Ben's plea, but without him at the helm, I had no interest.

"You know I'd love to help you," I said. "But let's talk in a few weeks when things settle down."

ELLEN WAS DUE HOME soon, and I couldn't keep from pacing the length of the apartment. Between Ben's struggle with the State of California and Damian's with the Feds, I was anxious to talk to her but wasn't at all sure she'd be sympathetic—and I was in no mood for an "I told you so."

When she finally walked in the door, I poured us both a glass of wine as usual, and as usual we headed to the living room to chat about our day. After a few minutes of catching up and connecting, I decided to dive in.

"Hey, I want to talk to you about my company," I began.

"Sure. That's a nice surprise. I'd love that."

"So, things have been going well as you know, and after all this time another inquiry came in from that original mailing. Anyway, mostly things are great but something happened and I'm thinking about dropping two clients."

Her brow wrinkled and she leaned forward. "What happened? Why would you do that?"

I told her the nitty-gritty details about Damian's contaminated flour and Ben now wanting me to work with his grandson.

"Okay, well the bakery thing's not good. But why resign them? From what you're saying, it's too soon to know how those situations are going to turn out. Maybe that was just Damian's first reaction, and so what if you work with Ben's grandson? They're paying clients and you need the income."

I'd anticipated this kind of response, but it was still jolting to hear the words.

"True, the money's important," I said after a sip of wine. "Very important. And I'm not walking out on either of them. Not when they're in the heat of their problems. But this issue goes back to when I conceived of my company and how I wanted it to be different. Good relationships with clients, caring about them, and feeling good about their products. That's at the heart of it. And now—"

"You know," she interrupted, her tone gentler, "I've always had trouble with how you choose clients. I treat all kinds of people and as long as I do my work with integrity, I figure I'm fine. Working with people is messy. Things are rarely black and white. And you know, there are certain things you have to do, especially when you're getting started in your own business."

"Look, I know you've never agreed with my views on this, but I see my work life as a reflection of my inner life, and that makes things even more complex. So yes, working with people is messy, and none of this is black and white."

I watched her lips form a slight, and I thought, triumphant smile.

"So maybe . . ." she said as she stood up, "maybe I've been right all along?"

Ellen walked behind my chair and threw her arms around me. Then before she left for the kitchen, she turned and told me that she felt closer after our talk.

I couldn't begin to respond.

There was no arguing with her logic, and I took some of what she said to heart. It just wasn't the level at which I wanted to have the conversation.

inner gyroscope

This turn in my path was so much more destabilizing and threatening than I could express. And more complex than I could articulate.

On one level, I was simply facing isolated challenges, each with its own unique sets of circumstances. On another, I felt like I'd taken a hit from a torpedo, as if the seminal intention of my business was under attack.

The stabilizing factor in that situation, and in others when I'd felt I was suffering an unbearable loss, was an invisible core somewhere inside me—a kind of inner gyroscope that could get pushed from one side to the other but always found its way back to true center.

When I finally restored my equilibrium, I saw the message within the difficulties. I was being pushed (kicking and screaming) into a more refined, more flexible, interpretation of what I'd set out to do.

Fundamentally, I was on a quest to translate my epiphany experience of transcendent love into day-to-day materiality. That was my true center, the nucleus around which everything revolved. And my trust in it was redemptive.

So, with this fresh understanding, my business strategy shifted. I would work with clients and products I felt aligned with. Period. That meant my choice-making needed to honor this hard-to-articulate feeling, this sense of inner alignment, rather than relying on my thoughts and assumptions about what it was supposed to look like.

The journey had taught me some of this before, but clearly, I hadn't learned enough.

chapter thirty

Get a Job

I was exhausted from an unusually jammed day of unusually intense client presentations, plus meeting a new prospect. It was good to be home. I put two wine glasses on the counter, poured mine half full, and then went into the bedroom and switched on CNN. Ellen would be home soon and I wanted to decompress. We'd planned to catch an early movie and do some light grocery shopping afterwards.

Fifteen minutes later I heard her key in the lock and shouted a cheery, "Welcome home, I'm in here!"

She entered the bedroom all aglow but as her eyes met mine, her bright smile disappeared. She dropped her purse on the chair and marched out of the room. A moment later she was back. She kicked off her shoes, threw her scarf onto the floor, and then retreated to the bathroom. The door slammed and from inside I heard her sing a phrase from a late 1950s doo-wop classic: "Get a job, sha na na na, sha na na na, getta job!"

Then she turned on the faucet full force as if to drown out anything I might say in response.

"What the hell's bothering you?" I bellowed, jumping up from the bed.

The water stopped and she reemerged, pausing in the bathroom doorway.

"I feel like I'm the only wage earner around here!" She brushed past me. "I work hard! I go to my office, put in five, sometimes six

full days a week, often nights, and when I come home you're lounging around my apartment with a glass of wine in your hand and, God
help us, watching TV!"

She stormed back into the bathroom and slammed the door again.

"You assumed the worst from the minute you walked in," I yelled,
wanting my anger to pierce the wall between us. "I had a very productive day. Up since four-thirty, then two big meetings with current
clients, then coffee with two new prospects. And by the way, I got
home not more than fifteen minutes before you did!"

"Yeah, well, every day's a big day for me!" came the reply. "And
then I come home, and there you are lying around like a—"

She halted her tirade mid-sentence, as if to stop from saying
something she'd regret.

"Lying around like a what?" I yelled back.

After a few long moments, the bathroom door opened.

"Seeing you lie around . . ." she gestured toward the bed. "I just
hate you wasting your time—*our* time—and not getting anywhere."

Ellen stared at me, then shifted her body sideways to avoid
touching me as she walked by. The anguish on her face was unmis-
takeable.

Then just outside the bedroom, she turned around. Her eyes
were red with anger. She went to the kitchen, filled her wine glass,
and plopped down in her favorite dining room chair.

Years of disappointment came tumbling out—about not earning
as much as her credentials warranted, about falling for men who
loved her but couldn't provide the life she wanted, and about our
living like *this* when all of our friends lived so well.

I'd heard it all before, yet something was different. Or maybe I
was more open to hearing it. There was a plaintive desperation in
this telling, a deep sadness that found a tender home in my chest. I
felt the venom drain from my body and sat down next to her.

Her grievances then turned to the present—how growing your
own company takes forever, and how ludicrous it was for me to be

piddling around with small accounts. It was unrealistic, she insisted, and counter-productive to try to combine my spiritual sensibilities with my work.

"Obviously," she went on, "I'm more practical than you are. It's time to get on with our lives. But you're still trying to patch a business together with a bunch of dreamers and dropouts. At this rate, we'll never afford a house! And don't get me started on you spending mornings on that book of yours."

I bolted out of my chair, took a few steps, then stood there staring at her. I couldn't believe all that bitterness was pent up inside her.

"You're serious? All our problems are about me? I'm a little tired of hearing how unjust your life is and how it's on me to fix it. And when have you ever wanted to understand what I'm trying to do and why I think it'll work? You make tons of assumptions." I took a breath. "Besides, if this is really how you feel, why the hell are we together?"

"Because we love each other!" she said, now standing up and facing me. "And I want our life together to be wonderful."

"Well, you're not showing it!" I picked up my wine glass, went into the kitchen, and came back with water.

"Don, *you're* the one I want to be with. And you're absolutely right," she exhaled deeply. "A lot of this stuff is mine, and I shouldn't be looking to you to solve that. It's just that I *don't* think you're living up to your potential. And I get what you're trying to do in your business. I just don't trust it."

I shook my head. "I think you would've liked the me I was in Chicago better."

"I love you now! All I'm trying to say is that it's not such a good idea to live your life by what happened in that *one* experience. Sure, it was amazing. But I think you're making too much of it."

"Look," I said, my anger barely in check. "I know we're out of sync on this. And believe me, I know the pain and frustration of feeling one-down when we're with our friends."

I took a long breath and sat back down.

"Here's the thing," I said, turning to face her, "I love you too—and, I'm finally doing work I love. And what happened to me by the pool that day is a big deal because *that's* what taught me to trust love. And trusting love is what makes me want to be with you despite our differences. And by the way, I fully trust that the money will be there."

"Yeah . . . someday."

"Well, I think it's gonna be sooner than you think."

She said nothing.

"Okay, look," I went on, still seeing the disbelief in her eyes, "if we trust anything right now it has to be *us*. We love each other and that tells me we're on the right track. Together. We just need to trust that."

"Or what?"

Confused and surprised by her response, I hesitated to say what came into my mind. Then I said it anyway.

"If we don't trust love over everything else, then what do we have? How do we have a future together without that?" The words flowed from somewhere deep inside me, and I felt relieved.

She looked at me though tears and nodded. "I *do* trust our love. It's the most important thing."

I put my arms around her, and she buried her head on my shoulder. It felt like we'd walked to the edge of a precipice and stopped.

"Would you see a therapist with me?" she asked through her sobs.

"Of course."

"I'll ask around. Gabe and Daniel see a guy."

We were both drained and raw, but the distance between us was evaporating. We stood up and held each other a long moment more. Ellen then pulled some leftovers from the fridge and we snacked in silence at the counter.

"I don't know about you," I said, "but I'm too wiped to go to a movie."

"Tell me about it," she smiled lightly. "How 'bout we watch something here?"

"Perfect. Shall I make some popcorn while you find something to watch?"

She nodded and started toward the bedroom, but stopped and put her hand on my chest. "I know I've said it, but I really do love you and I want to be with you." Then she added, "We're going to have the best time in Greece."

chapter thirty-one

The Launch

Our trip to Greece would soon be upon us and I was increasingly edgy about the whole bean coffee test. Sales figures were just coming in and we'd scheduled a meeting to review them.

On the way to Pedro's office, I stopped to greet the founder of the company, the father of the siblings who managed it. He was sitting behind his desk, dressed in a white shirt and dark tie, reading the *Wall Street Journal*—just as he was each of the other mornings I'd visited the plant. In his late eighties and retired, he still came in early each day to inspect the quality of the green coffee beans as they arrived.

"Good morning!" I'd say, stopping at his door. "How are you today?"

He'd look up and smile, "I'm still here."

"Good." I'd say. "*Very* good!"

He'd hold my gaze for a moment, nod appreciatively, then return to his paper. I'd nod too, and then head to my meeting. He never joined us, although I knew he had a say in every major decision.

APPROACHING THE DOORWAY, I could hear the four siblings chatting. They seemed in a bubbly mood.

After a round of warm greetings, Pedro handed me a spreadsheet.

"It's obviously too soon to know for sure, but it *looks* promising." I scanned the numbers and saw he was right. All twenty-five test stores were showing an unexpectedly high volume of sales. In some locations our numbers were better than the competition's.

Before I could comment, Pedro handed me another spreadsheet. They'd already calculated costs for a more significant rollout. Assuming the test period continued with these results, they were ready to launch their new brand.

AFTER THE MEETING, José, who was in charge of sales, walked with me to my car. He talked excitedly about this and that, including how much his father liked me.

"Really?" I said. "That's great. I've been saying 'hi' and asking how he's doing, and he always says: 'I'm still here.' It's our little ritual."

"Yeah, he mentioned that you've been stopping by." Then with a playful grin, he added, "He also said each time he sees you, your beard reminds him of Fidel Castro."

"Holy shit," I said, lowering my voice. I looked at José and we both burst out laughing. "That's the last person I want to remind him of!"

José was still smiling when he turned to leave and said he'd see me soon. He didn't seem bothered at all. But I was. I stood there shaking my head. *Castro? Yikes.* Did I really remind the family patriarch of the man who impounded their coffee plantation? I had great affection for their dad, and he'd never given me any indication of discomfort and definitely no hint that I reminded him of the guy who'd plundered everything he owned and, for a while, ruined his life.

I could think of nothing else all the way home. I lived in my Birkenstocks, and I loved my jeans and my beard. This was the unvarnished me who had emerged after leaving my Brooks Brothers suits back in Chicago.

By the time I got to the apartment, the stellar news about initial coffee sales was gone from my consciousness. The first thing I did when I walked through the front door was head straight to the bathroom to study my face in the mirror. It was then that I realized how much this family had come to mean to me.

I pulled out the electric shaver, unused for almost a decade, and began my task.

A FEW DAYS LATER, I was back at the coffee plant. I greeted their dad in the usual way and waited for him to comment on my beardless chin.

But nothing.

Had he even noticed? I didn't know.

I did know, however, that the rest of the family noticed. The teasing started immediately. No one said anything about it directly, but it was evident that they understood the significance of my gesture and were touched by it.

THE BODHI TREE BOOKSTORE on Melrose Avenue had been a kind of metaphysical refuge during those years when I was trying to figure out what the hell was happening to me.

Walking in there now, the pungent aromas of incense and coffee curled into my nose, and I was incapable of resisting. I purchased a small espresso and sipped it while perusing titles on travel in Greece. I'd promised Ellen I'd look for some books that highlighted interesting places. After scouring the shelves, I picked up a small, well-illustrated volume and found several pages profiling the Minoan Castles of Crete. I remembered reading about the mythic king, Minos, and the labyrinths there, and made a mental note that this might be an interesting site for us to visit.

As our date of departure grew closer, Ellen and Daniel were still spending time on the phone, adjusting details within the still-fluctuating itinerary. Plans seemed to change every few days, but Ellen kept assuring me we'd have as much time alone as we wanted. We'd have the comfort and fun of traveling with good friends, but also have our romantic times. We mused about taking side trips on our own and enjoying intimate dinners at bistros by the sea.

It was comforting to watch my excitement build, and Ellen's. It helped that all my clients were prepared for my absence and seemed happy for me to have the time away.

JUST DAYS BEFORE DEPARTURE, I received an odd-sounding phone message from my Ojai partners. I called immediately and the conversation went in circles for several minutes before I learned what was on their minds.

"As you know," Terry said, clearing his throat, "our marketing plan calls for the purchase of significantly more coffee. But now, uh . . . well, we wanted to tell you, we're running pretty short of cash and we had this thought. How would you feel about loaning us money for the additional coffee? Think of it as an investment in our growth. We'd pay it back, of course, and at a good interest rate."

As he spoke, I assumed he and Dave shared the mutual illusion that after the sale of my house in the Hollywood Hills, I was sitting on lots of ready cash.

"There's no hurry," Terry went on. "No pressure. Just think about it and let us know when you get back from Greece."

After the call ended, I went over to the window somewhat stunned. I needed to think. Putting money into Dave and Terry's business, even as a loan, had absolutely no appeal. I had the resources to grow my own business, but investing in somebody else's? But it wasn't simply about the money. It would mean a level of involvement that I was sure would pull me off course.

As I gazed out the window I saw a red squirrel making his way carefully along a power line. He looked like he had an acorn in his mouth and was stopping every few steps to look down and around before moving forward. This furry little guy reminded me of a tightrope walker. He also reminded me of me.

A PHONE CALL THE following day changed everything.

"Sorry to call again so soon," Terry said in an alarmingly apologetic voice. "Things have gotten a little more complicated. The coffee growers offered us the money."

"Really?"

"Yeah. When they heard we were cutting the size of our coffee order they wanted to know what was going on. I told them about us being jammed up and they offered us the cash right away."

"What are the terms?" I asked, concerned for their best interests and my own.

"Well, there is a catch. They want a third of our business."

"A third? That's seems like lot. And are they aware I have a third?"

"They are now. When I told them, they said we should get the money from you."

"And if I choose not to invest?"

"They'll only give us the money if they get a piece of the company."

"I see your dilemma," I replied. "And theirs. It does complicate things. Let me mull it over a bit more and get back to you. I don't want to make a decision like this without some thought."

After the call, my mind went into overdrive. How could I best serve my partners' interests as well as my own? If I refused to step aside, I'd block the investment the Ojai guys sorely needed. I couldn't sell my share back to them because they had no way to pay for it. I could elect to sell my share to the growers, but then the money would go to me rather than to my partners, which didn't solve their problem.

FIRST THING THE NEXT morning I called Terry and Dave and asked if they'd had any further thoughts or new information. They assured me again that they would understand if I decided not to front the money. They'd decline the offer and simply postpone their expansion.

"I've decided to give you back my third," I said, now certain about my choice.

"What! Give it back? You've put in a ton of hours already and helped us so much."

"I know, and thank you. But I don't want to invest cash, and I don't want to stand in your way."

"Are you saying you'd just step aside?" Terry asked. "Like that?"

"That's what I'm saying. Let's call our partnership an experiment that's turning out differently than we anticipated."

"Tell him we can get along without the investment," Dave yelled from somewhere in the back of their office. "I'd rather have his marketing brains."

"Tell Dave I appreciate that," I said, smiling into the phone, "but your business needs capital too. And I'd like to see you get it."

"What about our relationship?" Terry asked. I could tell he was disappointed by what my offer meant and was trying to make the best of it.

"I'm not going anywhere," I told him. "I'll be here when you need me."

In the end, we agreed I'd continue working with them and that they could call me whenever they wanted. To compensate me for giving up my share in their business they'd pay my full rate going forward.

We'd created our partnership with a handshake, and now, we were dissolving it with a caring conversation over the phone. I would always be grateful to them for being my first client in my new venture. In that way, they'd given me more than they knew.

MY BUSINESS WAS MORPHING before my eyes and moving me in ways I couldn't have anticipated. Yet with each step I felt more on course. It was also nudging me to trust signals beyond those that could be measured.

chapter thirty-two

Greece

Our party of nine arrived in Paris.

After an easy walk through customs, we took taxis to our hotel in San Germain where six others joined us—a woman friend of Daniel's who lived in France, three Americans who'd arrived earlier that morning, and Ruth and her friend Mark, the physician who'd introduced me to Ron Scolastico. The following day, we all flew to Athens and made our way to the Britannia Hotel.

The general manager met us in the lobby. A few paces behind him was a photographer who identified himself as being from the local paper. They'd obviously been informed that a celebrity would be staying there. The manager cozied up to Gabe, and after several smiling photos took him and Daniel to a luxury suite that included a broad balcony overlooking the park. The rest of us were given tiny inside rooms that faced a bright yellow light shaft. As someone in our party quipped, "It was the night Gabe got the suite and the rest of us got the shaft."

Ellen and I were exhausted by the time we got to our room, but I was still looking forward to an intimate evening together.

"So where would you like to eat?" I asked while we dressed. "I noticed an open-air restaurant in the park across the street."

"Oh, I thought I told you . . ." she said offhandedly. "Daniel and I are going shopping. I'll probably grab something with him."

"What?" *Did I hear right?* "We're not having dinner together?"

"Daniel and I have been planning for months to go shopping our first night here," she declared, as if this fact would remove the sting from my chest.

"You're kidding me! On our first night in Greece?"

"Can't you eat with the group?" she shot back.

I stared at her.

"You like Mark," she went on, her tone now impatient. "Couldn't you just call him and Ruth? And maybe not be so silly about this?"

Ellen pulled her toiletries from the suitcase and retreated to the bathroom.

I was boiling with anger. She was so self-possessed, so sure of her rightness, that I began questioning myself. Was I overreacting? Had I exaggerated my expectations about this being our trip? Maybe, but the deepest cut was from the cavalier way she dismissed my wanting us to be together—as if that was a trifling afterthought.

Ellen finished dressing in silence then grabbed her purse and mumbled a curt goodbye.

"Well, at least I know your priorities," I muttered loudly enough for her to hear.

Without looking back, she was out the door and gone.

I hated the churning in my gut, and I hated being that angry. Part of me wanted to go downstairs and ask for a separate room, but I knew where such a dramatic reaction would take us. Instead, I tried to see it through different eyes.

Ellen's relationship with Daniel and Gabe was long and caring, well established before I showed up. She'd even asked their opinion before letting herself get serious about me. And with Daniel, it was as if they were twins separated at birth, so of course the two of them loved being together.

But where do I fit in all this? I wondered. *Didn't we just have a cathartic evening about what we mean to each other? About our bond of love? About this being OUR romantic trip?*

I stared out the window at the stack of red-geranium flower boxes that sat on every windowsill in the shaft, but my eyes found no place to rest. "Okay, Don," I said half aloud, "it's a huge misunderstanding, but it's one dinner. Why the hell are you so upset about all this?"

AFTER A FEW ROUNDS of pacing our small room, a fragment of insight emerged. Ellen's night out with Daniel was *not* the issue. It wasn't even her dismissive tone. It was what her actions revealed about us as a couple.

I sat down on the bed and with devastating clarity saw what I'd been trying to ignore. We were not who I thought we were. Not who I hoped we were. Our perceptions of what it meant to be in love, and to make love the center of our life together, didn't match.

Somewhere deep in my being, a spell was broken.

I was also pissed.

The phone rang. My head was pounding from fatigue and distress. I answered it anyway.

"Hey Don, it's Mark. Ruth and I were wondering if you two would like to have dinner with us?"

"Ellen's having dinner with Daniel," I managed to spit out.

"Really?"

"Yeah, really," I said, not bothering to disguise my resentment. "But I'd love to!"

"Great! It'll be good to have some time with you. Meet you in the lobby in twenty."

Heading downstairs, I noticed that I was looking forward to the evening. It was always fun to be around Mark. He could be unabashedly playful. And each time I listened to a Scolastico tape, I sent him a nod of appreciation for introducing me. I didn't know Ruth as well, but she felt like one of us from the instant we met. She was a nurse and Jungian therapist, and potentially a wonderful friend. I was grateful, not just for the dinner rescue, but for time alone with them both.

After a good meal and lively conversation, the three of us went walking, and of course we ran into Ellen and Daniel and their handfuls of shopping bags. I wasn't proud of myself but when they joined us, I more or less ignored her. Back in our room we undressed in silence and climbed into a large feather bed without a word or touch between us.

STILL HOLDING THE SILENCE, I packed the few items I'd pulled out the night before while Ellen struggled to accommodate the bounty from her shopping spree. We were the last to join the others on the sidewalk near the limos. Ellen and I ended up in a car with a couple we'd just met, and I let myself be absorbed by their breezy commentary about the scenes of Athens flying by us.

In a short time, we reached the Port of Piraeus and unloaded our luggage. I was still smoldering and thought my best chance of relieving the pain of isolation was to force myself to be present with the people around me. I moved down the wharf to connect with a few others in our party while Daniel and Gabe were in the harbor master's office handling the paperwork.

When the two of them reappeared, we saw bad news written on their faces. The gleaming, white Princess of the Seas, the yacht displayed in the brochure that we'd leased months earlier, was not in the harbor. The Italian businessman who had it the week before decided to keep it a few days longer. There was nothing they, or we, could do about it.

The harbor master emerged from his office and despite the pressure, managed a buoyant attitude as he apologized and offered us two options: one a cruiser, the other a sailboat. Daniel didn't buy it. He muttered something about bait and switch, wondering if the exquisite ship in the pictures even existed. But we all felt—as the harbor master no doubt was counting on—that either of these two options was better than none. Both were docked nearby so we walked the short distance for closer looks.

"This one was once chartered by the Beatles," the harbor master announced, pointing at a gray, slightly weathered cruiser. "And they loved it!"

Seeing little excitement in any of our faces, he moved us along the quay to what appeared to be a fishing boat. It was rigged for sails but looked more like a hardworking commercial vessel. We were assured that despite appearances it was a pleasure boat large enough to sleep fifteen comfortably, and that its twin diesel engines were in good working order in case we needed power. Best of all, it could be ready in an hour.

As we stood there, disappointed and undecided, a handsome crew member came out of the cabin and, as if following a script, took off his shirt and started hauling ropes on deck. His broad shoulders and dark skin gleamed in the sun. After several minutes, he looked up and saw us watching him. He waved and smiled and went back to work.

"Let's take this one," Mark said with a sly lift in his voice. The women laughed and quickly agreed, obviously thinking the same thing, and the choice was made. This wasn't the elegant yacht we were promised and was much less than we'd anticipated, but it was the better of the two.

MY DARK MOOD FROM the night before was lightening a bit. Still, I couldn't shake a layer of heaviness. We boarded the ship and found the accommodations better than expected from the look of the exterior. We tussled a bit to figure who got what cabin, but soon we were all unpacked and gathered for drinks on deck while the crew prepared to cast off.

Right after we set sail, I walked to the stern of the ship and leaned against the rail. I was watching the coastline growing smaller when Ellen joined me. She took my arm and told me how sorry she was about the mess-up with dinner. Her apology sounded genuine but, frankly, her attempt to connect reignited my anger.

My heart ached from the fissure in our relationship. I didn't know how or when to tell her what I was feeling, but certainly not now. To do so would ruin us. I draped my arm around her shoulder and we both focused on the ship's wake unfurling behind us.

LATER THAT AFTERNOON, a violent storm tested us all, including the crew.

It got so bad that our captain, a young man who'd spent his life at sea, had to relieve his stomach from the fantail. Everyone else found solace below in their quarters, except a few like me who felt better up on deck, eyes glued to the horizon. The storm showed no signs of abating, so the crew decided to put into port at the nearby island of Kea.

By morning the sea was calm again, so we resumed our course to Mykonos where we'd spend several days. We breakfasted and lunched at sea, and then docked in the harbor in time to go ashore for an early dinner. Mykonos was the group's most anticipated island, a place known for its nude beaches, artist colonies, glamorous crowds, and unending night life. It was here that I felt the most relaxed with Ellen, aided perhaps by healthy portions of Retsina wine. It was also here that Mark finally cajoled me to get up and dance with him.

With each new island it seemed that the white-washed buildings grew brighter, more immaculate, while the spectacular blues of the domes and the ocean grew more varied and rich. My camera and I were helpless in the face of it.

As for Ellen and me, we immersed ourselves in the group. We were cordial with each other, even kind, but rarely alone.

WHEN WE LEFT MYKONOS, we were given the option of making a side trip to Delos, a small island sanctuary once sacred to the mythical god Apollo and goddess Artemis. We wandered through gleaming marble ruins and found our way to the island's featured relic—the eroded mosaic floors from a house said to have been Cleopatra's.

Each place we visited was more wondrous than anticipated, but most astounding was the island of Santorini. Arguably one of the most beautiful spots on the planet, it was breathtaking to sail into the harbor on the side of the caldera formed by a huge, once-active volcano. Towering above us was an unbroken line of gleaming white homes clinging to the edge of the ancient cliffs, and above that the sky was bluer than I'd ever seen. Something about being in that caldera was startling, even unsettling, but it was the next and final leg of our journey where I had the most compelling experience of our trip.

WE SAILED BACK TO Piraeus and caught a plane to Heraklion, capital of Crete and birthplace of the mystical painter El Greco and the important Greek writer and philosopher, Nikos Kazantzakis.

On our first day there, we visited the Palace of Knossos, a reconstruction of the largest Minoan castle on Crete. After roaming this remarkable structure for a short while with a handful from our group, I entered a room by myself and suddenly felt lightheaded. In front of me was a wall painting of several young gymnasts leaping over a charging bull. Gazing at this scene, I experienced an oddly personal connection to it, as if I'd somehow taken part in the drama myself.

It took a moment, but I regained my equilibrium and continued on. After that, everything in this reconstructed maze of rooms seemed starkly familiar, leaving me enrobed in a sort of extended déjà vu.

When I caught up with Ellen, I casually mentioned my experience but she turned away, apparently preoccupied with other things. In this uncomfortable vacuum, I wondered who I could discuss reincarnation with and immediately thought of Mark and Ruth—and my skincare clients back home.

OUR LAST FEW DAYS on Crete were a welcome contrast to island hopping.

We visited an array of historic sites, but my odd experience at the Minoan palace kept returning to the forefront of my mind. At a local store, I found a book explaining how the Santorini volcano probably created a tidal wave that reached Crete, destroying everything in its path. My heart ached at the thought of that original palace being engulfed by the sea and smashed to ruins. The images stayed with me on the flight from Heraklion back to Athens.

In Athens, we boarded a plane to London, then to New York. On the flight home to LA, I finally fell asleep, the volume I'd picked up at the Bodhi Tree Bookstore about the Minoan Castles of Crete still on my lap.

palpable distinction

I hated what happened that first night in Athens and the shadow it cast on the rest of our trip. But it did bring new clarity. It helped me see that love had become the context in which I lived—or was trying to live—in my work and my relationships (although I was obviously better at the work part).

By contrast, in my old life, love and a loving relationship would've appeared on a list of what makes up a good life, along with family, friends, a financially stable career, a comfortable place to live, and maybe a dog.

The distinction was now palpable. Love was no longer an item on a list. It was, for me, the totality of all life—of who we all are—and the center of how I wanted to be in the world. And now it was impossible to ignore that this wasn't being expressed in my relationship with the most important person in my life.

When we first met, I knew something significant was happening. I felt a strong attraction toward her, soul and body, and sensed that this was a person with whom I could find a depth of love not possible earlier in my life. Although those feelings softened over time, that original love was still alive for me.

Yet I was torn. In the stark light of our many differences, I couldn't help but wonder what had really drawn us to each other. And why?

I sometimes glimpsed the magnificence of who we could become together if we both made love our central priority. Other times, I wondered if our relationship was just a taste of our yearnings for love, rather than the fulfillment of them.

chapter thirty-three

The Modem

It was our first morning back in LA, and instead of luxuriating in closeness from our much-anticipated romantic trip, I woke up in uncomfortable territory. The love between us, which was once so tangible, now seemed beyond our reach.

To Ellen's credit, immediately after that awful first night in Athens, she made some serious efforts to be loving and attentive, albeit surrounded by the group. This helped patch the rift, but for me, it didn't heal the source. I wanted us to talk in depth about what happened, but somehow we never did. Perhaps we never wanted to. Or maybe we just didn't know how.

A few fleeting insights while we were away had eased the pain, but there was still much for me to understand and digest.

Ellen headed to the office early to reorient herself and prepare for patients, and I was happy to be alone. After an unsuccessful attempt to meditate, I watered my bonsai and trimmed a few dying leaves, then sat down at my desk.

The coffee family was very much on my mind, and I was hungry for details about our new product launch. Their file topped the neatly organized stack on my desk, but I refrained from grabbing it. I'd had the foresight to make notes about each client, including recent choices and likely next steps, and had told them I'd check in shortly after our return. I was determined to avoid my old habit of jumping right back into the fray, making things more urgent than they were. I also wanted solitary time to put finishing touches on my manuscript—a choice I was happy I'd made.

THERE ARE FEW THINGS more dispiriting after spending weeks away than having to confront LA's morning rush hour. After suffering the endless pauses between stopping and going, I arrived at the coffee plant late and jittery, and to a completely full parking lot and no openings on the street. I finally found a spot a couple blocks away, which was probably good because the walk gave me time to center myself. Then, as I reached the front door, a jolt of apprehension hit me. What if something had gone wrong with the launch while I was away?

Thankfully, my fears were short-lived.

When I joined the family in the president's office, they were buzzing about the new project. They greeted me warmly, asked how the trip was, and proceeded to show me the numbers. Sales had continued to accelerate, and they were having trouble keeping up with the orders. The company had experienced years of steady but limited growth, and this solid reception in a major supermarket chain was an exciting breakthrough.

It was also a breakthrough for me. In Chicago I'd been part of many successful new product introductions, even at the center of some, but this was wholly different. During those years, even when I led the group, I was always a team player in a giant agency, often working under killing pressure to produce results for faceless clients with vast budgets, each of whom had been assigned to me from above. By comparison, the modest budgets and personal flavor of my relationship with the family tasted particularly sweet.

MY POST-VACATION RE-ENTRY plan worked. Each time I scheduled a client meeting, instead of dreading it, I was excited about connecting again. I was even happy with Paige's suggestion that we meet this time in Newport Beach.

At first, I'd been taken aback by her choice of the Four Seasons, but walking into the hotel, I was pleasantly surprised at the understated elegance of the place. Unlike many luxury properties, this one seemed to have been designed to fit nicely into the locale.

We'd agreed on a 7:30 a.m. start time, and traffic was considerably lighter than I'd planned for. I checked the restaurant to see if she was early too, then wandered through the lush hotel gardens and around the shimmering pool before asking the maitre d' for a table by the window. My first cup of coffee was being freshly poured when I saw Paige's joyous smile from across the room. I waved and stood to greet her.

"Nice hotel," I said, signaling for the waiter.

"Glad you like it! We love it here. It's always quiet and gentle, and breakfast is quite modest compared to the ambience. Besides, I don't believe in avoiding nice surroundings just because my business and I are on a spiritual path."

"Agreed!"

"So, how was your trip?" she asked, after ordering tea.

"It was amazing, as you can imagine."

"Tell me. I know virtually nothing about Greece."

"There's so much to say. And we got to sail to so many islands, and the views from the ship were often spectacular. You've seen those iconic pictures of whitewashed buildings contrasted against blue roofs and ultra-blue skies? It's even more striking in person."

"I'll bet."

"Another standout was visiting a reconstruction of an Minoan castle on Crete."

"A castle?"

"Yeah, I know it sounds strange and it was. Walking around the place I kept having this feeling that I'd been there before, walked the halls before. Maybe even lived there. That kind of thing."

She nodded but said nothing.

"In this one room, there was a fresco on the wall of young men leaping over a charging bull. For some reason, that image had a huge impact on me, like . . . this might sound crazy, but like I might have been one of those young men."

"Or maybe the painter who painted them? You're an artist, right?"

"I didn't think of that, but yeah," I replied, encouraged by her openness. "It was a visceral kind of thing, not just a passing thought. And that sensation kept being there as I walked the rest of the palace. I tried talking about it with a few folks on the trip but no one seemed interested."

"Ouch."

I nodded, recalling the isolation I'd felt that day, but stopped myself from saying more. "So, shall we get started on your plan?"

"Oh yes, I almost forgot," she laughed. "We're on my dime."

She pulled out a document and handed it to me. We'd agreed by phone that I'd arrive early and that she'd drop off her updated marketing plan for me to review. Then I'd join her and Tim at their home to finalize details before she introduced their product line to spas.

Paige finished her cup of tea and left me to my task. I ordered some fruit and toast and began.

Like the partial draft she'd shown me previously, this version was thorough and sophisticated, now with just a few loose ends. About an hour later, I drove to their house and told them that once they resolved a few open questions about distribution to spas, we were ready to go.

Paige seemed relieved at my assessment, and neither she or Tim tried to hide their excitement. Back on the 405, this time heading north, I hoped that this, too, would be a successful launch.

AFTER SPENDING SO MUCH time swimming in an ocean of words, I couldn't believe I had a finished draft of my manuscript. It wasn't perfect, but it was readable. I ordered six copies printed and bound, and on my way home from picking them up I stopped to send one to Jennifer. She was the first person to encourage me to write a book, and the only one I'd shown chapters to while it was in progress.

Jennifer was often on my mind these days, and I wondered if it was simply because she was my best hope for insightful comments.

That evening, I presented a copy of the manuscript to Ellen. I had qualms about her reading it, but of course wanted to share it with her. She'd stopped objecting to how much time I spent on it and assured me she wanted to read it when it was done. I also needed the feedback. (As a writer once told me, criticism from an unfriendly reader is worth ten times the praise from a friend.)

"Oh, good," she said, setting it near her purse. "Congrats!"

Over the next few days, I distributed copies to our closest friends and tossed the remaining one in the bottom drawer of my desk.

I was no stranger to presenting creative work to others, important clients and astute critics alike. Sometimes it was scary, sometimes not. Sometimes I won, sometimes I got sent back to the drawing board, literally. It was all part of the risk, part of the process. But now as a new author, I felt vulnerable in a way I'd never experienced before. The book was a memoir—a universe away from all the writing I'd done in advertising and even from the stories I'd crafted for screenplays. This book (if it ever become one) was about my struggle to leave the allure and security of a big job in a large corporation in hopes of closing the gap between my soul and my work. It revealed brutal details about my career disasters and personal dramas before getting to the good stuff at the end.

Giving such an intimate account to our friends, all of whom had dazzling careers . . . I felt like I was jumping off a cliff.

I gave it to them anyway.

EARLY THE FOLLOWING WEEK, Paige and I began working on a press release for spa trade publications. We agreed that to save money she'd write the initial copy and send it to me for feedback. By now I'd given into her cajoling and had purchased a Mac, but I was still fumbling around learning to use it. Since I hardly knew what the word "modem" meant, Paige had to lead me through the process by phone.

"Is your modem turned on?" she asked. "Is the display lit?"

"Uh, well there's this little green light in the—"

"Good! That's it. Do you have your modem software open? You should see a window on your desktop."

"I think that's what I'm seeing."

"Great. You're doing great!"

Phew! I thought to myself. *We're underway and I haven't made a fool of myself. Yet.*

"Now," Paige prompted gently, "on the menu bar under Status, be sure it's set to Receive, not Send. It'll work better that way."

"Menu bar?"

"Oops, sorry. Yes, the menu bar is that string of words along the upper edge of that window you opened."

"Oh, okay. Receive is selected." I felt like a newbie pilot being coached through the pre-takeoff checklist.

"Now hit the button that says 'Ready.'"

"Done."

"Great. I'll send now. You can just sit back and wait."

I relaxed into my chair, relieved. Then a few seconds later my computer emitted an eerie, high-pitched techno squeal. "Eel!" I exclaimed. I couldn't tell if this was supposed to happen or if my equipment was self-destructing. Either way, my mind was imagining our two modems coupling somewhere out in hyperspace.

"Eeeek?" Paige asked. "What does Eeeek mean? Are you okay?"

"Just Eeeek!" I laughed, a bit embarrassed but still delighting in the strange murmurs of this midair union. I didn't know if it was just me, or maybe it was a guy thing, but those two computers connecting in the virtual heavens had a distinctly carnal feel.

Then the sounds shifted to a higher octave. "Ackkk! What the—"

"Ackkk? Is that the same as 'Eeeek'?" Now she was laughing too.

"Totally different. It's Greek!"

We both giggled. I was glad she was having fun with this too, but doubted that she shared my vision of two machines in some erotic rendezvous in the ethers between Los Angeles and Orange County.

"Is it downloading?" Paige asked as the buzzing continued.

"I guess so. Little lights are flashing on the modem and a bar on the screen is filling up." A few minutes later my Mac was quiet again.

"Okay, that's it. You should have the file now."

She was right. The file was exactly where she told me to look, safely on my computer. I opened it and assured her we'd succeeded.

"Boy, that was amazing," I said, a bit lightheaded from the experience.

"So, you *do* like technology," she teased. "C'mon, admit it!"

"Well, I'm not ready to say that, but it sure was an adventure."

"It's fun to see you so excited," she said. "I don't think I've ever heard you squeal before."

"That makes two of us."

chapter thirty-four

Feedback

Therewas an unexpected side benefit to the growth of my
business. It provided a compelling distraction while waiting for feedback on the manuscript. In addition, having to juggle more than a
handful of clients with projects in various stages of development was
good for my bank account—and my ego too.

It took several months, but I finally had comments from each of
my friends.

Gil got back to me first. He'd quit reading midway because "as
a therapist" this kind of book was too much like his work. Daniel
responded next. He thought it was "really interesting," presumably
a polite alternative when you don't want to say what you really
think. Beth said she liked it and returned the manuscript with typo
and grammar edits, making her feedback the most useful of the
bunch.

Ellen also said she liked it and wondered about my plans for it.
But before I could tell her that a screenwriter friend of mine had
offered to connect me with a New York literary agent, she shifted
the conversation to our weekend plans. Beth told me later that Ellen
was embarrassed by it.

She wasn't the only one who was embarrassed. All in all, instead
of being buoyed by usable critiques and at least some reassurance, I
felt stupid for having let my friends see it—humiliated actually.

There was one friend left to hear from but it seemed pointless to care. Tired of looking at the stack of returned manuscripts sitting on the corner of my desk, I finally tossed them into a bankers box that sat in the corner behind my filing cabinet, making a mental note to trash them as soon as I could bring myself to do that.

A week later, I heard back from Jennifer. Her message announced that she'd read the manuscript and wanted to talk. As I was dialing her number, I reminded myself that she'd surely find some way to be encouraging. Although, she was always straight with me, so I didn't know what to expect.

We spent a few minutes catching up before she asked if I had time to hear her notes. She then went into great detail about her reactions, some of which were positive, some negative, and suggested a number of solid edits, including that I omit a few chapters to sharpen the story line.

I couldn't believe what I was hearing. Real feedback. Insightful. Specific. Useful. She even offered to do a deep read of the next iteration.

Our conversation left me hopeful, but most restorative was that someone I respected understood the subtle inner process I was trying to communicate.

Still, within hours of that call, the negative comments were swallowing the positive ones. A few days later, I woke up realizing I'd completely lost my appetite to do any further work on the book.

IT TOOK A WHILE, but Ellen followed through about couple's counseling and did some research. Ultimately though, we decided to go with her first instinct and made an appointment with Gabe and Daniel's therapist, who was a psychiatrist. I was unconvinced that a science-based doctor could sympathize with my spiritual orientation, however I welcomed the opportunity to air our differences to a professional who would hopefully offer us something constructive.

In our first session Ellen described me as air-headed in my approach to business, and I described her as too single-minded in her focus on material things. Ellen told the doctor she was afraid I'd lost my drive and ambition. I told him she seemed more interested in my financial success than in me. Ellen responded by saying I was bumping along with less income than I could, and should, be earning. I made the point that I was working on building a new business that could eventually bring in a great deal of money *and* the kind of meaning I'd always wanted from my work. Ellen insisted that when we first met I'd duped her into thinking I was well-to-do and gainfully employed. I responded that she knew quite well what was happening and that we could've saved my house if she'd been willing to move in with me. Ellen suggested that I wasted too much time meditating and writing. I countered that she was impatient and no longer provided the level of support and understanding she once did.

He says, she says, back and forth it went. We were honest, which was good, and it seemed to me that our differences were clearly drawn and addressable.

At the end of the session, the doctor suggested that Ellen see him alone a few times and said he'd get back to me at a later date.

IT WAS GABE AND Daniel's custom to celebrate Christmas at their beach house in Hawaii. We were invited to join them for the fourth straight year, an invitation that was impossible to resist. If this year's celebration was anything like the others, the Christmas tree would almost reach the second floor landing and would sag with precious ornaments. Daniel and Gabe's presents to each other would be stacked knee-high around the tree, and Christmas music would be cranked up from dawn to dusk.

This invitation meant being hosted in their beautiful seaside home, and naturally brought with it an unspoken obligation that we add to the lavish Everest of gifts.

Unlike the trip to Greece, I had no trouble informing clients I'd be away. December was my slowest month, and they were all either on vacation themselves or engrossed in Christmas sales.

Ellen and I used the time to hunt for the perfect presents for each other and our hosts, which wasn't an easy task. Given the quality of their gifts to everyone, our contributions needed to be up to the occasion without being excessively expensive.

Our preparations were falling into place—until the day before we were to leave. A slightly urgent-sounding message from Paige came in. When I called back, she announced that she had something to send me and needed to know where. It had always been my policy to give clients a small gift at Christmas, not the other way around. But rather than argue the point, I gave her the address on Oahu.

Then she dropped a bomb, albeit playfully.

"So, now that you finished your manuscript, where's my copy?"

How does she know it's done? Either she was having a prescient moment or I'd let it slip. But it didn't matter. I'd promised to let her read it at some point. I was cornered.

"Uh, okay," I said, my mind in turmoil. The problem now was bigger than the disasters the book revealed. My friends had essentially panned it. "Let's talk about it at our next meeting," I gulped, trying to deflect her interest.

"Not so fast," she laughed. "I was hoping to read it while you're away. As you know, Tim and I are going on vacation too. We'll be in Pebble Beach and I don't play golf, so I'll have lots of time on my hands."

A wave of humiliation from the feedback came rushing in—along with my fear that this could cost me a valued client.

"Well, I uh . . ."

"C'mon," she cajoled relentlessly. "I don't bite!"

There was a playful insistence in her voice. This quality had no doubt helped her in business, but in that moment I wished it was otherwise.

In the next few seconds my fear took me into the very center of myself. *How can I get out of this?* Then beyond the fear arose another question. Could the sensibilities that make Paige a different kind of client also make her a different kind of reader? Could she see it the way Jennifer had? Perhaps. In some ways our connection had the qualities of a friendship. Plus something was telling me her enthusiasm should be given some weight.

With that, it all turned. Fear gave way to a tentative trust, and the edifice of fearing that had been trying to protect me suddenly collapsed—just as it had when I finally decided to say yes to the coffee roaster.

"You know what?" I said, surprised at my quick turnaround. "I'm almost positive I can UPS it this afternoon."

"That'd be great! If you don't mind, maybe send it 2nd Day Air to be sure I get it before we go?"

The image of her having my manuscript in her hands literally took my breath away. I could still say no.

Then out of my mouth came, "Good idea. UPS 2nd Day Air it is."

"Yay! Thank you."

After our call, I was both alarmed and elated—and a little numb. I sorted through the stack of returned manuscripts for a clean copy but couldn't find one. Then I remembered the one I'd set aside in my desk drawer. I grabbed it and marched myself to the UPS Store. There I wrote a brief note on a yellow sticky, slapped it on the title page, and watched as the clerk sealed the manuscript into the proper envelope.

On the way back to the apartment, my trepidation resurfaced. *What have I done? What if she's disappointed? Or hates it?*

I figured she wouldn't hate it, but reading all that personal stuff would surely alter her impression of who I was. How could it not? And what kind of feedback would she have? And how awkward would it be for her to tell me she didn't like it or couldn't get into it?

I shook my head, trying to dislodge this litany of terrors, and steeled myself for whatever would come next.

chapter thirty-five

Oahu

At Gabe and Daniel's home in Hawaii, their massive Christmas tree was always the center of our festivities. This created another aspect of the annual ritual: plan our flights so Ellen and I could join the guys at the unloading of the last shipment of trees from the mainland. If we didn't time it right, we wouldn't find one tall enough for their spacious living room.

As usual, the two of them flew in before the rest of us to open their house. Ellen and I arrived the following afternoon. The next step was easy. Get to the harbor early enough the following day to have our pick of the shipment.

Daniel and Ellen thought they'd organized the morning perfectly, but when we arrived at the dock, the cluster of containers stood empty. The only trees left were small and scraggly. The four of us were standing there watching this sorry scene when one of the longshoremen recognized Gabe's famous face.

Once again, the powers of celebrity-hood were about to work their magic. The gentleman who'd spotted Gabe greeted him with a big smile and informed us that the trees had come in earlier than expected and were gone—except for a few that had been set aside for a special order. He paused a moment, told Gabe not to worry, and motioned to some workers to prop up the larger trees. While we inspected our options, this group of burly guys remained gathered, staring at Gabe with that astonished but happy smile that people often get in the unexpected presence of a star.

THAT NIGHT WE FORTIFIED ourselves with Christmas music and alcohol in various forms. After we finally got the tree positioned just right, Daniel directed us in the delicate process of layering it with endless strands of clear Italian lights. We held off adding ornaments until the whole gang had arrived.

We met Mark and Ruth at the airport as planned. It was the first time we'd all been together since Greece, and the sight of these good friends was a comfort but also a painful reminder of that catastrophic first night in Athens.

With the decorating complete, we immersed ourselves in shopping, cooking, and wrapping. Much of what took place seemed wildly extravagant, but Daniel's childlike joy raised the celebration of Christmas to an art form and I was grateful to be part of it. In the midst of it all, Ellen and I allowed ourselves to be swept up in the festivities and lose the sense of ourselves as a couple—something that had now become the norm when we were with friends.

EACH MORNING IN HAWAII, I followed the same pattern: arise in the dark and head out to witness the first light of dawn. I loved the solitude of those early hours and enjoyed sitting on the seawall that separated the property from the surf.

The subtleties of that liminal space between night and morning were impossible to ignore that day—the rhythm of the ocean, the faint fragrance of tropical flowers, the soft glow of the sun that would soon rise over the mountains behind me. Then suddenly, a thought stabbed into my calm.

A client is reading my manuscript!

A wave of dread washed over me. I stood up in a panic. I needed to walk. Any peace I'd made with sending Paige the book was gone.

The open gate to the beach caught my eye. I climbed down the rickety steps and felt my feet sink into the cool sand. Once at the surf's edge, I let the warm water squeeze up between my toes and started a brisk walk. It felt good to move my body but the healing waters of the Pacific couldn't pacify my foreboding.

"This sucks," I muttered then tried to calm myself from within. *Sure it would be awful to lose a client, especially this one. And I sure as hell didn't want another negative book review. But neither would be the end of the world. Why is this so damn—*

Then I saw it.

When I originally made my choice about how to build my company, I assumed that the spiritual part would unfold only between me and me. It was my private mission, an orientation that would *inform* how I worked with clients, not a topic I would discuss with them.

Then Paige came along. And over the months it became the most natural thing for our meetings to include conversions about how those larger energies related to her business, particularly her choices.

And now that she was reading about all my failures, I felt like a total imposter.

I'd been forthcoming about my background and candid about who I'd become, but I had not elucidated the messy details and dumb mistakes that were central to my transition—and that created my cocoon of transformation.

Bottom line, I was scared out of my gourd that her learning the whole story would sever the trust we'd built and derail this grand experiment.

Phew. Seeing all that made me feel better, but I needed something more. I turned around and headed back to the house.

Let's see, it's three hours later in LA. By now she's probably up and working.

When I reached the door, I heard stirrings from somewhere inside but didn't see anyone. So I grabbed the phone and let its long cord trail behind me as I walked out to the patio. My clients knew I was on vacation and didn't want to be disturbed, and now here I was breaking my own silence. I hesitated but dialed anyway.

"Morning, Paige," I said cheerily. "It's me, Don. Hope I'm not interrupting you. I was just having some illuminating thoughts about your business."

"Wow, hi! I thought you didn't want to talk shop while you were away."

"I usually don't but I had some, you know, thoughts about next steps that couldn't seem to wait."

I laughed, probably a bit too vigorously, and let the momentum of the call carry me forward. Fortunately, my mind was well-practiced in thinking ahead about a client's business, and a few suggestions unspooled easily from my brain. She seemed appreciative, but my ideas were running dry. *How do I bring up the book?*

"By the way," I blurted, "the manuscript got there, right?"

"Oh, yes, thanks again for the expedited shipping. I started on it," she added. "Tim and I drive up to Pebble Beach tomorrow and I assume I'll finish it up there."

"Great! Well, I hope you like it," I said, trying to tease out any morsel of opinion she might have. Or more honestly, some reassurance or even encouragement.

"I already do," she replied enthusiastically. "I've only read the first few chapters but so far they've grabbed me. Oh! Did you get the box yet?"

"You sent me something?"

"Just a little thank you, nothing much. It's my Christmas tradition."

"You didn't have to do that," I said, wishing she hadn't.

"I know, but I wanted to. You've been such a big help to our business and I . . ."

I didn't hear anything after that. The idea of Paige sending a gift, even a small token, all the way to Hawaii was deeply unsettling.

I couldn't put my finger on why, but this gesture felt . . . what? Intrusive? Too personal?

Paige's other line rang and I couldn't have been happier for the interruption. She put me on hold and came back just long enough to thank me for the call.

When I returned the phone to the kitchen, Mark was making coffee as quietly as he could and pretended to goose me as I passed by. I rolled my eyes playfully, glad for anything that would help me reenter the reality under my nose.

My mind, however, went straight back to Paige reading the book. I was relieved that she liked it so far, but the career messiness was still ahead of her.

chapter thirty-six

Heart-Shaped Muffins

After a late-night celebration, I woke up Christmas morning with a headache punctuated by the piercing sounds of feral roosters announcing the day. Adding to my pain was the all-too-familiar odor from the local chicken farm, which thankfully only reached us when the breezes were blowing the wrong way.

The house was dark and quiet as I eased out of bed, slipped on a T-shirt and shorts, and tiptoed through the living room to the foot of the stairs. Glancing up, I noticed light peeking through the slats of Gabe and Daniel's bedroom door. They and everyone would be awake soon, so I started a pot of coffee and opened several ripe papayas. Finished in the kitchen, I unlocked the sliding glass doors, walked barefoot across the damp grass to the seawall, and stood there inhaling the fresh air off the ocean.

Suddenly, Christmas carols erupted from the house loud enough to turn the heads of campers on the beach nearby. Daniel was definitely up, and he wanted everyone to join him. Back inside I saw the tree lights go on and found him in the living room singing along with the music, "It's beginning to look a lot like Christmas . . ."

One of the things I loved about Daniel was his ability to be shamelessly joyous.

Soon we were all gathered, albeit in various stages of wakefulness. After allowing a few minutes for pouring coffee and getting settled, Daniel positioned himself on the floor and started sorting through gifts, laughing, and calling out names.

"Here's one for Gabe! Here's one for Ellen! C'mon kids! It's time to open our presss . . . ieeess! And I'm ready so I'm going first!"

Daniel picked up the smallest, most beautifully wrapped gift, and Gabe watched eagerly as he opened it. To Daniel's utter delight, it contained an exquisite gem-studded Bulgari watch. I couldn't begin to imagine wearing such a piece, but Gabe and Daniel traveled in some pretty glamorous circles.

Gabe was next. Daniel tapped him on the knee and pointed to a large, bulky, awkwardly wrapped shape partially hidden behind the tree. Tearing off the paper, Gabe uncovered a gorgeous rocking chair handcrafted from the now rare and expensive Hawaiian Koa wood. Gabe pulled the chair away from the tree, settled himself into it, and began rocking with the glee of a little boy. A few seconds later he opened his arms wide, inviting Daniel to join him in a playful embrace.

Ellen and I took the moment to suggest they open our gifts to them: two cashmere lap rugs for cold nights back in Benedict Canyon. In turn, I received a handsome blue blazer that fit perfectly, a subtle suggestion perhaps that my jeans-and-Birkenstocks look needed a makeover.

Ellen's gift from the guys was a delicate gold bracelet with charms that marked the many places they'd traveled together. She fell in love with it instantly and jumped up to embrace them both.

Ruth and Mark exchanged presents next, and from there the one-at-a-time rule gave way to everyone opening whatever anyone handed them. Ellen and I unwrapped our gifts unceremoniously. Before the trip, we'd agreed on no surprises. She gave me a special set of Japanese bonsai tools, and I bought her the Ansel Adams print she'd been wanting.

The stacks of festively wrapped presents had morphed into piles of paper, ribbon, cards, and treasures of all sizes. The room quieted and mock resignation crept into Daniel's face.

Gabe said something about breakfast, but Daniel interrupted with a squeal.

"Wait! I almost forgot. A package came yesterday. For you, Don."

"Oooooo, it's for you, Don," Mark toyed, as Daniel left the room.

I squirmed at the kidding, which always transpired when Mark was around, but marveled at how seamlessly he could slip into his teasing persona.

Daniel returned with the box and hovered over me while he studied the UPS label. "Hmmm . . . looks like it's from a woman," he said, joining Mark in the fun. "From a Paige person. In Newport Beach. Fancy address, dude."

Ellen was seated next to me and I felt both of us tighten. I didn't know what she was feeling, but the tension was unmistakable. But why? She and I both knew this was just a Christmas gift from a client. The guys didn't know that, however, but even if they had, they never passed up an opportunity to play.

As Daniel handed me the box, the Christmas music stopped. As if preplanned, his playlist had come to its end, casting the room in abrupt silence. Everyone's focus was now entirely on me as I examined all sides of the mystery package looking for an easy way into it.

"C'mon, Don!" Daniel laughed. "Open it!"

I fought the shipping tape for an embarrassingly long time, and my struggles stirred far more anticipation than the box deserved.

"So, my friend," Mark started up again, wriggling his eyebrows. "Tell us . . . who *is* this Paige dame?"

"She's a client."

"Slash that tape already!" Daniel directed, as Gabe handed me the knife he'd retrieved from the kitchen. "The lady's gift is awaiting—and so are we!"

Despite the intense prodding, I got past the shipping tape and made my way through a crumple of Christmasy tissue paper. Finally I uncovered a single red box. I lifted the lid and found several individually wrapped presents nestled inside.

Oh my God, what did she send? The packaging itself was beyond a customary professional gift.

I was completely uncomfortable being center stage, but worse, I had no idea what Paige was capable of. I nervously unwrapped the first gift and found myself holding a tiny, furry toy mouse wearing spectacles.

"Awww, it's a Mouse House!" Daniel took it from me and held it up for everyone to see.

"It's a what?" I asked, relieved to have some help.

"Call the exterminator!" Ruth giggled.

"Silly people, it's a cover for a Mac mouse. You know, those new computers," Daniel explained to the roomful of digital novices. "Looks just like you, Don, with those reading glasses down on its nose."

"Oh, that makes sense," I said, my shoulders relaxing. "Paige and her husband have been helping me get functional on my new Mac." I took another look at the cute little thing with big ears and gold wire frames resting on its nose and couldn't resist grinning appreciatively.

Reaching back into the box I took out a large white envelope. Inside was an issue of *Macworld* magazine and a note saying to expect a year-long subscription. Finally, tucked into the corner of the box was a small brightly decorated gift bag with a note clipped to the outside: "Open carefully."

My nostrils told me it was something baked.

"Muffins!" I declared. I held one up for the group to see and caught a look of distress on Ellen's face.

"Not just muffins!" Mark squealed *"Heart-shaped muffins!"* he added, kissing the air, instantly transforming two innocent pastries into something deliciously suspicious.

"Whoooaaaa! So, who *is* this Paige?" Daniel asked again, amplifying the drama. "You've never mentioned her."

"Like I said, she and her husband are clients. I often get thank-you gestures from people I work with."

"Clients, right," Daniel mocked. "Read us the note!"

"Ooooh, she sent a *little note*, did she?" Mark chimed in relentlessly.

I pulled the card from the rumpled paper. "Merry Christmas to Don and Ellen. Hope you enjoy the little treats. Love, Paige and Tim."

I was relieved. A harmless greeting that should calm things down. But as I was stuffing the wrappings back into the box, another note tumbled out. Daniel snatched it up before I could reach it.

"The envelope please," he said tearing it open. "Thank you, Ms. Hepburn." Then in his most dramatic voice, he continued, "Hmmm, now let's see. It says here that they're homemade banana chocolate chip muffins, made without wheat or sugar, and that they taste best when nuked for thirty seconds before serving."

"Yummy . . . " Mark cooed, reveling in my discomfort. If the guys were trying to mortify me, they were succeeding. I felt like a specimen under a giant microscope.

"I'm sure she makes them for all her suppliers," I said, hoping to finally neutralize the commentary.

Daniel restarted the Christmas music but Ellen gave me a blank, chilly stare. Without speaking she got up, grabbed a few dishes, and marched into the kitchen. At that point, I was too knotted up to follow her.

HOURS LATER, I WAS sitting alone on the patio, my equanimity still shaken from group pillorying. I'd been teased by Mark and Daniel plenty of times before. We all had, and it was in good fun as it always was with them.

So why did I feel like I'd been caught with my hand in the cookie jar? I wasn't hiding anything.

Then it occurred to me. I *was* hiding something.

The people in that room knew the basics about my business, but other than Ellen, they knew nothing about the intimate connection between my work and my inner life.

But so what? I've always been a private person. Why do I feel so exposed?

Then a deeper truth hit me.

The client who'd sent that gift wasn't simply a client. She'd become a spiritual ally.

So there it was. Their kidding wasn't altogether off-base. They'd picked up a closeness I hadn't yet articulated to myself—just not the kind of closeness they'd teased me about.

chapter thirty-seven

Invisible Walls

Not surprisingly, the chill between Ellen and me persisted beyond Christmas.

We were in one of our patterns. Something would happen (in this case the gift incident) and we'd both go silent until the issue faded or we fought about it again and hopefully found some resolution. It didn't help that we'd had virtually no quality time alone since arriving on the island, or really since Greece, and without the distraction of our usual routines, I knew the freeze would continue if we didn't somehow interrupt it.

I asked Daniel if he could recommend a place where Ellen and I could be by ourselves, and he said he knew the perfect spot—the outside cafe at the Sheraton Makaha with its lush ocean and mountain vistas.

It sounded ideal to me, and when I suggested it to Ellen, her face softened into a smile.

THE MAKAHA, A NEARBY resort, was set high in a tropical canyon lined with rugged emerald mountains. The restaurant veranda offered a spectacular view over a luxuriously landscaped golf course that sloped down almost to the sea. We took a table, ordered drinks, and managed a few quiet comments about the surrounding beauty.

A short time later, a group of Japanese tourists arrived for lunch, and the ambiance around us went from laid-back to buoyant. I was happy for the change, especially watching the couple at the next table who were giggling in confusion over the English menu.

"How're you doing?" I finally asked, wanting to hear if she was still smarting from the ribbing I'd taken.

"Fine," she responded, half looking away.

"No, really, I want to know how you're feeling."

"Well," she began, looking straight at me for the first time that day, "I'm not sure where we're going."

"What do you mean? On this trip? Or in our lives?"

"Our lives. I don't understand why you walked away from those two clients."

"What? That's still bothering you?"

"Yes. And, well . . . that's part of it."

I sat back in my chair, knowing exactly where she was going with this. Frustration oozed between each word as she reminded me, yet again, of all the ways she wasn't having the kind of life she wanted and why.

"On top of that," she added, biting her lip, "that muffin thing yesterday . . . you gotta know how much it upset me."

"You and me both!" I said, sitting forward again. "I wanted to discuss that too. We both know it was just the guys having fun at my expense, yet here we are, all disconnected again, hashing over the same old territory. They were joking!"

"You're not getting it." Her eyes bore into mine as if to penetrate an invisible wall between us. "The kidding isn't what upset me. All of those people are *successful* and exchanging such beautiful gifts, and here you are with this piddly little client giving you that piddly little mouse cover. And homemade muffins? It was embarrassing."

Whoa! I thought to myself, both shocked and amused. Instead of jealousy over some mysterious Madame X or being frightened that I might be interested in another woman, she was offended by the low cash value of my client's Christmas gift?

"Why are you smiling?" she asked.

"Well, I . . ." I shook my head. I couldn't come up with anything to say that wouldn't start World War III, so instead I motioned toward the Japanese couple at the table behind her. "See those two? They had the hardest time making sense of a menu and they're still giggling about it."

Ellen turned around briefly. Their meal was arriving and the wife was clearly uncomfortable. With a friendly laugh and a few awkward hand motions, the husband asked the waitress to take his wife's pancakes back to the kitchen and bring a Japanese menu. The two of them noticed me watching and smiled graciously. I smiled back. Their ease in navigating a difficult situation was another reminder of how remote and clumsy Ellen and I had become with one another.

I turned back to Ellen. "So, you really think our problems would end if we had more money?"

"It would go a long way," she replied. "Just look at us. We're supposed to be building a life together, but we don't seem to be going anywhere."

"You're right." I exhaled deeply, relieved to hear us both speak the truth. "But our problems are deeper than not being able to afford a big house in Malibu. We really aren't in sync."

She closed her eyes and a tear rolled slowly down one of her cheeks. I was sad too. Neither of us was delivering what the other needed most. In truth, we were failing each other.

I reached across the table and touched her hand. "I know that I'm not giving you what you want, and I'm sorry. I want you to be happy, but—"

"I'd like to leave," she said, pulling her hand away.

"That's it?"

"I'm tired. Let's go back."

She clutched her bag and stood up.

"You don't want to talk about this anymore?"

"We talk in circles," she said, shrugging slightly. "I guess it was a mistake not insisting the therapist see us together again."

I nodded, even though I wasn't sure that a therapist was our answer, at least that one.

I gave the waitress my credit card and watched Ellen stand there staring at the view.

The usual question filled my mind, and like each time before, I had my ready answer: Ellen and I were still together because our feelings of love always carried more weight than our obvious differences. Beneath our conflicts we were bonded by a connection that had once been deep and breathtaking—and I'd always assumed that's who we fundamentally were and hoped we could experience that again.

But was I wrong? So much of what we had seemed to have slipped beyond our reach.

IN SILENCE, WE WALKED side by side down the steps of the verandah into the parking lot. To get to our car we had to make our way around a Japanese tour bus that was blocking the crosswalk. The driver was standing by the door jotting something on his clipboard while his passengers waited in the shade.

As we passed the group, I noticed the couple from the restaurant. We smiled at each other once more, and with that goodbye I felt a wave of sadness that was bigger than the moment.

chapter thirty-eight

Woman in the Temple

G abe was still in the afterglow of another hit. Many scenes had been filmed on Oahu, and this led to our being invited to the Mochitsuki Festival at a Rinzai Zen temple in the mountains above Honolulu.

When we arrived, the main event was already underway—a group ceremony in which a mound of rice was hammered with a huge mallet on what looked like a tree stump. It was the ritualized making of *mochi*, a glutinous rice mixture pounded into a paste and then molded into a cake or cookie-shaped confection.

The crowd was jovial and focused but immediately stopped when Gabe appeared. They greeted him vigorously, and unlike so many times we'd accompanied our celebrity friend in public, each of us was warmly welcomed too. After the formalities of introduction, the men in our group were encouraged to take part. Gabe was first. He raised the heavy wooden mallet with ease but let it fall rather clumsily on the rice mound, stirring a ripple of laughter. Daniel, Mark, and I then each took our turns, and the locals giggled in delight at our diligent, but equally awkward efforts.

While the mochi-making continued, a friend of Daniel's, the one who was instrumental in our being there, asked if we'd like a tour of the grounds.

This remote compound was located near the crest of a mountain pass, and the vista seemed to transport us into another time and place. As we walked toward the temple past several shrines, low clouds crossed the peak and then rolled toward us with a fine mist trailing in their wake. Soon, the temple ahead of us was engulfed in billowing fog, and a delicate rain transformed the surrounding trees and buildings into the pale silkiness of a Japanese painting.

A few paces from the temple door, a flutter of desire rose in my chest and with it the long-dormant enchantment with monastic life that had so attracted me in my early years. It had been such a serious calling that I'd gone on several retreats at Gethsemane, the Trappist monastery in Kentucky, believing that full commitment to a contemplative life was my future. Crossing the threshold into the shrine, these yearnings were alive in me again, and I felt a quiet reverence for the holy ground on which I walked.

Once my eyes adjusted to the darkness, I caught sight of a beautiful Asian woman seated off to my right. Her back was straight as a sword yet somehow relaxed, and her delicate hands rested gently in her lap. I couldn't see if her eyes were closed but assumed from the slight, rhythmic rise and fall of her shoulders that she was deep in meditation.

Seeing this exquisite creature, all my thoughts stopped. I stood there breathlessly for an uncountable span of time until I finally shifted my weight. My movement made no sound, but the woman turned toward me.

She smiled when she saw me. Her eyes glowed with deep otherworldly absorption yet she was fully present with me. She held my gaze, and I half expected her to greet me by name. Then with a prayerful nod, she turned away and sank back into herself.

And that was it. That was all that transpired. The encounter itself consumed maybe a minute or two, yet it left in my heart a strange promise of future happiness.

I GLANCED AROUND AND realized that no one from our group was there. They'd either left without my noticing or hadn't entered the temple at all. I walked as quietly as I could to the door and once outside found the landscape still dripping with moisture.

Pebbles crunched under my sandals as I moved along the path through the garden. Wafts of mist floated around me like ghosts, and I deliberately slowed my pace so I could absorb the experience.

I was savoring my ever-changing surroundings when I noticed a fog-shrouded form ahead. As I approached, an almost life-sized sculpture of a standing Buddha emerged from the haze. I couldn't help but smile at his robust belly and the joyous grin on his face. Then I noticed he was holding a staff and what looked like a loaf of bread and a wineskin—symbols of the merging of heaven and earth I assumed.

In that moment, this ancient sage, this awakened pilgrim, became my elder brother showing me that this merging was indeed possible. This expression of the transcendent nature within daily life was what I'd been trying to do in my business, finally with some success.

I took another step, then stopped again. Was *that* the message of this little side adventure in the temple—that this same merging was indeed possible in every aspect of life, including an intimate relationship?

Then suddenly, a voice emerged from somewhere other than my conscious mind.

"I want to live my life as a prayer," I uttered to the garden, then immediately looked around to be sure nobody heard me.

At first these words embarrassed me. But they couldn't be more true. I *did* want to live with the single-minded purpose of a monk— but I wanted to share that with a woman who craved the same.

The thought of it took my breath away.

That simple statement named all the urgings that drove me. It was undeniable. The merging I so longed for included a mutual melding in love with another person, the fullness of intimacy with a woman who yearned for that same unity. Not just with each other, but with all of life.

"I want to live my life as a prayer," I announced to the fog.

The volition, the vigor, of these words raised tiny bumps on my arms and the back of my neck. I wanted to understand all that this meant and figure out how to make it real, but my thoughts wouldn't go there. I was floating amid the billows of mist. Tears were rolling down my cheeks, merging with the wetness in the air.

Moments later, I heard the sounds of a joyous crowd. I looked up and saw that I'd found my way back to the festival. My walking meditation was over.

I reentered the celebration and scanned for our group. Ellen and Daniel were standing together. As I approached, I watched them laugh and chat, clearly absorbed in whatever had sparked their amusement. Both of them remained oblivious to my presence even when I was close enough to touch them.

REFLECTION

sacred feminine

*There was a not-so-hidden message in my encounter with the woman
in the temple. Simply being in her presence, I glimpsed a living vision
of an ideal relationship.*

*To say I was moved is not enough. I was altered. My body and
mind were inflamed with a desire for a deeper embrace of Love. Her
quiet beauty, her self-composure, her meditative practice, all told me
that being with her could bring an experience beyond any I'd ever
known.*

*Of course I understood that this wasn't about being with her. The
woman in the temple was a symbol, a reflection of a heightened
possibility mirroring itself to me.*

*As I'd stood there, an undefined aspect of my longing formed into
something discernible. My yearning was not to reignite something lost
but to experience something new—a sacred merging with a woman, a
passionate union in which we would both grow in our mutual
divinity.*

*But was that actually possible? I didn't know. It certainly didn't
fit any definition of a relationship I'd ever heard about. Yet, I couldn't
deny that I was swimming in an expansive perception of a union that
was dazzlingly attractive, one that I was helpless to resist.*

*Looking back on all that, what a perfect expression of divine irony.
As a young man my desire to know God drew me toward entering a
cloistered monastery. Then decades later, standing in another place of
worship, this same desire was drawing me into the arms of the sacred
feminine.*

chapter thirty-nine

The Meditation

After a raucous New Year's Eve celebration at the Honolulu Country Club, we all slept in and wandered blearily to the breakfast table as we pleased. Then once we were all adequately awake and the dishes were done, we moved our gathering to the living room for the group meditation that had become our tradition. This collection of holiday headaches in search of inner wisdom was our clumsy but well-intentioned attempt to usher in a healthful year.

It was late morning by the time we'd settled ourselves into something roughly resembling a circle of mid-century Hawaiian bamboo furniture. The tree lights were lit. Gabe and Daniel were in their usual places on the sofa. I was in my favorite chair. Ellen seemed cozy on a chaise next to me while Mark and Ruth were in matching love seats at the opposite ends of the sofa.

With a touch of his remote, Daniel changed the music to something soothing and smooth, and I sank deeper into my pillowy seat and closed my eyes. A few minutes later, the noises around me faded and I disappeared inside myself.

As in previous New Year's Day meditations, I began by offering a general "thank you" to all the good people who'd touched me during the past year, even in the smallest ways. Then as my thoughts softened and the doors in my chest opened, I gathered into my awareness the family, clients, and friends who were most meaningful to me. One by one, I extended my appreciation for their presence in my life and for allowing me to be in theirs.

At the top of my list was my daughter Sarah, and as always, I was visited by that familiar sense of sadness for having lived away during so many of her formative years. We'd both lost something vital by my not participating in her daily life, though we did our best with long-distance calls and brief notes sent with her weekly allowance. My solace was in knowing that I could now give her my love, and maybe even some wisdom, in ways that were impossible when my world kept falling apart.

After embracing Sarah goodbye, I extended my awareness to family and friends in far-off places and gave each one a part of myself. From there, I checked in with each of my clients and felt a glow of warmth and gratitude. All seemed healthy and vibrant, and I thanked them one at a time for trusting me to help grow their business and for their contribution to building mine.

Then I decided to visit my book. The moment I focused on it, I was moved by an upwelling of pride that belied all criticism—from others and myself. Then a wave of reassurance told me that my story had wings and was almost ready for flight. I tried not to reject the news.

Finally, it was time to visit those sitting in the room with me.

I started with Gabe and Daniel, sending them heartfelt thanks, as individuals and as a couple, for opening their home and their lives to me and for generously including me in so many adventures. As I was appreciating them, a strange thing happened. In some mysterious part of my mind, I heard the resonant sound of a Tibetan bell.

That's interesting, I thought. *A confirmation of our connection?*

Next, I offered gratitude to Mark for the uncommon depth in our friendship and even for his sometimes embarrassing brand of playfulness. And again, I heard that same satisfying tone of a Tibetan bell.

Hmm. Nice.

Visiting Ruth, I welled up at how fully we'd recognized each other as soul friends. The bell intoned again, and this time I noticed that the sound had grown clearer and more affirmative each time I moved my attention from one friend to the next.

Finally, it was Ellen's turn.

I inhaled a deep, slow breath, and gathered her into my heart and embraced her. Then instead of the Tibetan bell, I heard: "clunk!"— a distinct and dreadful "clunk."

It was so shocking, my eyes popped open. *Did anyone else hear that? God, I hope not.* It reminded me of the dense thud of the heavy mallet striking wood at the Mochi Festival. But there was nothing festive about that sound now.

I scanned the faces around me and closely studied Ellen's. She and everyone else remained quiet, eyes closed. Thankfully, the soundtrack of my meditation was private.

Relieved, I closed my eyes and attempted to calm myself. It took a few minutes and some concerted effort, but I found my way back into a peaceful inner world. Again I focused on offering love and gratitude to Ellen. She meant so much to me and had given me so much. But once more I heard the same distinct and dreadful "clunk."

This time, the sound slammed through my body, somber and declarative like a judge striking a gavel to punctuate a ruling.

Ellen and I still regularly expressed the love between us, but our differences had become so vivid that this "clunk," although excruciating to hear, filled me with an odd sense of relief. It was as if a power greater than my ordinary mind had stepped in to declare its opinion.

It wasn't a final verdict and definitely not a command. It simply reflected what felt like truth—a truth that meant a choice needed to be made, and at some point soon.

A moment later, the sounds of restless movement startled me back to ordinary awareness. I half opened my eyes, expecting that our group meditation was coming to a close. But everyone was motionless.

I let my eyes fall closed again and returned to my interior world, a world that felt more real in that moment than the chair I was sitting in. My body relaxed quickly but my mind kept busying itself about Ellen and me. At some point my thoughts shifted, and I was back in the garden at the temple, then back to the woman meditating there, again graced by her penetrating presence.

So where do I meet such a woman? I asked without intending to.

Then instantly—and unexpectedly—an answer appeared.

Clear as an image on a movie screen was the radiant face of a beautiful woman, smiling brightly, her hair flaming, her eyes dancing with kindness and vitality.

My heart jumped several beats. Then the image disappeared.

It was Paige.

The next few seconds unfolded in a blur of confusion. But before I could make sense of what had been shown to me, my rational mind jumped in.

Don, stop. Don't go there. She's a symbol, another sign. Do not take this literally. She's no more a real possibility than the woman in the temple.

Of course she was a symbol. So I asked again.

Where do I meet such a woman?

And once again Paige's radiant face floated before me in a pool of light. This time there was no denying it. I gave myself over to what it meant, and all the uncertainty, all the yearning was swept away.

Then serious objections began.

My God, she's married!

She's a client!

She's too young!

You don't really know her.

She definitely doesn't know you.

You're being absurd.

Have you lost your freaking mind?!

The force of these protests was so convincing, and facts so obviously true, that I couldn't hold my ground. It was true that Paige occupied a unique place in my business life, especially given our shared spiritual sensibilities. But that was all.

Still, how could I ignore this? It was as if my own soul had thumped me on my head to get my attention and then led me by the hand to this inner vision, insisting I consider it as an answer to my question.

Then the voice of resistance hit me where it knew I was most vulnerable. Guilt.

What about Ellen? You love her. How can you turn away from that love? She gave you love when you hit bottom. And a home. And friends. Besides, if you leave, she'll be crushed. Sure, you're in a rocky time, but it'll pass, especially now that your business is growing.

I was dizzy and even desperate from this onslaught when, mercifully, I heard rustling in the room. This time I hoped it was real. I opened my eyes and saw that the others were indeed emerging from their quiet. I glanced at Ellen and our eyes met. We both smiled. The moment was warm. Then I had to look away.

I couldn't deny what I'd seen. And something about it felt deeply true. I just didn't know what it all meant.

On the spot, I vowed to tell no one what I'd just seen, heard, or felt.

Ever.

chapter forty

Sounds and Images

The crowing of a rooster woke me up, and scenes from my New Year's Day meditation were right there. Partly shocked, but also not wanting to disturb this revisitation, I remained motionless. Ellen moved and I stayed still to avoid waking her.

Thoughts and feelings about what I heard and saw tumbled through my mind, but I had no appetite to engage details or analyze meaning. I wanted to just lie there to see if anything had clarified overnight.

One uncomfortable thing did. That impossible-to-ignore "clunk" had broken through an inner fog. Then my mind flashed on the conversation with Ellen at Makaha. Our relationship *really* could be ending.

At that moment, Ellen tossed again in her sleep and snuggled closer. The warmth of her skin, which for years I relished, made me want to pull away. In sadness, I shifted my body ever so slightly and inched my way out of bed. Silent as a shadow, I dressed and went to the kitchen. After a long drink of water, I slipped out the door for a walk on the empty beach. The sun was still low behind the mountain, but the glowing sky promised another clear day in paradise.

I crossed the damp lawn to the seawall and quietly opened the gate. Then just as my bare feet were delighting in the coolness of the sand, something completely unexpected happened. My spirit felt free. It was as if I'd been granted a reprieve, a pardon, permission from some higher source—it was okay to release myself from a part of my life that was in perpetual discord.

The sounds and images from the previous day merged with the freshness of the morning and lifted me into a sense of limitless possibility. I wanted to run around and splash in the surf, sway with the palm trees and fly with the gulls.

I felt love everywhere.

A FEW MINUTES DOWN the beach, my brain was pounding with questions.

What am I thinking? How's that one experience enough to get me to leave someone I love? Especially when love is the very basis of the life I'm trying to build?

The thought of moving my stuff out of Ellen's apartment filled me with both guilt and compassion. I ached to shield her from the calamity of yet another lost dream. Yet staying wasn't the answer. Neither of us had been happy with our relationship for a long time, for different reasons, but we were unhappy nonetheless.

My mind then turned to Paige, and I had to remind myself that her visage in the meditation was an archetype, an attractive symbol like the woman in the temple. But then, why not show *her* face? Why show Paige's? There was no romantic spark between Paige and me, and certainly no sense of intimacy.

She was a special client. But just a client.

Then, as if to insist I get the point, the reminders continued. The age difference. The fact that we didn't really know each other. It would be generous to say we'd spent a total of twenty hours together. And of course, the real coup de grâce, the killer of killers—she was married.

I stood there watching the ocean. Without rolling up my jeans, I took a few steps into the surf and resumed my walk, perhaps hoping the waves would wash this inner jumble from my head and heart.

THE AROMA OF FRYING bacon teased my nose. I looked up and noticed smoke rising from a grove of palm trees around the curve of the shoreline. Or were they roasting a wild pig? In the still-early light, I saw the silhouettes of several people in an enclave of tents and pickup trucks. Seagulls swooped through the spirals of smoke for a closer look, and a few adventurous birds attempted furtive landings on truck tops, only to be shooed away.

Not wanting to disturb their gathering, I decided to return to the house. Besides, I was hungry. Moving slowly back through the warm surf, it occurred to me that this could be my last predawn walk on this beautiful beach, my last vacation with Ellen and these dear friends, and the last time I'd hear Daniel's enthusiastic Christmas playlist.

When I reached the gate, I caught the familiar whiff of coffee from the open kitchen door. My feet savored each step across the grass damp with morning dew. Sounds from inside revealed that everyone was up and in their morning routines, and I felt a gentle tug of love for each of them.

Ellen and Mark were happily stirring waffle mix in the kitchen, and I was glad they barely noticed my greeting. I wasn't at all sure I could hide what was going on inside of me. I slipped by them, poured a cup of coffee, and went to our bedroom to change into dry clothes.

ON OUR FINAL DAY in Hawaii, Daniel's friend stopped by, the one who'd shown us around the grounds at the Buddhist temple. He was a clinical psychologist of Japanese descent and had just published a book on psychotherapy and Zen. I joined the others in asking where we could buy a copy. He had a few in his car, and when I saw he had enough, I requested two—the extra one to reciprocate Paige's gifts.

We were booked on flights leaving early the next morning, and that afternoon Daniel suggested we all take a last walk on the beach together. When I heard him say "last," a fresh wave of nostalgia and sadness moved though my body.

When our group returned to the house I packed a few things, then, exhausted from troubled sleep the last few nights, I dragged a lounge chair into the shade of some palms. After a passing thought about what the future might hold, I drifted into a blissful nap.

When Ellen finally woke me, the sun was low on the horizon. It was time to finish packing. Still groggy, I rose slowly. As I followed her inside, I was flooded with dread about the uncertainties that awaited us at home.

chapter forty-one

Back in LA

The morning after our trip, I felt like I'd crash-landed back into my life.

Ellen and I resumed our routines. We got up early, dressed, and went jogging. We engaged in small talk. We waved and smiled at familiar faces. We came home, showered, and dressed for the day.

I was impatient to have the apartment to myself, but Ellen seemed to dawdle forever in the kitchen. When she was ready to leave, we managed a sad little kiss at the door. I tried to smile as she walked down the hallway, but the kiss of Judas popped into my head. Did I really deserve such a judgment? I hadn't betrayed her.

I had, however, finally faced the fact that our relationship was on crumbling ground. *Had she done the same?* I didn't know. But I *did* know that at some point we'd have to find the courage, and hopefully a gentle moment, to talk about it.

I WARMED MY CUP of coffee and went to my desk. As planned, my calendar was meeting-free for the rest of the week—an especially welcome gift after this trip. I was in no mood to leap back into work. Then I remembered.

Paige is reading the manuscript!

I jumped out of my chair. She might even have finished it. *Yikes.*

I knew she liked the first part, but what about the parts where my career unraveled in a slow-motion train wreck? Even Jennifer found that middle section difficult. I shook my head. How had I let Paige talk me into letting her read it?

I picked up the phone. I needed to know what she thought.

No, I told myself. I wasn't ready.

Give yourself some time, at least a day. Go for a drive. Get your whole self back here first.

I grabbed my keys and headed to the post office. Sorting through bills would, without doubt, ground me. Later that day, I read through the client notes I'd made before the trip. Fortunately, I'd been thorough.

BY THE FOLLOWING AFTERNOON I was ready. I cleared my desk of everything except Paige's file. I stood up to fortify myself and punched in her number. Before it rang, I hung up. I wasn't as ready as I thought.

I paced the length of the apartment several times, rehearsing what to say. Then after exchanging my half-empty cup of coffee for a full one, I dialed again.

"Hi, this is Paige," she answered brightly before I had time to retreat.

"Hi," I said, my throat suddenly dry. "It's Don." I pulled the phone away from my mouth and gulped my coffee.

"Welcome back! How was Hawaii?"

Her voice was as warm and friendly as ever. It was an instant balm.

"It was great! Mostly uneventful." I wanted to say more but couldn't think of anything appropriate. "I've been thinking about you and your business," I plowed on. "We should probably find a time to meet."

"Definitely. There's stuff to catch you up on, and we could discuss your book too."

"Oh?" I held my breath. "You read it?" My heart pounded in my chest.

"Of course I read it. I finished it. And I really, really like it!"

What did she say? The Hallelujah chorus was playing so loudly in my head, I wasn't sure of her words.

"The *whole* book?" I asked.

"Well, yeah," she sounded surprised by my question. "It's good. Powerful, actually. I couldn't put it down. So, maybe we could meet socially . . . I mean, maybe at our next meeting we could talk about it off the meter, if that's okay?"

I laughed.

"Of course. Off the meter. Absolutely!"

"I should warn you though, I've made some notes. I hope that's all right."

"It's more than I hoped for."

My eyes fell closed, and I realized my heart was still racing. To disguise my emotions, I added, "As you know, every creative project needs feedback."

"Oh, good. I was well into it before it occurred to me you might not want that. So, does Tuesday next week work for you?"

I looked at my calendar. "I'm already booked that day," I said, trying to keep my voice from revealing disappointment. "What about Wednesday morning instead, the fourteenth?"

"Perfect. Better! I'll have more time. Oh, I don't seem to have your December invoice. Did you send it?"

"Thought I did but I'll bring it to the meeting."

"Great. See you next Wednesday."

I hung up, collapsed into my chair, and exhaled an audible sigh.

"Wow." I declared to the empty room. "Wow."

chapter forty - two

The Manuscript

Given the jitters in my stomach, you would've thought I was heading to traffic court. Or worse. *Just chill, Don*, I kept telling myself. *It's Paige.*

But that didn't help. Neither did the stop-and-go traffic. My edginess grew.

Paige was now one of maybe seven people who'd read my manuscript, and other than Jennifer, she was the only one who seemed to genuinely like it. She'd even made notes, lots of them apparently. I was eager for thoughtful feedback, but my shoulders tightened at the thought of a serious critique.

What kind of a conversation was I walking into? Were there parts of the book that seriously bored her? Or bothered her? Had my chronicle of career failures dented her confidence in my business abilities? That risk, that fear, was why I resisted giving it to her in the first place.

DESPITE THE SLOW FREEWAY, I arrived on time. I scanned the restaurant, but she wasn't there yet so I selected a quiet corner table that would be private for our book conversation. It was exactly two weeks to the day since that strange New Year's meditation, and I was still unsure how to interact with her.

A minute later, I saw the hostess pointing Paige in my direction.

I waved and watched her approach, her familiar smile intact. *A good sign*, I thought.

She put her case on a chair and I stood to greet her. Our hug felt unexpectedly warm (to me anyway). Then after we sat down, a strange thing happened.

When I looked at her, the image of the face from my meditation hovered between us. The exact same face, with the exact same expression, was floating as a translucent overlay that made the scene before me etheric.

What the—?

To say it was unsettling would be a massive understatement.

The waitress provided a well-timed distraction. Paige ordered her usual: two eggs sunny-side up, bottoms crispy, hash browns crispy, no toast, and hot tea. I ordered my usual too, then took the opportunity to give her the book by Daniel's friend that I'd bought in Hawaii.

"It seemed like a subject you might be interested in," I said, handing it to her. "The author signed it to you."

"Wow! I love the cover." She flipped through the pages, pausing at each chapter heading. "Thank you so much."

"We met him at a Zen temple we visited. It's tucked into the mountains above Honolulu and . . . well, it's really something up there. I'll have to tell you about that experience sometime. It was life-altering."

"Really?"

"Yeah, but tell me, how was Pebble Beach?" I asked, afraid I might wander too deeply into what happened in Hawaii.

"It was good. We . . . well, the setting was gorgeous, and I always love being near the ocean, especially along a rocky coastline. The room had a real fireplace and a view of the water. My travel writer friend arranged it, at a good rate and an upgrade to a suite."

"Sounds beautiful."

Paige opened her case and I was disappointed when she retrieved a packet of papers instead of the manuscript. After a rather thorough presentation of current sales figures, she was ready to discuss her most pressing issue.

When I saw that she'd brought brochure mockups, I called for the waitress and asked her to clear the table. Paige then laid out several design ideas and explained that each had a different version of the text.

"I've been playing. Hope that's okay?"

"Absolutely," I reassured her, trying to keep my focus on this display of brochures instead of the manuscript now jutting out from her bag. "A couple of these designs are nice. As for the text, I can read them at home. Or, I can look at them now."

"Now'd be great! I'm anxious to know what kind of shape we're in. Half hour or so? I've got some phone calls I can make."

PAIGE RETURNED TO THE table sooner than expected, but I'd absorbed enough to comment.

"It all looks good. The languaging needs a little help but I can work with this."

"Yay!" she smiled. "I wanna get this stuff out there. Hopefully within a month."

"That's doable. Assuming we can have another meeting or two."

"How about next Wednesday?"

"Sure, that works for me."

"So . . ." Paige smiled, inching the manuscript out of her case. "I'm ready to shift gears if you are."

My eyes fixated on the stampede of little colored tabs running along the edge of the pages. "It's gotten awfully noisy in here," I said. "I believe there's a nice restaurant somewhere in the hotel that should be quieter."

ONCE SETTLED IN A booth with seats that felt like glove leather, I watched Paige flip through the manuscript. My anticipation heightened, and I couldn't have felt more exposed. But what she said next was so simple, and with such overflowing genuineness, it fell on me like soft summer rain.

"Well," she looked up and smiled. "I *love* it."

There was something about hearing her words face to face, something about seeing the sincerity in her eyes, that was deeply healing. All those arid months of uncertainty and disappointment about my writing instantly washed away.

Our server arrived and we told him we'd need a some time before ordering lunch.

"I mean, I *really* loved it. Especially how feel-able it is. And how honest."

I wanted to respond but kept quiet.

"I'm tired of dry, how-to books," she laughed. "Too much thinking. Know what I mean? I do enough of that all day. The way you tell your story, you do a great job illustrating how you can learn from life's big disappointments *and* from those subtle inner signals."

I wanted to take notes. I wanted to somehow remember what she was saying. I reached for my briefcase but stopped. I didn't want to interrupt her flow.

"That banter between your Little Voice and the Chairman? I just loved that! It's so relate-able. Oh, and your dog . . ." she tapped her hand on the manuscript, "I absolutely fell in love with Stray. Anyone who's ever loved a dog will feel ya there. This book definitely has some Kleenex moments."

I almost couldn't breathe. A million questions tumbled through my mind.

"And another thing," she went on, "that's so unusual, at least for me, is to get that layer of . . . profound, almost esoteric stuff, while reading a fully entertaining story, and without it sounding preachy. That's quite a feat, I'd say."

We both laughed.

"Well, I'm glad to hear the story works," I finally said, barely able to get my voice above a whisper. "Judging by the comments from some of my friends, I thought it failed on all counts."

She winced and looked at me quizzically. "I don't understand that. There's so much richness in the story, in the journey you take the reader on." She sighed and sat back in the booth.

Watching her, listening to her, I felt an invisible lock somewhere inside of me being pried open.

The waiter reappeared to take our order—an untimely intrusion. After he left, Paige immediately continued.

"So, you know what else *really* got me? This might be just me, but I've never known anyone with an inner process, a way of working with themselves, so much like my own. You know, being aware of those quiet impulses, the unnamable fears, the almost microscopic inner adjustments we constantly have to make if we want to live our lives from love. It's subtle stuff, but you reveal it brilliantly."

Her grasp of what I was hoping to communicate, especially about the struggle between love and fear, almost overwhelmed me. In that moment, all my trepidation was gone. We were totally in sync. And in a way that I'd never experienced before. Not with anyone.

During the next hour, Paige alternated between comments on specific parts of the book and relating parallels from her own life. As she spoke, it became increasingly clear *why* she understood my writing so well. Her journey had taken her through many of the same challenges and she'd learned many of the same lessons—but without all the life-crushing dramas. Sure, her experience with *est* was intense, but the way she navigated it . . . I sensed that personal transformation came more naturally to her.

More time passed. More animated talk. More comparing of notes.

Finally, the waiter returned, removed our empty plates, and asked about dessert. It seemed like only seconds before he was back with a slice of dark chocolate cake and two forks. As we shared this wicked extravagance, the conversation kept flowing. We discussed mutual aspects of our inner lives, our failures, and the ways we'd learned to grow from crisis and collapse. Raised in different generations, our lives had unfolded on totally different tracks, yet somehow, we'd lived parallel lives and seemed to understand each other perfectly.

"On some pages," she said, tapping the manuscript again, "I felt like I knew what you were talking about even when it wasn't in the words. I know that sounds weird . . . and I hope I'm not being too presumptuous, but I made notes in some of those places."

"No, no, that's exactly the kind of critique I've been wanting."

She searched the pages then turned the manuscript toward me. "For instance, look at this."

"You wrote your comments in green?"

"Yeah, regular pencil was hard to see, and I wasn't about to use red." She shuddered for effect. "So, green it was. Is that okay?"

"It's perfect."

As I read her carefully written notes in the margins, I felt more seen and less exposed.

The quality of her perceptions, so intimate and personal, transported me into a state of silent euphoria. It was almost too much. At one point, I leaned back in the booth, my hands pressed to my chest.

"Are you okay?" She looked alarmed.

"You're breaking my heart," I said quietly.

"Oh no! Did I say something that hurt your feelings?"

"Gosh, no!" I sat upright. "Quite the opposite. It's just that you're the first person who understands everything this book is about. Everything. And that you've been able to put it into words . . . it's hard to hold."

Her nose reddened and tears glistened in her eyes. She had joined me in my joyous discomfort. I couldn't recall ever feeling so understood and so vulnerable all at once.

chapter forty-three

Side by Side

I t was the front edge of rush hour when Paige and I finished lunch. We'd both be hitting more traffic than either one of us wanted, but it was worth it—certainly for me, and I hoped for her too.

Waiting for the elevator to the garage, I was still lightheaded from our conversation. Paige's marked-up copy of the manuscript was tucked safely in my briefcase, which I was holding in front of me with both hands as if protecting the Queen's Crown Jewels.

The elevator doors opened and Paige slowly intoned, "Oh no . . ."

"What's wrong?"

"You're going to think I'm clueless."

"Why?"

"I have literally *no* idea where I parked."

"I hate when that happens," I chuckled.

Paige laughed too, and relaxed.

"Any idea what level? Or how many floors you drove up?"

"Maybe two. Or three?"

"Okay," I said, pushing the G2 button.

We traipsed back and forth, row by row through the typical parking garage labyrinth. One minute we thought we'd spotted her car, and the next we realized we hadn't. White sedans were obviously a common choice. After wandering around for about ten minutes, an alarming thought crossed my mind: I wasn't sure where I'd parked either. At that very moment, Paige squealed.

"There it is!" She sounded like a seaman sighting land, pointing toward a white BMW parked against the back wall.

I took one glance in that direction and started laughing.

"What's so funny?"

"See that gray Bimmer parked right next to yours?"

"Yeah . . ."

"That's mine."

"You're kidding, right?" She looked at me, eyes wide. "With hundreds of cars in what—four, five floors—we parked right next to each other? That's wild!"

"Isn't it?" I said, wondering what it meant, if anything.

OUR CUSTOMARY GOODBYE HUG had a different quality about it, and as I stood there watching her car disappear down the ramp, a tug of emptiness hit me.

I placed my bag on the front seat and sat there a moment before following the exit arrows. Then while paying the toll, I noticed Paige's car parked off to the side of the alley that led to the street. I pulled up next to her and lowered my window.

"Everything okay?"

"You forgot to give me the December invoice," she called out.

"Oh yeah. You're right."

I pulled the invoice out of my case and tried to hand it through the passenger window but our cars were too far apart.

"How about I just send it to you?" I shouted.

"No problem," she called back.

"Thanks again for your feedback on the book."

"My pleasure. I'm excited about what you're doing. It's an important message."

A driver behind me tapped his horn.

"I appreciate you saying that. Your opinion means a lot to me. I hope our talking so long doesn't get you stuck in traffic."

The next honk was less patient.

"If we're going to talk, maybe you should pull over," she smiled. "Then you could just hand me that invoice!"

I pulled in front of her to let traffic pass, then walked back to her car and slid into the passenger's seat.

"Here you go," I said, handing her the invoice.

"Does this include today too?" she kidded.

Suddenly, I was embarrassed about charging her at all.

"No charges for today," I said. "In fact, maybe you should invoice me for your editing services."

She laughed.

"Okay," I said, "I guess that's it."

I started to get out of the car but something stopped me. Maybe it was the fact that she'd pulled over to wait for me. I sat back in the seat and turned to look at her. Our gazes locked for a few seconds and my heart pounded so hard I could feel it in my temples. I sat there, speechless.

"Where'd you go?" she finally asked.

"I was just wondering if we were going to have an affair," I blurted out.

Oh my God! What did I just say? I couldn't believe those words had actually popped out of my mouth! I was horrified. I could only guess that because our conversation had been so personal, even intimate, that my emotions had overheated and somehow made me lose all damned sense of who we were.

"No," she replied gently but without hesitation. "I won't have an affair. Besides, it would ruin our relationship."

"I feel the same way," I nodded, hoping I didn't look like the stupid jerk I felt I was.

I so wanted to reel back in what I'd said, but I obviously couldn't. So I simply smiled, told her I'd see her next week, and climbed out of her car. Then, as I heard her engine start, I turned back and walked up to her half-opened window.

"I just wanted you to know that I wasn't suggesting . . . I mean, I don't have affairs either. I didn't when I was married and I don't with Ellen. I just wanted you to know."

"I assumed that," she said, still smiling. "I think what we're really talking about is how easy it is when two people have such a deep spiritual connection to not know how to contain that experience or just enjoy it. They don't know what to do with it so they sexualize it and get involved in ways that aren't appropriate."

"Well said," I nodded, amazed at her ability to think so clearly despite the awkward mess I'd created. Not knowing how to make a cool exit, I added, "I'll see you next week."

Back in my car, I shook my head and watched her pull away. My face was hot with embarrassment. I couldn't remember a more humiliating blunder. Thankfully, Paige had used a tender touch and her insightful mind to rescue me.

THE DRIVE HOME WAS benevolently slow. My system needed time to recalibrate.

I still couldn't believe I'd even used the word "affair" with a client. I remained horrified, yet in some mysterious reality, in some alternate universe, was it plausible? Not that we would have an affair, but that we could have something more.

Inching along the freeway, I couldn't help but wonder if over the past six months these and other moments had formed a path—one that was now taking us into new territory. Our connection had been special from the beginning, I'd assumed due to our mutual focus on elevated ideals in business. Now it was becoming different, somehow touchable, breathable, in a whole other way.

I didn't know what was happening. But whatever it was, it seemed to have a mind of its own and was having its way with me.

chapter forty-four

The Bud Opens

The following morning, Ellen left early for the office. Gabe had invited her to be his guest at a late-afternoon event at the Los Angeles Music Center downtown, and she wanted to see as many clients as she could before he picked her up. She'd been looking forward to this outing, and so had I. It meant having the apartment to myself for longer than usual.

I pulled Paige's manuscript out of my case, sat down in the rocker, and began reading her comments. It was mind-boggling to be so understood by someone I'd met, what—six months ago? She seemed to know me at a depth at which I barely knew myself, and her notes were little nudges urging me to go deeper in places where I'd only skimmed the surface. In some of those cases, I'd held back deliberately, imagining my corporate buddies back in Chicago getting hold of my book. Basically, I was afraid anything spiritual-sounding would make them think I'd gone off the deep end.

After an hour immersed in her sensibilities, I began to see the manuscript as a rosebush of unopened buds with Paige coaxing each one to flower. A renewed trust in the worth of my story surfaced and new ideas began to sprout. I stopped reading, got up, and went to my desk, ready to start the second draft.

AS I TYPED AWAY on my new Mac, I found that integrating Paige's comments flowed more easily than I could've ever anticipated. I became fascinated by how seamlessly her observations fit into the self-contained world in which I wrote.

Writing had always been my solo domain, a private aspect of my inner life where I mined my most delicately formed perceptions. Yet, there she was, right there with me. It was a deliciously uncomfortable invasion, but for some reason I didn't feel invaded.

With this kind of writing, I'd always believed that only I was the true judge—that only I could be acquainted with the growing edge of my awareness. So with Paige meeting me there with such pristine insight, it was as if she'd reached in and drawn the essence of the book to the surface and was writing it *with* me.

At one point, her presence became so vivid, I had to stop and capture what I was seeing. I backed up the file to a disk, pulled the dust cover off my electric typewriter sitting on the table behind me, and tucked in a fresh piece of paper.

Words flowed onto the page, and a couple of minutes later, I pulled the paper out and read what was written there:

It feels like she has always been part of me.

She is what drew me to California.

She was the mystery woman in the temple shadows.

She was the Tibetan bell in my meditation on New Year's Day.

She is love and I cannot stop myself or keep myself from opening to it.

She is within me and I have no will to dislodge her.

"Oh, God," I said half aloud. "This guy is totally smitten."

I sat there staring at this litany of perceptions. Each had flitted in and out of my consciousness at one time or another, but pulled together like this they revealed more than a man falling in love. They described a communion of spirits. I couldn't help but feel that something was being born between us, something that had been waiting for us to notice.

Strange, the places my mind was taking me.

Could Paige be having a parallel experience? I wanted to believe this was more than my own imagining, but hadn't she told me straight out that a romance between us was impossible?

Yes, she had. Just yesterday.

All she was offering was spiritual companionship and some damn good editing. Oh, and being a great client. It appeared that I was slipping so far over the edge that I was creating a fantasy.

And yet . . . isn't it possible that she . . .

I stopped myself. Paige had said it so well: "They don't know what to do with all these powerful feelings, so they sexualize them and get involved in ways that aren't appropriate."

There it was. *Remember her words, Don. Memorize them. She spoke them to you and she meant it. She's married. She loves her husband. Give it up.*

I pulled out some client files and forced myself to think about something real.

HOURS LATER WHEN THE phone rang, I was absorbed in reviewing new reports about recent coffee sales. I wasn't going to answer, but I needed a break, so I stood, stretched, and picked up the call.

It was Paige.

She started talking but her words were so uncharacteristically tentative, it barely sounded like her. *Something's off.* I sat back down, having no idea what to expect.

"Damn," she paused. "I can't talk now. Maybe I can just send you something I wrote after our meeting? It's a kind of stream-of-consciousness thing."

"Sure. Did you have more thoughts about the book?"

"I'd rather you just read it. It's sort of . . . I don't know . . . it's a journal entry but also a letter. To you. It's very . . ."

I waited a few seconds to see if she'd finish her sentence. *This is not like her.*

"Sure, okay," I said, completely baffled, "let me get my modem ready."

"I have to warn you, it's really weird stuff. It's gonna sound romantic, but it's not. Anyway, you'll see. I'm sure you'll understand."

I told her that my modem was ready, and soon our computers met in space and began their squealing connection.

"Did it come through?" she asked.

"I'm getting it now."

"Great. Gotta go. Talk to you later."

In seconds, I was reading her words on my screen. My mouth dropped open, and I looked over at my bonsai as if to reassure myself I was still in this world.

Thursday, January 15th

A most amazing thing is happening inside me and outside me. It emerged in my meeting with Don, and I was most acutely aware of it in my evening meditation last night. But it's always there, always felt, and it isn't subtle.

I feel awkward writing this, but this thing seems to have a life of its own and wants to be expressed, and writing this seems to be my best option.

Please bear with me gently. I'm feeling very vulnerable.

One more thing before I describe it to you. I'm starting to experience this so tangibly, so physically, so intensely in my body and my heart, it's sort of bypassing my normal channels. Usually my thoughts, the voice inside me, is most predominant. I don't remember ever feeling anything as visceral as this, so it seems foreign, yet, at the same time totally familiar.

There are several types of feelings going on in me. First, there's a layer of energy vibrating around my whole body—but it doesn't *just* feel like energy—it feels like you. It's a very alive, tingly, electric sensation, and it's both stimulating and comforting at the same time.

Another is in my solar plexus. It feels warm and active, vibrant and compressed. And it aches like it wants more room. It's as if I am holding you there, fully within my soul, and my heart and within my body. . . (I hope that doesn't frighten you . . . I feel apprehensive and totally at home all at the same time. Odd).

When I close my eyes, I see threads of white purplish-blue translucent light woven loosely together in an intense but gentle stream that fluidly moves within itself. It starts at this place in the center of my body and finds its destination as it envelopes you and moves through you gently, lovingly, and with vibrant aliveness.

The third feeling resides in my chest but isn't as physical as the other feelings. I can only say that my heart is open in a new way. It's a subtle sensation that isn't associated exclusively with you, as are the other feelings. But it seems to be happening in some response to knowing you, my relationship with you, and the energy that exists between us.

You know the crack in the porcelain bowl that you describe in your book at the beginning of your process? The connection isn't clear to me yet, but that image is with me now.

My heart was pounding. *A crack in a porcelain bowl?* That was the metaphor I'd used in the opening of my book to describe the end of my marriage, the end of an entire way of life. Here she was using it back at me. Were my imaginings not imaginings after all? Was something actually happening?

I had to put my restless mind at ease. My hand reached for the phone, but I held it back. She'd said she had just a few minutes right now. Then I heard the elevator clang to a stop. *Is Ellen home already?* The door to another apartment opened and closed.

I read and reread Paige's words, then sat there staring at the screen. "It's gonna sound romantic," she'd cautioned me, "but it's *not*."

Here was yet another admonition not to expect more than was there, and I had no good reason to disbelieve her. But what she'd written . . . the feel of it, the power of it, the scent of it was, well, overwhelmingly romantic.

But was it? Reading through her verses yet again I found it was true: she'd never mentioned "love" and there was nothing about us being together.

I flashed on how the mystics of all faiths had for centuries spoken in sensual, even sexual language to describe their ecstatic openings. My heart sank. She was obviously having some kind of spiritual experience, but even if it had been prompted by our connection, she insisted it wasn't "romantic."

Regardless of what was happening to her, something was undoubtedly happening to me. I read the words on my screen once more. Could I be alone in all this? Before, I would have said yes.

Now I wasn't so sure.

I TOOK A LAP around the living room. Pacing always helped me gather my thoughts. I kept concluding that I needed to talk to her.

I dialed. The phone rang once. Twice.

Paige answered.

"Hi, it's me, can you talk?"

"For a few minutes. Tim's out on his bike."

I told her I was feeling many of the same things and that I loved how she'd captured such ephemeral stuff in words that made total sense. I also told her I was impressed with her courage to share them.

"That's reassuring," she said, "I feel so unlike myself. I wasn't even sure it'd be understandable. Or if I'd said too much."

"Gosh, no. I'm happy to hear whatever you want to say."

"Well, if you're wondering if your book will have an impact on readers, take it from me, it will!"

We laughed.

I have no clear memory of what was said next, but I did discover that my conclusions were correct. Yes, she was having a transcendent experience, and yes she was *not* translating it into a romantic connection.

Our next scheduled meeting was the following Wednesday. I considered suggesting a time sooner, but then thought better of it.

"So, next Wednesday, right, this time Stouffer's?" I asked.

"Yes. I'm sure I'll be back to earth by then. At least hopefully I will! So maybe we can finalize my new media kit?"

"Of course," I smiled. "We can't ignore business."

REFLECTION

benevolent wave

Years earlier, my out-of-body epiphany transformed my understanding of love. And of life. Rather than holding love as one of several core emotions, I experienced love as Love, the divine essence and substance of all things.

With that new perspective, I believed I finally possessed the key to resolving the split between my work life and spiritual life. That quest had always been and still was a solitary one, a challenge to be reconciled in the privacy of my own mind and heart.

Then Paige became a client.

She, too, was on a quest to live that Love (rather than fear) in business, and I glimpsed the potential of two people working together with the same high resolve.

Then Paige read my manuscript.

And she entered my inner world so fully, so intimately, that any remaining sense of being alone on this path was shattered. She had unwittingly infiltrated the deepest recesses of my being.

So by some mysterious grace, I was no longer alone in the sublime reality into which my epiphany had initiated me. And once again, I found myself vacillating between feeling fully illumined and mightily confused.

Mercifully, one aspect of my experience was stable. I could still feel myself being carried forward on a benevolent wave that I somehow knew to trust.

chapter forty-five

"What Did She Say?"

F inally, it was Wednesday morning. For some odd reason, I arrived more than a half-hour early. I was on autopilot and almost drove to the Hilton where we usually met, but I made a quick U-turn into Stouffer's garage.

I checked the cafe wondering if Paige's drive was as fast as mine. Apparently not. Rather than sit alone at a table, I found a comfortable spot in the lobby where I could wait undistracted and watch the elevator.

We hadn't spoken in almost a week, not since that day she sent her writing. However, she'd been on my mind—a lot—and I couldn't help but wonder if she was backing away. The thought of it sent me into a fear-fest.

Did she freak out about letting me read her writing? Did it embarrass her? What if she thinks she crossed a line and wants to stick to business only? Or even stop working with me?

Ten minutes before our meeting time, I headed back to the restaurant. The hostess led me to a two-top off to the side, but I spotted a more isolated table alongside the wall of windows. Potted trees lined the walkway outside and I asked to be seated there. I picked the chair that faced the entrance, put my briefcase on the table and opened it, pretending I was prepping for an important meeting.

When I looked up, Paige was walking toward me. Her face was

beaming and her stride was full of feminine self-confidence. At the sight of her, all my apprehensions drained away.

She dropped her bag on a chair, and we embraced.

"Nice view," she said, gesturing to the greenery out the window.

"Glad you like it."

Words came comfortably as we chatted a little about traffic, a bit about the weather, and then how our Christmas vacations seemed months ago instead of barely a couple of weeks. We concluded that time was elastic.

Listening to her, looking into her eyes, my mind returned to seeing her face in my meditation.

To the people nearby, we probably looked like nothing more than friendly colleagues. For me, though, her every word meant more than its meaning. Every gesture was charged with hidden significance. Every intonation suggested the presence of a larger presence.

I don't know what I expected, but in those first few minutes, nothing about her journal entry was mentioned, and nothing about our subsequent conversation. The proverbial elephant was now in the room but I dared not point to it. And I certainly couldn't reveal that each time she looked directly at me I saw her face from my meditation.

"I started reading that book you gave me," she said, "and it reminded me, you wanted to tell me about something that happened in Hawaii, I think you said at a Buddhist temple?"

"Uh, sure . . ." I hesitated. There was so much about that experience that I did *not* want to disclose. "Do we have time?"

"Is it a long story?"

"Doesn't have to be."

The waitress arrived to take our order.

"Two eggs sunny-side up, bottoms crispy," Paige said.

"And hash browns, also crispy. No toast. Hot tea," I added, finishing her order.

She laughed. "Am I that predictable?"

"Not really."

"And I'll have the same, except eggs over easy. And make mine coffee instead."

Despite my concerns about what to say and not say about my trip, I was happy for the invitation to discuss something more meaningful than marketing materials. The Mochi Festival's rice-pounding ceremony seemed safe enough, so I started there and then included the offer to see the temple grounds.

"It was so beautiful that day, with all this fog and mist coming off the mountains. It was like walking through a series of Japanese paintings."

Paige's eyes widened, and from the expression on her face, she was seeing it too.

"Inside the temple was also amazing. I stepped through this low door, not realizing that the others had moved on. Once I adjusted to the darkness inside, I noticed a woman quietly meditating in the shadows. I just stood there in the silence feeling like I'd spent lifetimes in temples and monasteries like this. These kinds of places move me in ways nothing else does."

"Yeah," she nodded, "I remember you talking about those feelings in your book, and how you almost went into the monastery at, uh . . . Gethsemane was it? Where you literally ran into Thomas Merton? Great scene, by the way, but go on."

"Yes, the Trappists in Kentucky." I paused while our food was set in front of us. "Anyway, when I finally pulled myself out of the temple, I walked back alone through the garden. The place was so quiet, and so serene, the gravel under my feet was *excruciatingly* loud. The fog was still rolling in, and with it . . . well, there was this sense of being on sacred ground. And my longing to live like this—where every aspect of life is revered—was reawakened."

I stopped and looked at Paige.

"Wow." She smiled and shrugged as if at a loss for words.

With that, I let myself become absorbed again.

"So next, something happened that completely surprised me. I heard myself whisper, 'I want to live my life as a prayer.' Hearing myself say that gave me chills. And then I got teary. And then embarrassed."

Did I really just tell her that?

Paige stopped eating and put her fork down gently. She said nothing but was fully present in her listening.

I took a sip of coffee and realized that this was the point in the story where I needed to stop. But in the telling, my hesitation had vanished. In its place was confidence—a knowing that there was value in what I was saying—and since it appeared she was feeling the same, I continued.

"Those words, that utterance about wanting to live my life as a prayer, really shocked me. It came out of nowhere. But they were . . . what? True. They were true. So I said it again. This time deliberately—and with full voice—even though I knew I didn't really know what it meant. Not yet. Although I did know it *wasn't* about becoming a monk. Or about religion for that matter. And I certainly don't have a hidden desire for a life of silence, or poverty, or celibacy." We both smiled, and I recalled her comment at the Four Seasons about the lack of conflict between a spiritual path and abundant surroundings.

"So," I continued, "I think it's about wanting to live a regular life, meaning a secular life in a way that's sacred. That's why I started my own business. But on those foggy temple grounds, it was obvious that my focus was too narrow—that my success with doing that in business wasn't enough."

I paused to check in with Paige again. Her attention hadn't wavered but she didn't appear ready to comment. I looked down at my cold eggs and decided to go on instead.

"So then I'm thinking that the woman I saw meditating in the temple is part of all this. When I was watching her, she turned and looked at me, and I remember feeling like my soul was being seen. She turned away quickly, but something happened in that brief encounter. For whatever reason, her presence was a more urgent call from some timeless place to share that kind of life with . . ."

My hesitation was back, but I had no impulse to stop.

"So, what I understood was how much I wanted to share that kind of life with that kind of woman."

I gulped some water and sat back in my chair. I needed to breathe. Paige was pouring more tea in her cup. There was something in the way she was listening, and something about her look . . . She seemed far away, yet so with me, I felt safe letting myself be seen by her.

"I'd like to tell you about a meditation I had a couple days later, back at Gabe and Daniel's." The words were out of my mouth before I realized that I was about to tell her something I'd vowed to keep to myself.

"This group of friends who are staying at the house has a tradition of gathering on New Year's morning to meditate together. And one of my personal traditions is to start that meditation by visiting the people close to me and thanking them for being in my life. So, we're sitting in a sort of circle in the living room, and I close my eyes, and soon I'm in this peaceful place. I start with Gabe and Daniel. After I visit them and thank them, I hear this lovely sound in reply, like the pure tone of a Tibetan bell. I take this to mean that all was well between us. Next, I visit Mark, and then our mutual friend, Ruth. And again I hear that same affirming tone, although now I've noticed that it's gotten clearer and more resonant with each person." I exhaled.

"Finally, I get to Ellen."

You'd have thought that my inner voice would be yelling at me to stop at this point, but I was getting no such signal. I kept feeling that doors were opening and that for some reason, it was important to reveal the truth.

Paige remained silent, her eyes connected to mine.

"Ellen's sitting beside me, so close I can hear her breathing, and I open myself to her like I did with the others. But instead of hearing that beautiful tone . . . this time I hear—*clunk*!"

Paige's mouth dropped open and our eyes stayed locked. It seemed we were both mesmerized by my story.

"I mean, it's a loud *clunk*! Just like the sound that big mallet made up at the Mochi Festival when they were pounding the rice. And it's so loud—you can imagine hearing that in the middle of meditation—that my eyes pop open. I'm *sure* the others heard it too, but everyone's still sitting there, looking peaceful.

"So, I lower my eyes again, and once I'm settled, I open myself to Ellen again, and again I hear this same dreadful *clunk*! It still shocks me, but this time I know what it means. It's insisting I hear something I'd been avoiding."

Paige looked like she was absorbing everything, even breathing with me. I'd never seen her so quiet, or so still, for so long. I had no idea how she was taking this, but there was no sense of being judged or blocked. Instead, there was this subtle sensation of being encouraged to continue, to let the rest of it flow just the way it happened.

I took a sip of my cold coffee and reentered the story.

"As you can imagine, it takes me a while to get back into my meditation, but once I'm there I ask the powers that be for some illumination. Immediately, I'm reminded of the words I'd spoken in the garden at the temple: 'I want to live my life as a prayer.' But this time I hear: 'I want to live my *whole life*, not just my business life, as a prayer. My relationship included.'"

I stopped talking and gazed into Paige's large, brown eyes. If I was going to stop telling this story somewhere, it had to be here. To go further would put us both in a very awkward place. But she was still right there with me, her presence completely open and receptive.

I took a deep breath and went on.

"At that point I'm imagining a relationship lived like a prayer, and that woman in the temple comes to mind. So I ask a question I'm pretty sure won't be answered, but I ask it anyway. 'Where do I meet such a woman?'"

I paused.

"Then on the blank screen in my mind . . . *your* face pops up."

I paused again, expecting her to finally say something. But the only response I could discern was a slight tilt of her head. She kept gazing at me, breathing quietly, her eyes smiling. *Did she not hear me? Or did she just not grasp it?*

So I said it again. "When I asked where I could meet such a woman, your face appeared. In full color."

Our eyes were still locked, her expression the same except for a subtle nod. Then she looked away. Time was moving slowly, or maybe not at all.

"So?" I asked almost in a whisper. "What do you think of all this?"

Everything in me fell silent. It was as if I'd been following a luminous cosmic thread, and this is where it led me. I'd found a true place in myself. I'd spoken from that place. Now I waited.

Paige just kept breathing—I have no idea for how long—her head now turned slightly as if peering out the windows or off somewhere else.

Finally she looked back at me. Then simply and exquisitely, as if drawing her words from the ethers, she said, "I'm yours."

chapter forty-six

Grabbing Lightning

S*he said "I'm yours," right?*

Yes, that's what she said.

Flooded by a wave of confusion and joy, I just sat there. We both just sat there. A roar of emotion pulsed through my body, obliterating all my other senses. The simplicity of her response revealed something I could feel but not understand.

She seemed to have taken a huge leap beyond me, and I was suddenly struggling to keep up. It was breathtaking. The future was a blur. I hadn't stopped to anticipate her response, but I would never have guessed *this*—or that my whole world would be knocked off its orbit.

The silence at the table continued. But the silence was far from silent.

After a few seconds—or was it a few minutes?—Paige stood up.

"I'll be back," she said. Nothing else.

I watched as she headed toward the ladies' room. *Is she upset? Does she just need to gather her thoughts?*

She was gone for what seemed like hours. The waitress was refilling our water glasses when Paige returned wearing a faint smile.

"You okay?" I asked.

"I am. Yes," she said softly.

What was I supposed to get from that? Her face radiated warmth without the slightest hint of what she was thinking. I couldn't read her. She seemed both subdued and highly vibrant. And her expression . . . was it acceptance? I hoped so.

A portal had opened somewhere in the universe—or so I imagined—and she'd walked quietly through it. Or had *we* walked through it?

No question, I was confused. Moments before, I was brimming with more words than I could utter. Now I was speechless.

THE RESTAURANT WAS NOW empty and it felt like it was time to leave. We gathered our things and I took care of the check.

Paige was still silent, which was now disconcerting. She wasn't a nonstop talker, but she was always engaged and responsive. She seemed engaged now, even responsive, except without words.

How can someone say: "I'm yours," and not explain?

We found a secluded sitting area off the lobby. Words came slowly at first for both of us but then flowed—just nothing about the word-bomb she'd dropped.

I don't recall how the conversation started, but we spent the next hours getting to know each other. Until that day we knew certain things—about our business aspirations, our values, bits of our histories. Now, in this new universe with the cloak of professionalism gone, we slipped into the back and forth of people in their first blush of attraction.

We meandered through our stories: where we were born, grew up, went to school, why we'd made certain choices, piecing together how we'd arrived at the moment Scolastico told Paige she should call me. All the hard and soft statistics of two lives. What dreams remained unfulfilled? What were our favorite colors? What movies did we like?

Our bodies didn't touch, but our quiet conversation braided us together, no less intimately than the murmuring of lovers on their first night in each other's arms.

Hours went by and soon we were hungry.

We went back to the cafe but it was noisy with business lunches, so we decided on the Italian restaurant upstairs. It was barely occupied, and as we stepped into the quiet elegance, I felt us both relax. We settled into a booth that had high leather backs where we could easily rest our heads. Our conversation continued seamlessly from topic to topic—some sublime, some ordinary, some even silly—letting a full array of life's moments and memories circulate between us.

When the waiter asked about dessert and coffee, both of us glanced at our watches. How did it get to be midafternoon?

"Just the check," I beamed, "thank you."

I was reeling with joy, but my logistical mind was also kicking in. In all our back and forth, neither of us had raised the obvious question. What do we *do* about all this? I couldn't fathom just driving away and imagining the possible outcomes and next steps, but I didn't know how to raise the issue. I certainly didn't dare ask what "I'm yours" really meant.

"So, where should we live?" I asked instead.

A brief, quizzical look darted across Paige's face. Then without hesitation she responded matter-of-factly. "I guess LA. My business is more mobile than yours."

She turned her head toward a painting on the wall, then almost immediately back to me, her face charged with surprise.

"My God," she breathed. "I'm married!"

I could only watch and listen as the circumstances of her life jolted back to the foreground and her sense of responsibility took over. She had a husband, and they had a company together, and a house, and friends. And a father and mother and a sister she was close to. So many beloved people, possessions, and routines, all carefully woven together to create a life, had been abruptly turned askew.

Of course, her litany made me think of Ellen, our friends, our life together. A part of me had seen this coming. I'd been unsettled and apprehensive since that nightmare in Greece. No, it'd been longer than that.

Paige was silent again as if looking thoughtfully into herself. Minutes before, everything was pristine. We'd been swimming in eternal timelessness—no musings about the future, no talk of what would happen beyond that day, beyond that hour, beyond that table. Now, the realities of our everyday lives were back, sharp and clear.

My inquiry about where we'd live had broken a spell. Or had it catapulted us forward? I had no idea, but I was battling a barrage of questions. *Where exactly will we live? When will we move in together? What can we afford?*

Inexplicably, I didn't think to question whether or not this would happen, only how and when. Still, a heaviness had set in and was about to bury us, when we spontaneously reached across the table and found each other's hands.

With that simple touch, the weightiness vanished. We reentered the realm of our togetherness, and nothing else mattered. We made no plans, but it felt like we were merged.

WE WALKED HAND IN hand to the garage, and it was impossible to feel where my skin stopped and hers began.

At her car, we embraced intensely without a kiss, but with anticipation for an uncertain future that felt illumined by the heavens.

We'd both grabbed lightning, and I knew we'd never let go.

Paige's reflection

We've told a few people this story, and this is the point where someone turns to me and asks, "What the hell were you thinking?!"

My most honest answer is: "I wasn't!" There was no thinking involved, but here's what I was experiencing:

Going into that breakfast, I was already in somewhat of an altered state. Something in me had shifted while reading the manuscript. I didn't know what or why, but I was buzzing in ways I'd never felt, essentially walking around in a shimmering hum.

So while Don's describing what happened in Hawaii, I'm sitting there just listening and listening. But it's not my normal listening. At first, I follow the details of the story, then without noticing, something shifts, and I'm no longer thinking, which is inconceivable for me.

Somehow, my persistently active mind has retreated into stillness. Pure stillness. I'm no longer hearing his words, but their meaning is pulsing in my chest. I'm joined with him in every scene, every feeling, every sensing. I'd never experienced that before, but it was so vivid, so real. Pristine. And utterly unforgettable.

Then "I'm yours" emerges to be spoken, and it's a simple statement of fact. It's a statement of truth, not the answer to a question, not a promise of what would be. It's simply the set of words that reflects what I now know to be true. It's the description of the reality I'm perceiving beyond the boundaries of my normal being: we are one, we are together, we are joined.

That trip to the ladies' room (I'd been drinking a lot of tea) is one of those odd times when every detail is burned into visceral memory. I can see the exact stall I sat in and recall the precise thought that floated up from inside me: *I guess I'm creating a love affair for another lifetime.*

Then the thinking stopped again, until later when he asked me where we would live. *"I guess LA because my business is more mobile than yours."* Talk about not thinking!

Also burned in my memory is turning my head toward my left and seeing the painting hanging next to me. That's when I was hurled back into all the practical circumstances of my life — including that I was married.

Somewhere in the middle of that, our hands touched across the table. The frenzy of fearing evaporated, and I was in that transcendent realm again where there's no urge to control. No urge to protect or defend. No urge — no thought really — about the future, and certainly no compunction to plan. Only vibrant love, and a trust in all goodness and the goodness of all.

This might sound impossible. (I still shake my head in wonder.) But I was in a world that simply was. A world filled with expansive perceptions and intense awareness, but with no linearity, no sense of anything unfolding in time or space. It was all happening in total nowness and peace.

So what was I thinking? Lots was happening inside me, but as I said, it wasn't what you'd call thinking.

chapter forty-seven

Alternate Reality

I was crazy in love with a woman I barely knew.

She was driving home to a man she'd fleetingly forgotten she was married to, while I was driving home to a woman I loved but with whom I now knew I could never spend a lifetime—all because I'd described a strange meditation that I'd vowed to keep to myself.

Then there was her response: "I'm yours." These two words propelled us across an invisible abyss into a new life—an alternate reality—inconceivable just moments before.

Yet neither of us had made any commitments. Or had we? She was clearly in no mind to plan, and I felt I needed to respect that. *But respect what? A future that can't be put into words? Besides, it was all so . . . unreal.*

My thoughts gyrated in my head until one thing emerged as real. I fully believed that Paige had become mine. And I knew I had become hers. We were in this together, inextricably united in one of those no-turning-back realizations when you know your life has been transformed.

Beyond that, I was mired in confusion. Like the idea of driving "home." Where was home now? Emotionally, home was our togetherness. However, we still needed a physical place to land. I was pretty sure we decided to live together. But when? And where?

I know she said she'd move to LA. But was that before or after she remembered she was married?

Inching along the freeway, I wondered if she'd recall our day together the same way I did. She was definitely in some kind of altered state.

My mind was now a blur. My heart was clear but I felt as though someone had stuffed cotton balls into my head. Did we decide on *anything*? Didn't we at least need to coordinate our timing?

I think we decided nothing.

My mind froze. Then it rambled.

What happens when she tells Tim about this. What if his reaction makes her change her mind? What if he's so furious he throws her out? Where will she go? Here, to LA? And what if she tells him tonight?

That last thought made me shiver.

In the midst of transcendent love, I was having a full-force fear attack.

WITHOUT HAVING TO THINK, I exited the 10 Freeway at Fairfax. The closer I got to the apartment, the shallower my breathing got and the tighter my shoulders.

What would I tell Ellen? *When* would I tell her? And how? Was there a time, a place, a circumstance that would soften the impact? Could I even describe what happened to me in a way that she could hear? If there was, I couldn't find it.

She'll never believe me, I thought. She won't buy that this just came into being today, let alone that my first real hint of it was during our New Year's meditation—two weeks ago. She'll be certain that Paige and I have been having an affair for a long time. Could I blame her? The reality of it made no sense.

I knew Ellen's mind would latch onto the handful of past comments about enjoying my new client, and that no matter how thoroughly I told the whole truth, it would sound like a fabrication. That little box of Christmas gifts in Hawaii, and how everyone *knew* something was going on, would be her indisputable proof. In the end, our friends would believe Ellen's version of the story and support her perceptions, and her.

None of them would believe me. None would be able to support me.

My stomach twisted, and I felt like I was going to be sick.

My fear then moved past these nightmarish prognostications into old familiar territory. Guilt.

How dare you do this to Ellen? I scolded myself. *This is all your fault, all your choice. You'll be off starting fresh with another woman, and she'll have to cope with yet another devastating romantic loss. And it'll all be on you.*

A rush of sadness shot through me. I cared deeply for Ellen and, in some ways, still felt love for her. The last thing I wanted was to cause her the distress of another failed relationship. Part of my hopefulness about our turning things around had been fueled by my desire to avoid precisely that.

I let out a deep sigh and managed to compose myself a bit. I reminded myself that love is what mattered and that all these fears, no matter how compelling, didn't get to steer my choices. More than that, my love for Paige had a different quality to it, what felt like a larger dimension, and I couldn't imagine not honoring that.

Whatever was next with Paige, the truth about Ellen and me was that we were already living a failed relationship. We'd both been unhappy for some time, and staying with it wasn't going to help.

Rather than try to squeeze into a tight parking space in front of the building, I opted for a large one about a block down the street. By the time I'd walked back to the apartment, the aftershocks of fear had dwindled, at least enough to breathe a full breath. I also knew that whenever the time felt right to talk with Ellen, I'd be honest and kind.

I took the elevator upstairs and let myself into the apartment. It was too early for Ellen to be home, though I never knew the exact time she'd finish her day. Would she intuit a change the minute she saw me? I couldn't imagine that my guilt wouldn't somehow be on display.

The light on my answering machine was flashing. I set my briefcase on the desk and started to listen, but the clatter of the elevator arriving on our floor pushed a gag of nausea into my throat. When I heard footsteps head in the opposite direction, I exhaled and restarted the message. It delivered a temporary reprieve. Ellen had an evening meeting with her colleagues and would be home quite late. Surely, I'd be asleep by then.

AT FIVE A.M. SHARP, my eyes opened wide. Everything felt normal for a split second. Then I thought of Paige and it hit me. *Was it just yesterday that she said I'm yours?* I was stunned. Adrift. But filled with joy. My whole being was overflowing with Paige's presence while my rational mind was faltering from the fear and uncertainty of it all: *When? Where? How?*

Ellen shifted in the bed beside me. I recoiled, not because she was there, but because my system reacted to her as if she was the other woman.

Life was morphing right under my nose.

Still lying there, I forced myself to consider my morning. *Let's see, it rained last night so no jogging today.* That was reason enough to be glad for inclement weather.

I got up slowly to avoid disturbing Ellen, then brought her coffee while she dressed. I touched her shoulder gently as I was leaving the room and realized I was trying to comfort her. Some part of me needed to quell the upheaval that would soon be hers. I knew full well that the road ahead would be harder for her than for me and that there was little, if anything, I could do about it.

She dressed in a hurry, and we barely spoke. Minutes later she was out the door and on her way to work.

I WENT STRAIGHT TO my desk to gather materials for two meetings that afternoon. My business had been growing and client relationships were deepening just as I'd hoped. This provided me a welcome sense of stability, and at that moment, a welcome diversion. My emotions needed a break.

Mornings alone in the apartment were usually my favorite time, but today Ellen's absence made it feel strange. Empty. Then I realized that the apartment was back to being her place, not ours.

In her absence, I became aware of an even more uncomfortable feeling. I was, second by second, living a lie. Trying to be real with Ellen had always been important to me, but how could I claim any personal integrity when I knew my future was elsewhere?

chapter forty-eight

No Compromise

T he following day, Ellen was buoyant as we dressed to go jogging and particularly talkative as we made our rounds at the track. Then, walking back to the car in a light drizzle, she took my hand like she used to.

In the past, I would've rejoiced at her unexpected touch. Did this sudden show of affection signal a change? Had she finally resolved the anger and resentment that had spewed out in Hawaii? Or was she just feeling her usual Friday morning lift?

Everything else was routine. Ellen showered and dressed while I made coffee. As she poured her to-go cup, she suggested we go out for a nice dinner to celebrate the weekend. And to talk.

Talk? I'm sure I frowned, but there was no plausible way I could say no. I agreed when she recommended we try the trendy new seafood restaurant on Ocean Avenue in Santa Monica.

We hugged goodbye, and it felt like she held me longer than usual. Did she want to discuss our relationship? If so, I had no idea what I'd say. We needed to talk soon, really soon, but I wasn't ready. Some part of me trusted what was unfolding, but another part was spinning so wildly, my cells couldn't absorb it.

I DOUBLE-CHECKED MY calendar. No meetings, just some creative work for client presentations the following week. I was free to work on the manuscript—if I could get my mind to focus. As soon as I sat down at my desk, the phone rang. *Could it be Paige?* I hoped so. How could we have been immersed in such closeness and then no contact for three days? Excitement and fear danced in my chest as I grabbed to catch the call before it went to voicemail.

It was her, but she couldn't talk. It had just started drizzling again and Tim would be back from his morning ride any minute. She was calling to say that she wanted to send me some notes, some things she'd written. With a surge of anticipation, I set my modem to receive.

Minutes later, the document was on my Mac and open.

Thursday, January 22nd, 8:00 p.m.

I feel like that cartoon character who runs out over the cliff but stays aloft, oblivious to the fact that the earth is no longer there. But it feels safe, and kind, and I don't fall.

I feel thoroughly, totally connected with you—and something about what's happening feels like it's moving me to a whole new level of existence. My thoughts don't even try to keep up. Suddenly this active, creative mind is at a loss. The detail and power of deep subtleties that are usually elusive are now so real and tangible, they've taken over my normal channels of thinking, feeling, deciding. Thought-possibilities that should frighten me exist now as if faded fragments of an old dream.

Unless this passes quickly and I awaken to find I've been dreaming, or deluded, this is the freedom and love I've longed for in the quiet, unspoken depth of my heart.

The words 'no compromise' have come to visit. Life seems more precious. I feel like God has asked me to honor life and

myself, and you and God within each of us. The door has been
opened wide to cross into a world of impeccable trust.

As our friend Ron would say: "I am infused with love."

I exhaled deeply, relieved to feel our connection again. Then I
closed my eyes to more fully feel what she was feeling. There was
something about her "no compromise" that had struck a note. A positive note. Although I didn't know why.

I looked back to the screen and noticed more writing below.

Friday, January 23rd, 3:00 a.m.

I'm <u>never</u> awake at 3am unless I'm <u>still</u> awake or spinning with
worry or anger, neither of which is even remotely the case
now.

I check for sadness, remorse, regret, impatience, fear, but
none are there. And I wonder if the choice to be with you
could be so right that these 'to-be-expected' emotions—the
negative ones—will find no place in my heart. Or is it just not
time yet? Maybe, but it doesn't really matter.

I love watching and feeling this receptive, open side of me
come forward. I like her. I like how she feels. It's very relaxing
in here, and creative, but right now there's nothing to do,
despite the challenges I know are ahead.

I feel grateful, alive, passionate, and quietly safe. I'm safe
and at home in the deepest way. It's all new, and it's all
familiar.

I love you.

I closed the document on my screen and leaned back into my
chair.

Never had anyone been so open and unprotected with me. Never
had anyone received me so completely or given themselves over to

me so wholeheartedly. And, never had I been so fully open to receive such a gift.

It felt natural and real, but also impossible. Yet, there it was in front of me. "I love you." The words that had, in the past, so often made me feel trapped now made me feel free.

THAT EVENING ELLEN WAS running late with a patient, and rather than risk losing our dinner reservation she decided to meet me at the restaurant. I waited at the bar with a glass of wine, still churning over what I'd say if dinner was about discussing our relationship.

When I saw Ellen at the maitre d' stand, a wave of sadness washed over me. As she walked toward me, I knew that regardless of what she wanted to discuss, it would be beyond unkind to break the news in a bustling restaurant or any location from which she'd have to drive home alone.

Before I could get the bartender's attention to order her a glass of wine, the hostess appeared to show us to our table. Ellen was chatty about her day, and despite some difficulties at work, she was in an upbeat mood. The food was as good as we'd heard, and we got through dinner without either of us bringing up anything heavy.

After the table was cleared, we ordered two short espressos, and our waiter enticed Ellen into a decadent chocolate something. The minute her dessert arrived, she excitedly announced what had been on her mind.

"The guys are talking about another big trip!" She went on excitedly and wrapped up by assuring me that the destination hadn't been set yet, but she wanted to be sure I knew well in advance.

"Thanks for the heads up," I said, hoping the look on my face read as simple surprise. "I'm sure you and Daniel will come up with something wonderful."

The image of her going on that trip alone made my heart hurt, but was that really what she wanted to talk about? Another trip?

Once again, our minds were in different worlds. It so mirrored our life together.

I paid the tab, then gave our parking stubs to the valet. Waiting for our cars, about to drive home separately, I saw the two of us standing silently at a crossroads.

chapter forty-nine

Unsettled

It was Ellen's turn to cover the office on a Saturday. As always, I was happy for time alone to work on the manuscript, and it left me open for Paige in case she reached out. I considered calling her, but that would've been completely out of character on a weekend. Besides, my guilt rose and squashed the urge.

I immersed myself in the book until right before noon when the phone rang. It was Paige, but her tone was different. Upbeat, but hollow. She sounded like she was talking to a new business associate. After a brief, cordial exchange, she asked if she could send a file.

As soon as my eyes met the words on the screen, I felt like I'd stepped into a cold shower instead of the warm embrace I expected.

Friday, January 23rd, 8:45 p.m.

This evening was rough. I lost touch with the bliss and security of the love I've been experiencing. I felt the heaviness of challenges I see ahead. I find myself checking inside to make sure I stay open and loving and aware of the other human being whose life I am disrupting.

A voice inside says: be kind and gentle, but do stay true to yourself. And I take that advice to heart.

She went on to say that she'd been visited by some "curious thoughts" about our life together. That sounded innocent enough, plus she'd clarified: "even the not-so-fun ones are fun to think about." But as I read more, I realized she was grappling with some serious questions, fears even, which stirred my own fear.

> Will we fight? Who will our friends be? Are there hidden challenges that will match the magnitude of our love? How will we handle money? Who will cook?! You've said you get angry. I can see you getting angry, but I only see it melting. I do wonder how I would feel if you really exploded at me.

I felt a sharp jab in my chest. I couldn't imagine that level of anger erupting in her presence, let alone *at* her. But anger was not foreign to me. My heart sank, but I took a breath and went back to reading:

> And what will it feel like to embrace your love fully without hiding? And what will it be like to unreservedly express how I feel for you?
> As I hear myself, I'm a bit in awe that amid the fleeting concerns and fears, I'm so peaceful. There's so much to materially worry about here. I'm amazed that that part of my mind hasn't jumped in. (This is highly unusual for me. I've been a very good worrier.)

And that was it. I closed the document and moved from my desk to the rocker. After removing a few dead leaves that had fallen from my bonsai, I closed my eyes and was immediately met by an image of Paige and me on a high wire. We were utterly vulnerable.

Until now, I'd been struggling with turmoil and guilt, and some logistical questions, but mostly I'd been trusting a sense of certainty that I didn't dare question—as if we were being led toward an exquisite light. Still, this could go badly in so many ways.

Could our connection turn out to be just another fleeting flash of hope?

Paige wasn't saying any of this, of course. She seemed peaceful in the face of her concerns. But I heard them as a bundle of understandable fears, and that left me wrestling with my own demons and a history of failed dreams. A demoralizing advertising career. A painful stint at Fox. A dismal time at Disney. Unsold screenplays and the screenplay that was bought on a Friday and un-bought by Monday. Then there was the soul-wrenching bankruptcy of Quantum Leap. And finally the loss of my beautiful house—and my beloved Stray.

Could this new love really be the early stage of another . . . ?

A calmer voice reminded me to slow down and breathe. To trust my inner sensing and move at an even pace. *This is different*, I told myself. *Qualitatively different. And fear isn't trustworthy.* Hadn't Paige said as much at the end of her note when she talked about being peaceful despite all the concerns?

It was clear that she was feeling something strong between us. Yet rereading her words I kept feeling that she could be slipping away. The absence of practical plans had me beyond unsettled, but was that it?

Then I realized what was bothering me—not knowing *when* she'd be ready had me wondering *if* she ever would be. The thought of it sent a shot of terror into my gut.

But wait a minute, how can such boundless intimacy exist between two people and they not end up together?

But if we're going to end up together, shouldn't we making plans?

chapter fifty

Apartment Hunting

I paced around the apartment several times then went back to my desk. I thought I was ready to get my head into some client work, but I couldn't keep myself from reopening Paige's document. Instead of scrolling to the top to reread, I accidentally scrolled down and discovered something I'd missed.

Saturday, January 24th, 6:00 a.m.

I've been awake since 4:30. I think I understand why morning people cherish this time. It's like a clear, cool lake that lies completely still after a night of peace.

I can see the sky lighten through the droopy tree out the front window, and I think I'll put on my walking shoes and go out to see what it's like. I wonder if this change in my timing is permanent? I hope so. I've always wanted to be awake and mobile by dawn, but it never felt like my energy and my body would support that desire.

About ten minutes into my walk I realize that it's the first time I can remember going out with nothing to listen to. But this morning I am very happy just to be with myself, alive and vital in a way I've never felt before. I wonder what has really changed that I feel so different?

> Remember the movie "Harvey" with Jimmy Stewart and his
> big, invisible rabbit? Well, like Harvey, you were with me,
> walking right by my side—but in something that resembled
> *your* body, not a rabbit's! Mostly I experience you as a warmth
> of energy, and I'm aware of the presence of a new emotion
> joining the expansiveness I've been feeling. It's a light and
> happy joy, and I'm very glad to have it.

Wow, I thought. She might not be ready to talk practical details, but she's definitely not pulling away. Then I noticed asterisks and scrolled down some more.

> It's pretty intense around here. Nothing spoken, but the air is
> thick with sadness and hurt. But I don't have the courage to
> talk to Tim yet . . .

Ouch. I leaned back into my chair, aching at her predicament. She hadn't said it directly but rather than slipping away, it sounded like she was on the verge of telling him.

I bolted upright. I needed to get serious about finding somewhere to live. I'd checked the listings for short-term, furnished apartments, hoping to find something nice, but that was it. And nothing looked even remotely promising. Besides, even if Paige was slow to tell Tim, or even if she never did, I needed a place for myself.

A few hours earlier, things were moving too slow. Now they were moving too fast.

The bulk of the afternoon was still ahead of me, so I shut down my computer and spread the classified section on the table. Soon I discovered how unprepared I was for apartment hunting in LA. When I moved out here from Chicago, I contacted a realtor who helped buy my house in the hills—and from there I moved in with Ellen.

MY FIRST STOP WAS at a small residence hotel on Wilshire in Beverly Hills. I'd heard some nice things about it and thought it was probably a good short-term option. Except when I got there, the bouquet of fake flowers in the lobby turned me off, as did the price.

Next were several month-to-month rentals in Santa Monica. It would be wonderful, I thought, to find something closer to the ocean. The first option was too small and cramped, not to mention on a very noisy street, and expensive. The next was affordable but had shabby furniture. My final stop was a condo that looked appealing in the ad, but when I saw the building, I couldn't go in.

Sure, I hadn't thought this would be easy, but I didn't expect to feel so defeated. The only sunshine in an otherwise dreary afternoon was that one way or another I was about to move.

THAT NIGHT ELLEN GOT home later than expected and was exhausted. She ate lightly and went to bed early. I was worn out too, but woke up a few hours later and couldn't get back to sleep. Living between two worlds was taking its toll.

My mind was chaotically trying to figure out the housing expenses that lay ahead. Ellen and I had always shared monthly costs, and the only thing I knew for certain about Paige's finances was that the income from her business wouldn't be enough to support her and Tim if they lived apart, at least not anytime soon. And who knew what would happen to their business after they split.

I shuddered at the rough financial seas Paige and I would be sailing into and was hit by an image of the two of us struggling to survive on a makeshift raft tossing about on a surging ocean. The winds were rising, and the raft was dipping and bobbing amid crashing waves. I was trying to tie everything down, but we were hopelessly vulnerable to the elements.

I got up and went to my desk. It was the only place in the apartment that felt like home. After a few minutes there, I walked over to the bank of windows and gazed at the distant skyline, wondering where my bonsai and I would live next.

chapter fifty-one

Heartache

Early Monday morning I was trying to convince myself that it was reasonable to call Paige well before business hours. Didn't I need to confirm this week's meeting and review priorities right away so I could start prepping materials? But each time I picked up the phone, I put it back down.

It had only been five days since I heard the words, "I'm yours," but each day, each hour, seemed like a whole universe of time creeping along. Thankfully, clients were happy to schedule meetings with me despite their post-holiday regrouping. I needed the distraction—and the income.

With all my other client calls complete, I picked up the phone and punched in Paige's number. After four rings, I considered hanging up.

"Good morning, this is Paige."

"Whoa . . . it's good to hear your voice."

"Yours, too!"

"Can you talk?"

"For a minute or two. Enough to send some more writing. The weekend's been pretty intense, and . . ." Her voice trailed off but her sadness spoke loudly in the silence.

"Sorry to hear, but yes, modem's ready."

"This one's kinda heavy. Are you sure this isn't getting too overwhelming?"

"Definitely not," I said, wanting to reassure her.

"That's good to hear. I've gotta make this quick because—" Paige interrupted herself, I assumed to focus on what she was doing. A few beats later the transmission was complete.

"Okay, it came through. So, this week it's Thursday, not Wednesday, right?"

"Yes. Can't wait! Maybe we can talk sometime between?"

"Call whenever you can," I said, opening the file. "Unless I'm out at a meeting, I'll be here."

Sunday, January 25th, 9:00 a.m.

We had a blowup last night. Tim's hurt and fear erupted as anger. I listened quietly, not knowing how else to respond. I felt soft and secure but also closed down. I couldn't get my heart fully open to him. I saw the anger and understood his desire to lash out, but mostly I was aware of him trembling. As I watched myself, I wished I could feel his pain and do something about it, but I couldn't. Partially afraid to feel it, but also so saturated by . . . well you know, whatever this blissful transcendent thing is.

I told him I was sorry for pulling away and that I knew the distance was painful. I told him that a soft light was growing inside me and that it needed my private attention—that it was time to reevaluate what I want, how I feel, what's important to me. I told him I made the choice to withdraw even though I knew it would hurt because I needed to look at my life freshly and without the influence of us and our history.

As he understood a little, his anger turned to sadness, and he asked me to be more considerate by letting him know when I would be out with a friend, or needed to be alone, or when there was time for him. He asked me for some warmth and tenderness. And I asked God to help me open my heart to him.

It was late and I was drained when we quietly crawled into bed. I wanted to meditate and be alone but felt I should hold him in his sadness. Was I doing this out of guilt? I almost got up but didn't. Being there was painful but important, probably for both of us. My heart opened a bit, and from a place of trust and love, I chose to give him my caring presence.

Awake at 6:30 this morning, I feel a little disappointed to have missed the early morning quiet. But a deep sense of truth is here, I think in response to my silent request for help last night. If I want to open my heart to this dear one I'm hurting . . . make my choices from love, not convenience or fear, and tell and trust the truth. But even with that, I still feel torn between worlds. In some ways free and in motion. In other ways rooted and immobile.

I closed the file. These glimpses of Paige's inner life—her heart openings and her heartache—were precious. I had a strong desire to help but knew it was impossible. Tim was grieving and I hurt for him. And what about Ellen? I had no idea what she was feeling but couldn't imagine she wasn't sensing something.

This was the most wrenching piece of it all—the tearing apart of relationships. I couldn't begin to rationalize it, or avoid it, or make excuses for it. Or make it better. I also couldn't turn back.

Still, the dichotomy was hard to hold. On one level, I was steeped in the most joyous experience I could ever have imagined. On another, my heart ached for the people whose lives were being dismantled by the very source of that joy.

chapter fifty-two

Crouching Tiger

I paced the living room. It was Wednesday. Paige said she'd try to call sometime before tomorrow's meeting.

I hated that we couldn't talk when we wanted. I hated being out of touch especially when I knew things were rough for her. I hated this antsy feeling and not being able to do anything about it. Keeping my body in motion was my only relief.

I glanced at the LA skyline barely visible through the smog. On my next lap around the apartment, I stopped to straighten a picture, probably crooked from the latest tremor. Then I checked my watch, closed a drawer, picked up a piece of lint from the carpet, and then another one, then I checked my watch again.

At some point the pacing made it worse. I went to my desk to find something to occupy my mind. I'd just pulled out a couple of client files when the tiny red light on the phone lit up. I answered it on the first ring.

"It's me," Paige said.

"Are you okay?"

"Yes and no. It's been—"

"What happened?" I interrupted.

"Wide swings," she paused. "I'm exhausted, but it's good to hear your voice. Say, how's the book coming? Still able to read my notes on the manuscript?"

"Yeah, they're great. Still writing in your journal?"

"Every day. That's how I keep sane. That, and a couple late breakfasts with my good friend Donna at this little cafe in Corona del Mar. My comfort food order is hot chocolate and a yummy croissant sandwich with poached eggs and brie. It's a treat in the middle of all this—and really a lifesaver. You'll have to meet her sometime."

"Glad you have that kind of friendship," I said, aware that I didn't. "And sure, I'd love to meet her sometime. So, do you have some recent writing to send me?"

"A couple days' worth."

"My Mac's ready when you are."

A few minutes later, another file was on my desktop. "Got it."

"Hey, you've gotten good at this! I'll call later today if I can, but if not, I'll see you tomorrow morning."

Monday, January 26th, 10:00 p.m.

At the end of my meditation, I saw a very clear, simple vision. I saw Tim and I about to complete this part of our journey together, with honor and understanding and love. I saw us as caring, courageous battle partners. The last years were among many we've fought as comrades. The battle is now over. We won. And now it's time for us to walk proudly and respectfully off the field. Tim will walk his next chosen path of fulfillment, and I will walk mine, joining my beloved, for the last time, for all eternity.

Tuesday, January 27th, 8:00 p.m.

Yesterday, when the phone rang I knew it would be you. As I listened to your voice and its caring and love, I could feel the lightness reenter my body. And I felt both calm and quiet and a spark of wonderment. Our love became real again and I was awestruck at its power to rejuvenate me. It's so very precious.

All day I knew that you knew how I felt, and that helped me maintain a foundation of trust. I'm very grateful for the open channel that bonds us through distance. It doesn't surprise me anymore, but I'm still thanking God for this gift, many times a day.

I'm tired and drained. I felt sick earlier—my stomach was unhappy and tight, but I knew it was just old fear dragons come to visit. Every minute gets heavier and heavier. I can't live this lie. I think it's time to let go and jump.

My head was filled with the image of a tiger crouching, poised to leap. So much had happened in the last three days, I could barely breathe.

I stood up to go to the kitchen but sat right back down.

Wednesday, January 28th, 5:00 a.m.

Why have I not told him? This question keeps prodding me. I think I'm trying to acclimate, trying to find some sense of ground. It's not even two weeks since everything changed, since whatever blinders I've been wearing were removed.

But I can't do this anymore. I'm avoiding Tim while at the same time trying not to hurt him. It's to the point where it's disrespectful and cruel. I'm afraid I've been choosing from terror, not love. I know he knows I'm leaving and only his fright and maybe a fragile strand of hope keeps him from confronting me.

I think I know what Thomas Merton meant in his journal when he said, "What have I to do with all that has died, all that belonged to a false life? When you know it's false, you can't keep living it even if you don't know what's next."

Yes, even when I don't know what's next.

I can feel myself well up with sadness, in my eyes and in my heart. I feel like I need to let everything fall. Everything. My relationship, my friends, my family. (Telling them will be as hard as telling Tim. Almost.) And my business, my home, this area, even my thoughts and standards, likes and dislikes—all the things that defined me forever.

And I don't know where I'm going.

Will you still love me, and I you, when this distance is gone and we immerse ourselves in a new routine? What if making love isn't what we think it will be? Will our new reality even come close to our dreams? And what if it all falls flat and I find that I gave up what I had for less?

I'm truly afraid. I feel like I'm walking into a . . .

As I moved into that thought, I heard myself say: *into a dark, unknown void*, and immediately the tightness in my chest released and the sadness is now gone. The darkness isn't true. That's just the fear, the past holding on.

I don't feel like I'm walking into a dark, unknown void. I feel like I'm walking into the safety of a long-forgotten home. It's light and airy with a lovely bluish-white mist. It feels like the soft, moist breezes in Hawaii that I cherish so much as they gently lap over my body and caress every bit of my soul.

So, I'm ready. I want to take a deep breath and tell the people I need to tell. I want to tell them the truth. Even if they don't understand, I need to remember the largeness of who they are and trust that telling this truth will lead back to love.

I shut down my computer. When I stood up this time, my stomach tightened into a powerful coil. Not in pain, but in readiness.

chapter fifty-three

Telling Tim

J ust back from jogging, I unlocked the apartment door and heard the phone on my desk ringing. Ellen brushed past me, heading for the shower. I hurried to my desk and realized it was my business line. It was too early for a client call.

"This is Don," I said, feeling a stab of dark anticipation.

"Sorry to call so early but I wanted you to know . . . I'm at the hotel, in case—"

"You are?" I interrupted trying to sound less alarmed than I was.

"It's okay if you can't come sooner, but I told Tim last night." Her voice was shaking but controlled, like that of a journalist reporting from the center of disaster. "We cried for hours and hours. After he finally went to bed, I . . . well, I couldn't stay there. And I didn't want to go to Donna's in the middle of the night, so I got in the car and drove here. The hotel offered me a half-day rate if I'm out by noon."

"It'll take me a little while to get out of here," I said, my world spinning wildly.

I listened to make sure Ellen's shower was still running. It wasn't.

"Take your time," she said, weariness slowing her words. "I've been here since . . . about four this morning. I waited to call, thinking seven would be okay."

"This is perfect, but it'll take me a while to get there. I haven't showered yet, and traffic will be a bear."

"Whenever is fine. I need to get some sleep. I'm in room 423."

Hanging up the phone, I jotted her room number on a sticky and gathered our meeting materials from my desk. A sound behind me let me know that Ellen had entered the room.

"Something's come up," I said with a quick glance. "Paige wants to meet earlier."

Ellen looked puzzled but didn't pursue it.

THE HOT SHOWER CALMED me down a bit. I dried off and went to the living room to get dressed. I wondered how many more mornings I'd be getting dressed standing in front of Ellen's entryway closet.

"Should I make toast for you too?" Ellen called from the kitchen.

"No thanks. It's a breakfast meeting." I picked up my briefcase and checked my pocket for my keys. "Are you still planning to be home around the regular time?"

"Yes. Why?"

"We need to talk," I blurted out. I then opened the front door and looked back to see her standing there, frozen.

Her face had crashed.

The elevator ride down was excruciating. I couldn't believe what I'd done, what I'd said. Even worse was the offhanded way I'd said it. And then I just left? What a dreadful thing to do. *I should go back and apologize.* All day long she'd be agonizing about what would happen that evening. But I couldn't go back. Everything would unravel and make it worse.

THE FREEWAYS WERE AS slow as anticipated, and I had to keep telling myself to stay cool and think rationally. *But there's nothing rational about this!* It had been only about a week since I'd told Paige about my meditation. *Are we nuts?*

An hour later I entered the garage at Stouffer's. I parked at the first open spot and rushed for the elevator. Room 423. I knocked softly. Paige appeared and we melted into each other's arms.

Our embrace was like none before. She was limp and drained of energy, and I could feel sobs tremble through her body.

She sat down on the bed with her back to some pillows. Her face was red and blotched, her eyes puffy. I pulled up a chair next to her and held her hand. She cried as she recounted her bare-all conversation with Tim and his uncharacteristic bursts of anger that just as quickly surrendered to waves of sorrow and panic. His biggest fear was that we'd been having an affair. Once he understood that we'd never shared that kind of intimacy, they talked and listened and held each other much of the night, mourning their mutual losses. Then raw from the emotion and exhaustion, she escaped into the early-morning darkness. Her first sleep came only after she'd called me from the hotel.

"I haven't told Ellen yet," I said when she became quiet.

"That's okay. You don't have to tell her anything," Paige replied. "Not now, not ever. I did what I did because I know my marriage is over. It's over, no matter what happens with you, with us, whether or not you leave Ellen."

I was shocked that she'd even consider that I might stay with Ellen. Yet, as we spoke I began to understand. Her choice to end her marriage was what she called a "separate truth," something that needed to happen even if we hadn't met.

Yes, her feelings for me had influenced her choice, but only the timing. She'd had plenty of time to reflect, one of the side benefits, she said, of our not being able to talk that often. With limited access to what I was thinking and no certainty about what I would do, she made her choice independently. Her decision demanded nothing of me.

She'd realized that she and Tim had been living with a deep, almost invisible discontent, probably unnoticed because their challenges rarely erupted in conflict or anger. They were great friends and colleagues, but that was it. Not enough to sustain a marriage.

When I finally let that sink in, I relaxed into a sense of freedom I hadn't known was missing. But it changed nothing about what I wanted.

"I will always be with you," I said, squeezing her hand.

A slight smile touched her mouth and we lingered in each other's eyes.

"What about you?" she asked gently. "Are you okay?"

"When I left this morning, I told Ellen we had to talk when she got home tonight."

Paige winced. Fragile from bearing Tim's suffering, she understood the agony and emptiness Ellen was surely feeling and could well imagine the encounter we'd likely have to endure.

Paige adjusted her position on the bed, trying to get more comfortable, then shifted from slumped to sitting up and asked if I'd mind rubbing her shoulders a bit. As soon as I began massaging her neck, her body was familiar to my hands. A hint of passion rose softly within me but I let it pass. Now was *not* the time.

WE CONSIDERED ROOM SERVICE but Paige needed air, so we decided to go down to the cafe. She asked if she looked presentable and I told her she did, but that she might want to think about combing her hair. She laughed and fluffed her curls with her fingers.

"Combing it would make it worse," she said with a smile. "This will have to be good enough."

It was comforting to be back in our favorite meeting place. We were among strangers, but by now, the restaurant felt homey. Paige ordered her usual breakfast and the color soon returned to her face. She told me that she'd arranged to stay with her good friend Donna and her husband, for a while if needed, but that she could leave Newport Beach anytime.

"Well, *after* I tell my family," she clarified. "My parents will be at my sister's this weekend and I'm going over for dinner tomorrow night."

As we spoke, it became clear that she needed a few days in her "old" life, and that I was free to do whatever I needed. We'd continue to let things unfold as felt right. We still didn't have firm plans, but at least we'd discussed what was next.

Just before noon, we went to the front desk so Paige could check out of her room. From there, we went our separate ways. She was heading home to pack an overnight bag and be there for Tim as best she could. I was heading back to the apartment to pull some things together and wait for Ellen's return.

Our only other plan was to move in together somewhere on LA's Westside. Beyond that, we were stepping onto a midair platform that didn't exist but that we trusted with all our hearts.

chapter fifty-four

Telling Ellen

I got home to a message from Ellen. She was running late, but it was just an unexpected appointment with a longtime patient needing help. There were no signs of trepidation in her voice, but she had to be feeling it. The look on her face that morning had said it all. I still couldn't believe how thoughtless I'd been. I organized a few things at my desk and began to pace.

My mind, my emotions, my whole system was jumbled. I kept trying to find a gentle way to tell her but soon realized that there was no honest scenario that would limit the heartbreak.

I let out an audible sigh and pulled a small piece of luggage from the closet. In it went a change of clothes, a Dopp kit, and a jacket. Feeling sick to my stomach I pushed the bag back into the closet and closed the door. There was nowhere to turn for comfort. I allowed myself a single glass of wine.

A LITTLE OVER AN HOUR later I tensed up at the familiar sound of the elevator slamming to a stop. Moments later Ellen's key was unlocking the door. Her face was pale. She looked exhausted.

She knows. Of course she knows.

The light was gone from her eyes. Her movements were limp and heavy. She dropped her keys and purse on the dining room table and went to the refrigerator. After standing in front of the open door for the longest time, she closed it without pulling anything out. She poured herself a glass of water and lingered there, sipping it.

Finally, I asked her if we could sit in the living room. She nodded and curled up in the overstuffed white flannel chair. It was her favorite. I positioned myself on the edge of the sofa facing her, and she grabbed the side pillow and held it against her chest.

There was no cushion for what was about to happen, and any soothing effect from the wine had vanished.

"I don't know how else to say this," I said to the anguished look in her eyes. "Paige and I have fallen in love."

Ellen stared at me. Then her body convulsed into sobs.

"I don't believe it!" she cried, rocking back and forth, clutching the pillow. "I don't believe it. I don't believe it! Not again. Not again."

I knelt by her chair and took her into my arms. After a few minutes, she embraced me in return and we sobbed together. I was crying for Ellen who, in almost-childlike surrender, was having to absorb the bitterness of another devastating loss. I was also crying for myself, the part of me who'd made her worst fear come true, but also for the part of me who was wounded on the same battlefield.

Being both executioner and victim had become one excruciating reality.

IN THE FOLLOWING HOURS, we talked and cried and hugged and talked some more. Some part of her kept trying to reject that this was real. With confusion creasing her forehead and a faraway look in her eyes, she murmured again and again that she couldn't believe it. How could she be abandoned once more? How could she lose another man she'd dared to love? She cried in a wail that boiled over with loss and bereavement.

I held her as if holding myself, knowing that nothing I could do or say would soften this blow. I'd assassinated who she thought we were and shattered the life she believed was hers.

AT SOME POINT—I don't know how or why—the throbbing emptiness that had engulfed us lifted. In its place was a flood of unconditional love, a fierce encounter with a tenderness that was perhaps the holy root from which all love is birthed.

Here it was at last, the sacred center of ourselves. No barriers, no defenses. No pretenses, no masks. And in their absence we were vulnerable enough to love again, and to being loved. The emotionally naked union I'd yearned for during our years together had finally arrived. How sad, I thought, that it came in our final hours and in this way.

MORNING BROUGHT A STARK reversal. We'd fallen asleep holding each other, but sometime during the night, Ellen's openness turned to anger. She came at me like an animal fighting for survival, storming around the apartment in an outrage. It wasn't fair, she cried. This relationship was supposed to last. She felt ripped open, devastated, betrayed. And she spewed out her bitterness about life, about God, about me.

I wanted to scream back at her, to remind her that she was as culpable for the failure of this relationship as I was. I wanted to overwhelm her with my own bitterness but glimpsed the downward spiral that would surely follow. So I took a deep breath and resolved to listen as best I could. I knew it wouldn't be enough, and maybe she would have preferred a fight, but I didn't want to go there. Besides, I wanted to at least try to show her the respect I'd have wanted if I were in her position.

AFTER A TIME, THE apartment was finally quiet. Ellen had retreated to the bedroom, I'd guessed to get ready to go out. I decided to brew a pot of coffee as I always did each morning. There was little else I could say or do. Part of me wanted to leave, but I also wanted to be there in case she needed something from me.

I heard the bedroom door slam shut and set the cup I'd poured for her on the kitchen counter. After a few minutes, I went to take it to her, but as I reached to open the bedroom door I heard a muffled conversation. It sounded like she was canceling an appointment, perhaps rescheduling another—hard to say. Then a heated conversation started. I assumed she'd called one of her friends.

I carried her untouched cup back to the kitchen. A few minutes later the bedroom door flew open. Ellen walked up to me and looked me straight in the eye.

"I'm going to Beth and Gil's for the day," her tone now stiff and bitter. "He was still home when I called, so I talked to him too. Here's what I want. I'd like you out of the apartment before I get back this evening. You can use it during the day for your office."

I nodded.

"How quickly can you move out?"

"I'll start packing right away."

"I want you gone as soon as possible."

"Of course."

She headed back to the bedroom and emerged a few seconds later with her purse and a sweater. Without looking at me, she walked out of the apartment and shut the door without a slam.

chapter fifty-five

Hopefully Tomorrow

My mind was focused and alert—a stark contrast to the last several weeks—and I fully trusted that Paige and I would be together soon. I took my coffee to my desk and gathered my client files into one stack. I needed to keep organized. My clients were my financial life force.

Paige and I hadn't spoken since we'd separated at the hotel, and I wanted her to know that I was free to make a move. It was probably too early to call her, but I dialed anyway and waited.

"Good morning, this is Paige," her voice was like music.

"Hi!" I said, my love pouring itself into the phone.

"Hi! How are you? Are you okay?"

"It was hard. But beautiful too, at least last night. I'll tell you more about it later. I can use her apartment during the day but need to leave before she gets home."

"Yikes. Where will you—?"

"I thought I'd call Larry," I said before she could finish her thought. "He stayed at my house in the hills many times reading scripts, sometimes showing up unannounced. Are you still having dinner with your family tonight?"

"I am, but I don't quite know how to break the news. But basically, I figure I'm just going to tell them the truth. That I'm feeling so much love, and that even though I've never shared details with them . . ." It sounded like she gulped some water. "They've known that Tim and I have been struggling."

"Well, I'll be anxious to hear how it goes."

"I think it's still best if I call you," she suggested gently.

"Of course, of course. I'll be here packing." Then came the question that had been off limits before. "So, when do you think you can come to LA?"

"Soon. This weekend I hope. I have to pull some business things together to make sure it keeps functioning, and that could raise some issues with Tim."

We talked a bit more, and our goodbye was sweet and optimistic. But after I hung up, I told myself to rein in my expectations. The two of them were breaking up a business and a marriage. A shot of fear pulsed through my body, remembering how difficult my own divorce had been.

LARRY OPENED HIS FRONT door with a wide smile and handed me a glass of wine. We finished the bottle together, and he was such a sympathetic listener I ended up telling him the whole story. Despite so little contact in the past few years, he remained a soulful friend.

The following morning, Larry had an early meeting at a film studio but left a freshly brewed pot of coffee for me. My first thought was to check in with Paige about how it went with her parents, but then I remembered that she'd call when she could.

ELLEN'S APARTMENT SEEMED eerily quiet, and I was reminded of how small it felt when I first moved in. I assembled a fresh moving box and began packing.

Three boxes later the only thing left on my desk was a framed photo of Ellen and me standing with Daniel and Gabe at the Acropolis in Greece. I assumed Ellen had already told them, but I wanted to connect with them myself, and soon. Beth and Gil too. Ellen was at their house, but I could reach Gil at the office. First, though, I needed some toast to settle my stomach. When I finally dialed, I was lucky to catch him between patients.

"So, you know what a mess she is," he jumped right in.

"Yes," I said quietly. "How's she doing?"

"Not good. Tell me, is this final? Or is this some . . . temporary thing?"

"It's real," I replied. "But Ellen and I are hoping a friendship will survive. At least at some point we were."

"I don't think so," he said sharply. "I told her what I tell my patients—when someone steps on your foot, and it hurts, you push them away!"

Hearing this, I understood Ellen's change of heart the previous morning. I wanted to tell Gil he shouldn't butt his nose in when he didn't have the whole story, but they were her friends before me, and they'd be there for her after me.

Our exchange wasn't what I'd hoped but I was glad I'd made contact.

WHEN I ARRIVED AT Daniel and Gabe's house, Daniel was outside feeding his two rescue dogs. I'd hoped to see Gabe also, but he was filming that week. Daniel was upset, and over coffee proposed a myriad of ways to patch things up.

It took some back-and-forth but when he finally understood that repair wasn't an option, he sat back and listened. I was in the middle of explaining what had happened when Daniel's face lit up with a quizzical grin.

"Is this the woman who sent you those heart-shaped muffins in Hawaii?"

"Yes, but it's *not* what you're thinking," I chuckled, unable to keep myself from matching his grin.

"C'mon, baby" he prodded, "I *knew* something was up with those muffins! And that adorable little mouse thingy!"

"No," I protested. "Really, there was nothing between us until two weeks ago!"

"Two weeks? And you're running away with her? You're no kid, Don," he teased.

"Yeah, I know. And I know it sounds nuts. But it's more real . . . and more precious than anything I've ever experienced."

"But *two weeks*?"

"We've been working together since August."

"Oooh, let's see now, that's . . . six months? That makes a *huge* difference!"

We laughed, and it felt good.

"Okay, but seriously," he said, dropping the kidding. "You know I understand, don't you? It happened almost that fast with Gabe and me."

Daniel and I started to reminisce, but we stopped ourselves when it went from fun to sad. Besides, it was time for me to leave.

"One last thing before you go," he said, as we were releasing from a long hug.

"What's that?"

"I envy you."

Getting into my car, I was flushed with gratitude for Daniel's openness and warmth, and for his invitation to come over so we could talk in person. I was also glad that at least one of my conversations with friends had gone as I'd hoped.

BACK AT ELLEN'S APARTMENT, I was so focused on getting my stuff packed before she returned that I jumped when the phone rang.

"I have some news!" Paige announced, sounding lighter than I expected.

"It went well with your family?"

"I wouldn't say that exactly. Mom and Dad were shocked at first,

Then they . . . well mostly Mom, started in about this being another one of my impulsive choices. Plus, they were so sad for Tim and worried about him. He's become like a son."

Paige went on to explain that in her family, she had a reputation for being rash when making big life decisions—even though in reality she always researched things thoroughly and thought them through. She just never included her parents in that process. Though in this case, she conceded, it was as sudden and unplanned as they all feared, and even more impossible to explain.

Her parents were also distressed that Paige, barely in her mid-thirties, was involved with a man in his early fifties. Her aunt, her mother's sister, had outlived two older husbands, so the potential for that kind of loss was not theoretical. It had been less than a year since they'd buried her second spouse.

"Whoa, I guess their concern is understandable," I said, feeling a tinge of regret about that likelihood for us. "So . . . what about your sister? How'd she react?"

"That was interesting. She said very little and seemed uncomfortable, but not critical, so that was a relief. But one of the best things about the evening was her saying, 'I just think you should be happy.' I could tell she meant it."

Paige's voice choked a bit, and she began talking more slowly.

"After we hugged goodbye, my parents told me to tell Tim he wasn't losing them and to be in touch soon. That's when I lost it. My mom retreated to the kitchen, but my dad . . . he put his arm around me and said we'd all get through this."

Hearing about her evening made me sad. Mostly though, I was happy she had that kind of support.

"So, ready for the news?" she asked still sniffling, but now upbeat.

"Uh, that wasn't it?"

"Nope. I think I might be able to get up there tomorrow."

"Really? Tomorrow!?"

"Yeah, but I can't be sure yet," she cautioned.

"Not sure?"

"Yeah, I need to . . . you know . . . with Tim. I'm hoping it'll go smoothly, but . . ." She was obviously holding back tears. "I don't think I told you, but he's being amazing. Even when I can tell he's angry, he's not dumping it on me. There's a lot of sadness and having to breathe deeply. It's such a big loss to absorb, and so sudden. I'm not sure I could be so understanding in his shoes. And I'm so grateful that our closest friends are still *our* friends and that they're supporting us both."

Now I was the one holding back tears. I was also in awe of the delicacy with which they were handling this, especially compared to the gulf between Ellen and me.

"And guess what else?" Paige chirped, bringing me out of my thoughts. "I called my travel-writer friend, and she can get us a good rate at a hotel in Santa Monica. It's just a Holiday Inn, but it's close to the ocean, near the pier I think. Is that okay?"

"That's great," I said, a little embarrassed that I hadn't worked this out myself. "So, tomorrow then?"

"Hopefully tomorrow. I still need to see how Tim responds when I start packing."

chapter fifty-six

Beloveds

I t was a bright Sunday morning. Larry was in the kitchen pouring my coffee into a cardboard cup. Paige's arrival time was still unknown, and I wasn't even sure she'd make it that day.

My suitcase and bonsai were waiting at the front door. I called the Holiday Inn. The reservation was still in place, but no, no one had checked in yet.

"I feel like I'm about to step off the planet," I said to Larry, trying to put words to an unfamiliar sensation. "Like I'm moving into a life that feels real, but that hasn't given birth to itself yet." By now he knew the whole story, but I hadn't articulated one underlying truth: that even though I'd met Paige just months before, she now possessed my soul.

Larry often kidded me about the risky choices I tended to make, but this time his warm familiarity was precisely the grounding I needed. So was his thoughtful carrying of my suitcase to the car while I cradled my bonsai.

"Thank you for these last couple days, my friend," I said, opening the trunk. "I'm sure I wasn't easy."

"Nah, you were just being you," he teased. "It was fun hearing about your new life and new lady. You're like a kid waiting for a parade. You can hear the band playing, but it hasn't quite come into view."

We laughed and hugged. And with my bonsai strapped into the passenger's seat, I drove away feeling grateful for the stability and fondness in this friendship.

I HAD NO DESIRE to sit alone at the hotel, so I parked on Ocean Avenue near the Santa Monica Pier and took a stroll along the bluffs.

The scene was like entering a living postcard. Steep cliffs overlooking miles of gorgeous, sandy beaches and the mighty Pacific, calm and endless. People were already gathering in bunches near the water, spreading their blankets to stake out favorite spots. The air was crisp, but under the warm Southern California sun and cloudless sky, it was a perfect 68 degrees, nothing like Fe*brrr*uary in Chicago.

I felt blessed to be there that morning, blessed that my professional life had finally taken root, and deeply blessed by the gentle forces that kept expanding my heart. Even more, I felt the undeniable presence of the mysterious influence, the invisible guidance, that had brought Paige and me together.

How was it possible that we'd found our way to each other in a world of unpredictable timing and impossible distances? Our souls had birthed us almost two decades apart, launched us into different cites, given us different heritages and backgrounds. Our educational and career paths couldn't have been more dissimilar. We had no friends in common and knew none of the same people—except Ron Scolastico, the only person who could have introduced us. Yet, all of these seemingly divergent elements were now being revealed as integral threads shaping a shared destiny. Perhaps we're always living two lives—the one we're creating choice by choice, and the one being invisibly shaped for us.

As if to punctuate my communion with divine forces, the distinct sound of church bells interrupted my reverie. I glanced at my watch and guessed it was the noon service at St. Monica or one of the other local churches.

Noon! What if she's already at the hotel? But she might not even get up here today. Maybe I should've checked in . . .

THE HOLIDAY INN WAS less than a mile away, but with the streets now crowded with traffic and pedestrians, the drive was painfully slow. I pulled into the first open space in the hotel parking lot, retrieved my bougainvillea bonsai from the front seat, and grabbed my overnight bag from the truck.

The man at the front desk was alone. I put the bonsai on the counter, gave him my name, then reached for my driver's license and credit card.

"You're checking in for how long, sir?" he asked, his eyes fixed on his computer screen.

"A few days. Has Paige checked in yet?"

"Let's see. No. One or two keys?"

"One, please. Ah, no, two!"

He slid the plastic keycards across the counter, still not looking up.

Riding the elevator to the top floor, I found the room at the far end of a dark, low-ceilinged hallway. The smell of a slightly run-down property followed me into the room.

I put my things down and opened the window to a gush of clean, crisp air. Leaning out to the left, I saw the Pier and the Pacific Ocean beyond. I left the window open and turned my attention back to the room. It was sparsely furnished and not pretty, but it was clean and the bed was well-made with new pillows and a fluffy comforter. After centering my bonsai on the chest of drawers, I relaxed on the bed and waited, eyes closed. It was already the longest day of my life.

I HADN'T PLANNED TO fall asleep, but sometime later the phone rang. Startled, I moved slowly at first, trying to open my eyes. Then realizing where I was, I scrambled to answer it.

"Who can this be?" I inquired playfully.

"Hi, I'm here!"

"Wow, you're here!" I couldn't believe this was actually happening. *She's here!*

"Yup. Downstairs."

"I'll be right down."

"No need. Just tell me where I'm going."

BY THE TIME I got to the elevator it was stopping at our floor. The door opened and Paige was there, looking quite petite next to her large suitcase. She stepped out with her case in tow and we kissed for the first time. A real kiss. Then lingering in each other's arms, I held her close, resting my head on hers.

Once in the room, the flowering bonsai caught her eye.

"Oh, how beautiful!"

"It's my faithful bougainvillea. She's got quite a story to tell."

"Can't wait to hear!"

We set Paige's bags next to mine and couldn't help but embrace again.

My meditation in Hawaii was a month ago to the day. Before that, she was a like-minded client. Now she was perfectly new to me, yet perfectly familiar, like a returning lover in my arms again. In that moment, something indescribable opened between us, something so daringly exquisite it shortened my breath.

We drew back enough to gaze into each other's eyes. I saw something spectacularly alive and waiting there, and could feel she saw the same.

Standing became unbearable. I quit trying to balance myself and pulled back the comforter. We sank onto the bed, her body warm and willing next to mine. Heaven seemed to open for us as we surrendered ourselves to each other. We breathed deeply, rhythmically, and entered the new universe we were creating together. No words were uttered. The boundaries of our bodies disappeared.

IT WAS DUSK WHEN we went in search of food. I remembered a Mexican restaurant on Wilshire Boulevard a few blocks away. It wasn't great, but like our hotel room, it didn't matter. We ordered soft tacos. I had a glass of house white wine, Paige had water. We laughed. We glowed. We held hands across the table. There was no uncertainty, and thankfully no more waiting, and no more distance between us.

And so we began the endless process of discovering each other by doing the simplest things. Eating, walking, being, working side by side, sharing stories, lying closely in each other's arms.

Everything was important, yet nothing mattered. I was with my beloved and she was with hers.

Not the end.

epilogue

Fast-forward thirty-two years and our path of love is still unfolding—in our relationship and in business.

We spent our first two years in an apartment and were then able to buy a home in a beautiful canyon in the Santa Monica Mountains. It was there that we were married in a private ceremony in front of the fireplace. It was also in this home that we finished the manuscript that brought us together. That book, *Executive in Passage*, was launched about a year after we moved into the house.

About ten years after that, we conceived of this book, *Grabbing Lightning*, but its gestation period was achingly long. Over the decades, some of our close friends and family would tease us, wondering if they were ever going to get something to read. So when we finally had a finished manuscript, we shared it with those folks, plus a few newer friends. We also asked if they wouldn't mind pointing out typos and anything that didn't track.

They indeed found typos and passages that we agreed were confusing. They also asked questions. Several readers identified strongly with Ellen and Tim and wanted to know how they fared. Others asked what happened to my original intent to build a love-based business and whether that part of the strategy held up.

Everyone was curious about our relationship after such an intense start, especially whether we hit the typical obstacles that tend to plague couples over time. Our favorite version of this question came from Rebecca, a lovely woman in her early thirties who's been in a relationship for almost a decade:

"So, did your relationship just go from bliss to bliss to bliss—or did you run into all the usual crap? And how'd you manage to trust that love and keep it going?"

We all laughed and said we'd try to address that and other questions as best we could in the epilogue.

Here goes.

What happened with Ellen and Tim?

As you might imagine, the fact that our togetherness came at the cost of two people's pain was a prominent and challenging part of our early time together. The distress we caused was hard to hold, and the thought of it now still prompts a sorrowful wincing in our bellies.

My relationship with Ellen was greatly influenced by that initial advice from her therapist friend: "If someone steps on your foot, and it hurts, you push them away." Ellen refused to speak to me after I moved out, but I trusted what she told mutual friends—talking to me wouldn't help.

We did, however, meet over coffee a couple of years later and were kind and caring with one another. When we were parting that day, she said she preferred this be the last time we connect, and it was.

Things with Tim went quite differently. He was overwhelmed at first, vacillating between anger and despair. Still, he and Paige managed to speak regularly, and not just about the practicality of it all. They mourned the loss together, as gently and respectfully as they could, and slowly crafted a friendship. As Paige describes it, the form of their relationship changed, but their mutual bond of caring did not.

Tim's inner process was well described during a session with Ron Scolastico. He was told that indeed, it was as if he'd been handed a sack of horse manure. But rather than angrily throwing the stench on everyone and everything, including himself, he was courageously choosing to fertilize his new life. We still marvel at his strength of character and are grateful that we're all friends to this day.

What happened with trying to build a love-based business, and did that part of the strategy hold up?

Bottom line, my handcrafted, oddly initiated business experiment worked. The company's success was more than I set out to achieve— not just the measurable kind, but the kind that lives true in your heart. But it was not without struggle.

After Paige and I were together a short time, it made sense for her to contribute her obvious skills to the business. We persevered in our efforts to integrate our ideals, spiritual and otherwise, into all aspects of our work, but quickly discovered that making choices from love (rather than fear) was a more multifaceted undertaking than anticipated.

We stumbled often, made choices that backfired, and kept having to refine our understanding of what this commitment to love meant in the practical world of producing results. Thankfully, in time, this once-perplexing process became an almost unconscious healthy habit.

One thing that was particularly fulfilling was what happened with the coffee roasting family. From the early days onward, the sense of mutual trust grew, and that relationship was, in many ways, the ideal I initially imagined for my business. And as it turned out, their new brand, which we named after their father, caught the early wave of the coffee revolution that introduced Americans to the pleasures of freshly roasted whole bean coffee. The success of this brand ultimately brought national recognition to this good family and buoyed their fortunes (and mine) for decades to come.

So yes, the love part of the strategy definitely held up. While there's no way to know what would've happened if we'd strayed from that core commitment, from my point of view, love was the critical factor. My ultimate measure? In addition to the client relationships being warm and durable, those were my happiest and most financially rewarding years in advertising.

Even so, at some point, my inner signals started nudging me again. It was time for another change. Paige and I would periodically talk about my feelings of being done with marketing, but it never felt like it was time to act on them.

Then, on New Year's morning, while we were in the middle of our annual ritual of musing about the upcoming year, I found myself asking if she wanted to run the company herself. Paige's response was immediate, which surprised me because other than when she said, "I'm yours," she's usually thoughtful and deliberative about big choices.

"Nope," she said, "at least not the marketing part." She did, however, want to grow a small but rewarding aspect of our work that had sprouted from readers' responses to *Executive in Passage*. We'd unexpectedly, yet happily, found ourselves offering workshops and private consulting for small business owners and executives who desired more fulfillment from their careers. This included a focus on their communication, and that's the part Paige wanted to develop.

I was a little disappointed at first, but I also felt a lift.

Several months later, Paige entered the Human and Organizational Development program at Fielding Graduate University in nearby Santa Barbara. Their multidisciplinary approach seemed a good fit, and with much of the learning done remotely, it wouldn't disrupt our lives too much. Plus, earning her master's degree would take less than two years. Perfect.

Six years later, Paige emerged with two master's and a PhD.

To accommodate this new timeline, I slowed my exit strategy but took every graceful opportunity to reduce my client roster while Paige immersed herself in studying and developing her research. This lighter version of our business gave me time to enjoy the school's policy of welcoming significant others to partake in the learning. It also gave me time to write in the mornings again—imagining and drafting *this* book.

One of the best things about our journey through Paige's doctoral studies was her research on the impact of fear in the workplace. She dove into the emerging bodies of literature on the neurobiology of fear and the neurobiology of love, and looked at their impact on human connection and communication. Then, in a flukey turn in her course schedule, she fell in love with a cutting-edge communication theory called CMM (Coordinated Management of Meaning), which holds communication as a creative act rather than merely transmitting information. Paige even had the privilege of being mentored by CMM's originator, Dr. Barnett Pearce.

Paige's research was ultimately published under the title: *The Enactment of Fear in Conversations-Gone-Bad at Work*. After graduation, there was another fortuitous meeting—this one with Dr. Dan Siegel, founder of the then-new interdisciplinary field of interpersonal neurobiology. For the next four years, Paige participated in his local, small-group learning sessions, which expanded her understanding of love and fear and their impact on relationships and well-being.

Paige's going back to school indeed created a turning point in our work, but it didn't turn out as we expected. Shortly after graduation, we were invited to do a workshop for an adult education group at a large parish in Santa Monica. "On what topic?" Paige inquired, thinking it odd that a church would want to host something business related. "On relationships," came the answer, and that's what prompted us to develop the workshop that evolved into the program we now call "The Love Conversation."

Did your relationship just go from bliss to bliss to bliss — or did you run into all the usual crap?

Yes, and yes.

During those first few years, our new world was so radically loving so much of the time that we felt transformed as human beings—

as if our love had somehow eradicated all our usual troublesome patterns. This was, of course, an egoic delusion that got busted pretty quickly!

So yes, we definitely ran into the usual crap. Old habits returned, begging to be understood and transformed. In fact, our journey from "bliss to bliss to bliss" included some shocking plunges into excruciating chasms of misunderstanding and hurt.

But there was a benefit. These disruptions were so sharp and so painful, we simply *had* to get back to the fullness of our love—right now!

With time and lots of trial and error, we kept learning how to do this relationship dance. Old patterns that once triggered us mightily lost their power over us. But as you might expect, some were more stubborn than others.

For instance, I'd sometimes feel criticized by something Paige said and would snap at her in anger—and she'd collapse into a world of hurt. We'd fight for a while, then withdraw in frustration. At other times, the hurt would hit, and we'd go straight into silence. Either way, a video camera would have found Paige in another room behind a slammed door, sharply muttering while reorganizing a drawer. And it would have captured me at my desk pummeling my keyboard or stomping out the door to walk it off.

We were seeing fear in action like never before—irritation, anger, hiding, pouting, and fighting to be right. Even worse, although illuminating, was the palpable experience of ineffable love being extinguished by what should have been a relatively inconsequential mishap.

In those dark moments, we both glimpsed the perils ahead if we failed to master our own fears and the disruptive patterns being formed between us. And had we not persisted in developing some form of self-intervention, we would have indeed lost everything.

And how'd you manage to trust your love and keep it going?

Ultimately, love itself became our best intervention. This relationship felt so precious, it was torment to hold any distance between us—not just in separate rooms but with any shield over our hearts.

In the early days, it was Paige who'd make the first move. She'd come toward me and just look at me, love pouring out of her face. Then she'd reach out and gently touch me, and whisper, "I'm sorry for my part." It came from such a true place in herself, I couldn't *not* join her there. I'd reply, "I'm sorry for my part too," and we'd fall into each other's embrace.

We humbled ourselves like this again and again so that love could win again and again. This practice—each of us repeatedly neutralizing our own fear reactions and returning to love within ourselves before returning to love together—put us on the path of ever-deepening dimensions of love.

But that part of the dance was only the prelude. Once we'd restored our connection, we each brought our vulnerability into a full conversation about what happened, why it went so wrong, and how we could do better next time.

For years, we had to deliberately and conscientiously repeat these steps, sometimes a few times a week, often a lot less, but we were learning what worked for us and what didn't. In time we found that this practice didn't just *restore* our love after one of those nightmarish glitches, it opened new realms of love, trust, and intimacy that were deeper and more viscerally felt than we'd known to reach for.

Even when life was difficult, some core part of our inner worlds remained peaceful—so much so that we started sensing gentler stirrings, sweet, subtle experiences that we couldn't have noticed before. We trusted love more. We loved each other with more abandon. There were more prolonged periods of uninterrupted joy. Challenges hurt less and penetrated less deeply. Old behaviors that used to trigger us barely showed up, and when they did, the problems were solved more easily and without drama. We also experienced a heightened sense of being in tune with a benevolent flow that seemed to enable us and all things around us.

Over time, these subtle experiences became more vivid, more pervasive. We were no longer just husband and wife, nor simply each others' partners. As we shared our most vulnerable, unvarnished selves with each other, we seemed to shift into a different orbit, into a way of being and loving for which we had no words.

One manifestation of this is that we found ourselves naturally being in full service to the well-being of the other. Paige's problems, concerns, and desires were mine, and mine were hers. And as we joined together to deal with our challenges and to create our life, we discovered both the restorative and generative powers of boundless love.

Plus, somewhere along the way, we realized that we'd unwittingly opened access to an experience that before was only a concept—the unmistakable alchemy that arises when two people merge themselves in transcendent love. Perhaps that's the natural outcome when you grab lightning, not just once, but again and again and again.

As you can tell, it gets fuzzy trying to describe this. Overall, these experiences are well expressed in something Ron Scolastico said in one of his last two readings with Paige and me, which happened to be his final readings before he passed:

"All human beings, whether they know it or not, desire that merging, that experience of the divine manifesting through a beloved one with whom they share their heart."

And that brings us pretty much up to date. Getting this book done is a big completion for us. And it opens another new chapter. We're not sure exactly what that will look like, other than that love will surely be the point.

So again, not the end.

Love is not a mere sentiment.
It's the truth at the heart of all creation.
—RABINDRANATH TAGORE

about the authors

PAIGE AND DON now dedicate their time to helping clients experience extraordinary love in their cherished relationships. They make their home in a verdant canyon in Los Angeles.

DONALD MARRS spent decades in advertising serving Fortune 500 clients. Disheartened by conflicts between his integrity and his work, he opted out of big corporations and ultimately chose to help family-owned companies with similar values—a story he shares in his first book, *Executive in Passage*.

PAIGE MARRS, PhD, holds a doctorate in Human & Organizational Development. Her approach blends cutting-edge communication theory, interpersonal neurobiology, and spiritual wisdom to help clients overcome troubling patterns that repeatedly undermine their relationships at home and work.

If you'd like to connect with Paige and Don or sign up
for their newsletter, you'll find them here:

theloveconversation.com

CPSIA information can be obtained
at www.ICGtesting.com
Printed in the USA
FSHW020459261119
64513FS